A STUDY IN CREATIVE HISTORY

THE INTERACTION OF THE EASTERN AND WESTERN
PEOPLES TO 500 B.C.

by

O. E. BURTON, M.A.(N.Z.)

KENNIKAT PRESS
Port Washington, N. Y./London

A STUDY IN CREATIVE HISTORY

First published in 1932
Reissued in 1971 by Kennikat Press
Library of Congress Catalog Card No: 71-105821
ISBN 0-8046-1197-1

Manufactured by Taylor Publishing Company   Dallas, Texas

KENNIKAT CLASSICS SERIES

TO MY WIFE

WHOSE PRACTICAL HELP
SYMPATHY AND ENCOURAGEMENT
WERE INVALUABLE

PREFACE

To-day international problems of all sorts are looming very large. Their solution demands, among other factors, some knowledge of the complex of historical tendencies which have produced them. Many of us have had no other background than that of British or, at the most, European history, and yet we are grappling desperately with the difficulties resulting from the new contacts which during the last two centuries have been established with the peoples of the East. The purpose of this book is to move away from the conventional European background and to get, in a rough way, an international one.

The writer has aimed at producing a work which will enable the serious reader to get a reasonably clear comprehension of the main movements of thought as they emerge clearly into history. No attempt has been made to deal with any thinking that cannot be demonstrated by reference to authenticated source manuscripts. Practically no attention has been paid to civilizations, such as those of Cnossus or Assyria. Their influence on the thought of Greece, Persia and Israel may or may not have been very considerable, but the fact remains that any effect they may have had upon future developments comes indirectly. In the opinion of the writer the outstanding developments prior to 500 B.C. were the emergence of the Prophetic school in Israel, of Mazdaism in Persia, of Brahmanism and, subsequently, Buddhism in India, and of Confucianism in China. These have been treated in some detail, and fairly copious quotations have been made so that readers may get a reasonably clear idea of what the original statements of beliefs, so important and widespread, actually were. The importance of the period is realized when it is considered that Buddha, Confucius and II Isaiah—three towering figures—were practically contemporaries.

O. E. BURTON

Wesley College
 Paerata
  New Zealand

FOREWORD

While all artificial divisions are necessarily imperfect, it is at least possible to consider History as the interaction of the Eastern and Western peoples. The date, 500 B.C., selected as the end of an era cannot be rigidly adhered to over such a wide field, but in the two cases Buddhism and Confucianism, where the mark has been overstepped by perhaps fifty years, the freedom taken does not make for any confusion. Throughout, the attempt has been made to select such themes as are of importance to subsequent interaction and to neglect others, however interesting, which were of importance only to a single people. The writer believes that at about 500 B.C. the stage was set for international action. What has happened since and what is happening to-day is largely conditioned by the philosophies of life that had been worked out by that date. This book aims, above everything else, at setting out in clear form the ideas formulated by ancient schools of thought which are either of definite influence on men and affairs to-day or which have profoundly influenced other major philosophies that have emerged since 500 B.C.

CONTENTS

CHAPTER	PAGE
Preface	9
Foreword	11
I. The Movement of History	15
II. Egypt	18
III. The Phoenicians	32
IV. Assyria and Babylon	40
V. The Israelites:	
(a) Ideas of God in Early Fragments of Old Testament	58
(b) Ideas of God in Genesis (J E)	64
(c) Ideas of God in Exodus (J E)	71
(d) Ideas of God in Numbers, Deuteronomy (J E), Joshua	76
(e) Ideas of God in I and II Samuel	79
(f) Ideas of God in Amos	85
(g) Ideas of God in Hosea	88
(h) Ideas of God in Micah	90
(i) Ideas of God in I Isaiah	92
(j) Ideas of God in Deuteronomy	96
(k) Ideas of God in Nahum	100
(l) Ideas of God in Zephaniah	101
(m) Ideas of God in Jeremiah	102
(n) Summary of Pre-Exilic Ideas Concerning God	108
(o) The Exile	115
(p) Ideas of God in Lamentations	118
(q) Ideas of God in Ezekiel	119
(r) Ideas of God in II Isaiah	122
(s) Summary of Exilic Ideas	126
VI. The Medes and Persians	127
VII. Mazdaism	
(a) Gâtha Ahunâvâiti	130
(b) Gâtha Ustâvâiti	136
(c) Gâtha Spentâ Mainyû	138
(d) Gâtha Vohû Khshathren	139
(e) Gâtha Vahistâ Ístis	140
(f) Yasna	141
(g) Vendîdâd	144
(h) Yasts	149
(i) Summary of Mazdaism	155

13

CHAPTER	PAGE
VIII. INDIA:	
(a) Early History	162
(b) The Period of Rig-Veda	165
(c) The Sacrificial System	173
(d) Khandoga Upanishad	178
(e) Kena Upanishad	182
(f) Aitareya-Āranyaka Upanishad	183
(g) Kaushîtaki Upanishad	185
(h) Vâgasenyi-Samhita Upanishad	186
(i) Mundaka Upanishad	186
(j) Svetâsvatara Upanishad	188
(k) Taitirîyaka Upanishad	189
(l) Brihad-Āranyaka Upanishad	190
(m) Máitrâyana-Brâhmana Upanishad	195
(n) Katha Upanishad	196
(o) Summary of Early Brahmanism	198
(p) Revolt Against Brahmanism	202
(q) The Life of Buddha	204
(r) Buddhist Theory	212
IX. CHINA:	
(a) The Shû King	232
(b) The Shih Kings	246
(c) The Yî King	248
(d) Lao-Tze	252
(e) Life of Confucius	253
(f) Summary of Ancient Chinese Thinking	263
X. GREECE:	
(a) The Trojan War	266
(b) Hesiod	278
(c) Greek Migrations to Asia Minor	281
(d) Development of Greeks from 776 B.C. to the Outbreak of the Persian Wars	284
XI. ROME	292
XII. THE INTERACTION OF THE EASTERN AND WESTERN PEOPLES TO 500 B.C.	298
BIBLIOGRAPHY	314
INDEX	316

A STUDY IN CREATIVE HISTORY

CHAPTER I

THE MOVEMENT OF HISTORY

The "Problems of the Pacific" is the phrase most commonly used to-day to denote the special set of difficulties, dangers and opportunities which rise from the meeting of the Eastern and Western peoples. When, in the days before the dawn of History, the first few families of the human race set out on their task of subduing and replenishing the earth they at once diverged. They developed in process of time a diversity of language, customs, culture and religion. In a very general way they drifted some toward the East and some toward the West. From loose federations of clans and tribes meeting, mingling, separating again there evolved gradually the primary races of mankind. Stretching in a rough line from the Atlantic to the Pacific along the warm belt of the Mediterranean countries, Asia Minor, the Euphrates valley, India and South China, we find Iberians, Berbers, Egyptians, Sumerians, Dravidians and Semites—brownish peoples—who for the most part lived in settled agricultural communities. Toward the centre of Asia emerged the great Mongolian race, flinging off from its teeming homelands nomad hordes who became the Lapps, Esthonians, Finns, the Huns, Turks and Mongols, the Ghurkas, Burmese, Siamese and the Chinese of history. Originating probably in the vicinity of the Caucasus, but emerging clearly in the centre of Europe, the Aryan races reached the Baltic in the north, the Atlantic in the west and crossing the mountain barriers occupied Italy and Greece. They became known in their settlements as the Greeks, Italians, Celts, Scandinavians, Teutons and Slavonians. A long arm of the race reaching back to the East became the Medes and the Indo-Aryans. In Africa the negroid peoples developed with little influence from races occupying Europe and Asia.

At a very early period a clear distinction commenced to be drawn between the peoples of the East and the West, between the Asiatic and the European, between the Greeks, the first representative European nation, and the Barbarians. "These are the researches of Herodotus of Halicarnassus which he publishes in the hope of thereby preserving from decay the remembrance of what men have done, and of preventing the great and wonderful actions of the Greeks and the Barbarians from losing their due meed of glory; and withal to put on record what were their grounds of feud" (Herodotus, Bk. I). "For Asia, with all the various tribes of Barbarians that inhabit it, is regarded by the Persians as their own, but Europe and the Greek race they look on as distinct and separate" (Herodotus, Bk. I, c. 4). Human history, from about 1000 B.C., centres upon the problems arising from the interaction of the East and the West, resulting as it has done in the synthesis, extension and clash of religions, in the meeting of cultures, in the stresses arising from economic impact and in the dangers and difficulties inseparable from the ebb and flow of vast populations. There is a living historical process connecting "Croesus, son of Alyattes . . . lord of all the nations to the west of the river Halys . . . the first of the Barbarians who had dealings with the Greeks . . ." (Herodotus, Bk. I, c. 6) and such modern movements as Swaraj, Christian Missions to the East, the operation of Western capital in China and Hindu labour in Fiji. If we can grasp the ascending sweep of this great process wheeling and circling upward from the dawn of History to our own time we shall have a fuller knowledge of the immense problems men of our age are heir to, gain some ground perhaps for optimism and some guidance for our activity.

CHAPTER II

EGYPT

Egypt—the land of Kem—was the first country of antiquity to attain a high standard of civilization. From the most ancient times its people had lived on the rich soil of the Nile valley and delta, secured by the sea and vast deserts from the incursions of the migratory tribes who roamed over wide tracts of Europe and Asia. The legends of Egypt contain no reference to the Flood or to the general set of beliefs commonly held by Semitic and Aryan peoples. It seems probable that the Egyptians developed in isolation, and that at whatever period they branched from the parent stock of the human race it was at a time far beyond the reach of research.

Menes (*circa* 4000 B.C.), the founder of Memphis, is the first great historical figure known to us. Tradition represents him as having reigned for sixty-two years. He was successful in war and the chase, a great builder, a political organizer and law-giver. His immediate successor, Athothis, is reputed to have compiled medical treatises. Their successors of the 1st and 2nd Dynasties built pyramids and introduced the worship of the sacred bulls—Apis at Memphis and Mnevis at Heliopolis—also that of the Mendesian goat. This was no doubt a move to strengthen priestly authority, and also to do away with the inconvenience of an immense number of sacred beasts scattered throughout the length and breadth of the land. At this early period plague and famine had already made their appearance. In the reign of Binothris women were enabled by law to succeed to the kingly power. From the accession of the first monarch of the 3rd Dynasty (*circa* 3338 B.C.) we have inscribed contemporary monuments. Libya was at this time subject to Egypt. The country was prosperous and the arts developing with some rapidity. Senoferu, the last of this line, established military colonies in the Sinai Peninsula with the object of protecting copper mines and blue-stone quarries which were operated by Egyptian enterprise. Under the 4th, 5th and 6th Dynasties (*circa* 3124 B.C.–2592 B.C.) the monarchs seem to have enjoyed great power and authority. The pyramids were built. With the limited mechanical power available at the time the building of one of these vast structures must have absorbed almost the whole surplus effort of the people during the lifetime of a king. Around the tomb of the monarch were ranged those of his greatest subjects—landed aristocrats, often members of the royal family—who lived in ease and luxury on the labours of the toiling masses, who were no doubt as poor as the fellaheen of our own day. From the mummy case of Menkira we learn that at this period the myth of Osiris was firmly established. Ptah-hotep, a monarch of the 5th Dynasty, is alleged to have been the author of a moral treatise which has survived. The kings of the 6th Dynasty apparently embarked on predatory expeditions. Their army was levied from North Egypt, and in the inscriptions of Pepi we have lists of conquered peoples.

For some hundreds of years there is an almost complete gap in the history until we come to Amenemhat I, the first ruler of the 12th Dynasty, who established his rule over all Egypt about 2380 B.C. Monuments and tombs of the period indicate a period of prosperity and a general advance in culture and artistic skill. At this time the inundation was brought definitely under control. The power of Egypt was advanced steadily toward the south, and Nubia became a dependency. Amenemhat III devoted a lifetime, not to the erection of a vast and costly tomb, but to engineering works planned for the benefit of the nation. The flood waters of the Nile were carried to an immense artificial lake, from whence they were drawn as required for irrigation by means of a system of canals. At this point there is another break in the records, probably caused by the invasion and conquest of Egypt by the Hyksos. The invaders were wandering tribes of Semites who may have served as mercenaries in the Nubian wars. Attracted by the wealth of the land, whose defence was in its natural barriers of desert and sea rather than in the valour of its sons, the fierce tribes poured in from the south of Palestine and the interior of Arabia. The struggle was short and the conquest was complete. The men of the desert established themselves as a military aristocracy, and their chief ascended the throne of the Pharaohs. They would almost certainly adopt the culture and the religion of the conquered people, whose economic and social life would not be greatly modified by the change of rulers. The Israelites may well have come to Egypt during the period of the Shepherd Kings; and if these Hyksos were, as has been suggested, of Semite race the cordial welcome given to Jacob and his sons is understandable, also the ready assignment of lands for settlement. The new dynasty was far from being securely placed on the throne, and the wanderers from the desert were welcome reinforcements.

The story of Joseph may explain much subsequent history. The Hebrew minister collected great quantities of surplus grain during a period of abundance. Famine came sore upon the land and the people were compelled to drive hard bargains for food. Their money was exhausted. Cattle were mortgaged and then the land itself. The result was the speedy reduction of the whole people to economic subjection. One-fifth of the whole product of Egypt was the bargain which the shrewd Israelite drove with the starving people on behalf of the foreign Pharaoh. The Hyksos were now absolute. Mastery could scarce go farther than this. The pressure became intolerable. A great rising of the native people led to the overthrow of the foreign overlords, their expulsion from Egypt and the reorganization of the country under the rule of Aahmes—a Theban prince—the first monarch of the 18th Dynasty (*circa* 1600 B.C.). The Hebrews possibly shared the general hatred which attached to the Hyksos, and Joseph, whom they regarded with veneration, may well have been a very Shylock from the viewpoint of the Egyptians.

Under the kings of the new dynasty Egypt reached its highest point of prosperity and power. Military expeditions were carried out not only to the south but to the north and east. The soldier became an increasingly important class. Priestly influence was intensified. A new official class—the high civil servants of the State—exercised enormous power. They were grasping and unscrupulous. Heavy burdens fell upon the poor—the toilers in the fields, the sailors on the ships, the private soldiers in the army. Egyptian art reached its highest point and became increasingly devoted to religion. The great temples were built. Captives were now employed on public works. In the fifteenth century B.C. the Egyptian armies captured Nineveh and reached the Euphrates. The Exodus took place towards the end of the 19th Dynasty (*circa* 1450 B.C.). This probably strengthened rather than weakened the real power of Egypt. The power of the Empire, strong in its centre, fluctuating in all its extremities, remained comparatively stable until a period subsequent to the reign of Shishonk, whose armies ravaged Palestine 971 B.C., or perhaps somewhat later. From this time there is a steady decline in political power. A number of petty princes replaced the old central authority. As a result of this disorganization Piankhi, King of Natapa, to which city had fled the priests of Amen-Ra from Thebes, was able to invade and subdue the whole of the northland and to establish the dynasty of Nubian kings.

The new rulers were not strong enough to withstand the shock of Assyrian invasion. Shabak was routed at Raphia. His successor was saved only by the destruction of Sennacherib's army by sudden pestilence. In 672 B.C., a few years later, Essarhaddon marched into Egypt, routed Taharqa, the last of the Nubian kings, plundered Memphis and placed his own governors in the more important cities. Under Psammetichus there was a period of restoration to something like the old unity and strength. His son endeavoured to dig the Suez Canal, without success. Phoenicians in his employ circumnavigated Africa. For the space of two or three years he restored the Empire to its farthest limits, but the success was short-lived, and the victory of Nebuchadrezzar at Carchemish utterly destroyed the power of Egypt. From the period of the subsequent invasion the land of Kem has never again been really independent. The Babylonian, the Persian, the Greek, the Roman, the Arab, the Turk and the British have all in their turn swayed the sceptre of the mighty Pharaohs.

The external influence of Egypt upon other peoples was religious, artistic, scientific and economic.

In connection with Egyptian religion we shall consider in the first place the main beliefs concerning the persons and the character of the gods. In the very beginning of all things was an inert watery mass. There was neither heaven nor earth, gods nor men. From the abyss arose Neb-er-tcher —"Lord to the uttermost limit." He took upon himself the form of Khepera and became the "creator of everything that came into being." At first he was One. By words of power he laid the foundation of things and gathered together the members of his body. From him sprang the gods Shu and Tefnut, and from these again Seb and Nut, who brought forth Osiris and Heru-khent-an-moati and Set and Isis and Nephthys. The cry of Kephera to his eye caused men and women to come into existence; from his tears sprang up the plants and all creeping things. His one eye was the Sun, his other the Moon (History of Creation, A and B, *Legends of Gods*, pp. 4–13).

The gods appeared in bodily form amongst men. Ra, "the self-begotten and self-created," ruled over men, women and gods. In process of time men murmured against him: "Behold his majesty—life, strength and health to him—hath grown old and his bones have become like silver, and his members have turned into gold, and his hair is like unto a lapis-lazuli." A secret council of the gods was convened, while the blasphemers themselves fled to the mountains. In accordance with the advice of the council the eye of Ra in the form of the goddess Hathor was sent forth against the fugitives. She slew the men, and found mastery so sweet that she "waded about in the night seas in their blood," refusing to return even at the command of Ra; and it was not until by a stratagem, by means of which she became drunk, that "she gave no further attention to men and women." But the heart of Ra was still weary. The goddess Nut was transformed into a cow. The god mounted upon her back. The children of man, seeing that his departure was nigh, pleaded with him to remain. They seized their bows and shot down the rebellious ones. Pardon was pronounced to them, "for the slaughtering of the enemies is above the slaughter of sacrifice." Yet Ra would not be turned from his purpose. "I am departing from men, and he must come after me who would see me." Rising majestically to the heavens, he called into being . . . "a great field . . . an abode for multitudes . . . Sekhethetep." The guardianship "of the millions . . . which live in darkness" was entrusted to his children (Destruction of Mankind, *Legends of Gods*, pp. 15–41).

Amongst the gods themselves there were jealousies and intrigues. The goddess Isis "lived in the form of a woman who had the knowledge of words of power." The easy sway she exercised over "the millions of men" filled her with loathing. She aspired to rule over heaven and earth. Ra was old and falling into dotage. If by some stratagem she could gain "knowledge of the name of the holy god" his power would pass to her. Isis formed a magic snake, which she placed in the path of the great god. The reptile struck him "and the living fire" commenced to depart from his body. He cried out in agony, and the other gods rushed to him. Isis, standing before him, asked for his sacred hidden name. Ra replied: "I am the maker of the heavens and the earth, I have knit together the mountains and I have created everything which existeth upon them. . . . I am the maker of the hours and the creator of the days. . . ." But Isis said: "Among the things which thou hast said unto me thy name hath not been mentioned." The torment of the poison worked upon the god "stronger than that of a blazing flame." At last the hidden name was spoken and Isis, the great lady of enchantments . . . mistress of the gods . . . had knowledge of Ra in his own name (Legend of Ra and Isis, *Legends of Gods*, pp. 43-55).

The trinity of Osiris, Isis and Horus is perhaps the most important part of Egyptian belief. The degree of reverence paid to the various gods differs greatly according to the period. Sometimes the older gods were forgotten and faded away into the dim background. In a Hymn to Osiris that god has become "Lord of eternity, king of the gods." He is the creator: "Thou hast made this earth, with thy hand the waters thereof, the trees and herbs thereof, the cattle thereof of every kind, the creeping things thereof and the fourfooted beasts of every kind." The universe is maintained by him. "The height of heaven and the stars are obedient unto thee, and thou makest to be opened the great gates of the sky . . . and thy seats are the stars which never rest." The ends of the earth make supplication to him (Hymn of Osiris, *Legends of Gods*, pp. 97-105). Osiris ruled in Egypt and did much to civilize his people. Not content with this, he travelled through the world persuading men everywhere to live according to his laws. On his return his half-brother Typhon had him trapped and murdered. Isis was inconsolable. She flew round and round the earth uttering cries of grief. "She made to rise up the helpless members of him whose heart was at rest. She drew forth from him his essence and she made thereof an heir." The child was Horus. Through fear of Set, Isis concealed her son, but in vain, for while she was seeking food for him he was bitten by a scorpion, and when she returned he lay dead. "Calamity hath befallen the child . . . and the child hath perished." At the sound of the lament of Isis the sun stood still in the heavens. The god Thoth descended to the earth to bring the dead to life. After the utterance of words of mighty power Horus rose again to life. He grew in strength. Osiris appeared to him from the other world and pledged his son to avenge his death. This he did, and Typhon, the murderer, was overthrown by "the triumphant one; the son of Isis, the flesh and bone of Osiris" (Death of Horus, *Legends of Gods*, pp. 143-197).

Osiris from being the ruler and protector of a people became the Lord of Amenti—the place to which all men and women went after death. Before him their souls were tried, and he pronounced the judgment which gave entrance to the realms of the blessed, or which despatched the unjust to the dreary caverns of Tuat. Isis, who had not passed through death, but who had in a measure been victorious over it, was regarded as the goddess of living things. In the universe there was a distinct conflict between good and evil. Ra, Osiris, Isis and Horus were the supporters of the good principle. Ranged over against them was the fiend Apep, a personification of the destructive powers of nature.

Herodotus remarks that the Egyptians "are religious to excess, far beyond any other race of men" (Bk. II, c. 37).

Budge says: "The Egyptian might be more or less religious according to his nature and temperament, but, judging from the writings of his priests and teachers which are now in our hands, the man who was without religion and God in some form or other was most rare if not unknown" (*Egyptian Magic*, p. 243). What accounted for this preoccupation with religion? The Egyptian believed in the possibility of a future life. "They were also the first to broach the opinion that the soul of man is immortal" (Herodotus, Bk. II, c. 123). Nearly all religious observances and ceremonials are based on this fundamental position. The chief aim of every Egyptian was to make his future safe. Theoretically, life in heaven depended upon righteous living, but in actual practice it came to be a question of right ceremonial.

By the use of the proper formulae and the observance of special rites the individual was able to identify himself with the victorious principles in the life of the gods—especially Osiris. Thus they were saved from the fiend Apep, who went about destroying wherever the unhappy individual was not placed under divine protection. The whole process of embalming the bodies of the dead was intended to provide them with such safeguards and sanctifications that no assault of the destroyer could possibly be harmful, and also to engage on their behalf the utmost power of the beneficent gods. No pains or expense or time were spared by the rich in the elaborate ceremonial of mummification. As far as it was humanly possible the physical frame of the deceased was rendered imperishable. And yet "No Egyptian who believed his scriptures ever expected that his corruptible body would ascend into heaven and live with the gods, for they declare in no uncertain manner that it remains upon the earth whilst the soul dwells in heaven" (*Egyptian Magic*, p. 182). The explanation of the apparent contradiction lies unquestionably in the theory of the Ka. The soul was the double of the body. The rite which preserved some member of the one in a material way transferred in mystical fashion its virtue to the spiritual. The body made incorruptible on earth guaranteed the life of the soul in heaven. The gods were to the Egyptians "mighty ones"— the creators and sustainers of the universe—but men could obtain power over them. Nowhere in the history of religion did the priest exercise greater sway, not only over the lives of men but over the actions of divine personages. Initiated into the awful mysteries, knowing the hidden names, the magical spells and above all "the words of power," he was able to control the future destinies of the soul by commanding, not the suppliant only, but the powerful rulers of the universe. Where the Hebrew feared God and obeyed Him, the Egyptians feared but looked to command. Their religion, then, was an anthropomorphic polytheism. It contained one idea of great elevation—the immortality of the soul. This grand conception was, however, overlaid by the basest superstitions. Insistence on moral conduct is altogether lacking. The gods themselves are not identified with morality.

In the civilization of Egypt we find the beginnings of architecture, art and science.

The pyramids at Ghizeh (Cairo) are probably the oldest remains of buildings which can in a real sense be classed as the results of scientific construction. The Great Pyramid is the largest building in the world. While the general design is comparatively simple, the highest degree of technical skill would be required for the transport, the shaping and the accurate fitting of the immense blocks of stone which were piled one upon another to a height of nearly 500 feet. Scattered throughout the country are the ruins of temples, ancient tombs and statues of the gods and kings. Some of these are of immense size. They show great mastery over material combined with a simple design. All buildings were rectangular or square. The lines were plain and severe. The column was known and used, but its full capacity was never employed. We do not find in the ruins any traces of the true arch. It was no doubt the colossal size, the accuracy and the sheer triumph of men in the massing of materials rather than the essential beauty of the result that caused Herodotus to write: "I visited this place (the Labyrinth) and found it to surpass description: for if all the walls and other great works of the Greeks could be put together in one they would not equal either for labour or expense this Labyrinth, and yet the temple of Ephesus is a building worthy of note and so is the temple of Samos. The pyramids likewise surpass description and are severally equal to a number of the greatest works of the Greeks, but the Labyrinth exceeds the pyramids. . . . The upper chambers, however, I saw with mine own eyes and found them to excel all other human productions. . . . I passed from the courts into chambers, and from the chambers into colonnades, and from the colonnades into fresh houses, and again from these into courts unseen before" (Herodotus, Bk. II, c. 48).

The same vastness of design was shown in the greatest engineering work of the ancient world—the formation of the Lake of Moeris, into which the water was introduced by a canal from the River Nile. "The current sets for six months into the lake from the river and for the next six months into the river from the lake" (Herodotus, Bk. II, c. 149).

Egyptian art is displayed in statues, inscriptions, paintings on the interior walls of tombs and temples and decorative carvings on columns. The statues are frequently extremely large, a sitting figure of Memnon, for instance, being some 53 feet in height. All forms of art show technical skill, but throughout there is a stiffness and formality. The religion which called forth the effort of the artist had itself become stereotyped, symbolic and to a very large extent trivial.

Art was mummified and never burst the wrappings of superstition with which it was swathed.

Science was a strange complex of astronomy and astrology, chemistry and magic, good medicine and curious spells for exorcising demons. Moses, on his return from the wilderness, apparently engaged with the magicians of Pharaoh in what to the initiated was a first-class conjuring contest, to the ignorant a demonstration of the miraculous. As St. Stephen remarks: "He was learned in all the wisdom of the Egyptians." Much of this wisdom as practised by the leading scientists of the day—the initiated priests—almost certainly consisted in a repertory of wonders calculated to enhance their reputation in the eyes of the vulgar. Many of the vagaries of astrology and of other pseudo-sciences were the result of honest research along paths which were found ultimately to be blind. With all the error there was much positive achievement. Geometry must have been well understood, and the general science of mechanics or the pyramids would have been impossible. Metallurgy must also have reached a high stage of development to make possible the accurate cutting and engraving of the hardest materials. Medicine was much studied. As has already been mentioned, one of the very earliest kings is alleged to have composed a treatise upon anatomy. The recognition and treatment of disease had reached such a point of development that to the astonishment of Herodotus "each physician treats a single disorder and no more: thus the country swarms with medical practitioners, some undertaking to cure diseases of the eye, others of the head, others again of the teeth, others of the intestines and some those which are not local" (Bk. II, c. 84). The hieroglyphics of Egypt are amongst the oldest forms of written speech. The Egyptians never developed a truly great literature, but they gave letters—through the Phoenician traders—to Europe.

Egypt possessed a developed social and economic life centuries before any of her near neighbours had a settled existence of any sort. This, taken into consideration with the comparative isolation and the cramping effect of religious beliefs, produced a certain insularity. "The Egyptians are averse to adopt Greek customs or, in a word, those of any other nation" (Herodotus, Bk. II, c. 91). It was an abomination for them to eat with men of an alien race (Gen. xliii. 32). Apparently they themselves did not readily leave the country of their birth for foreign trade or travel. Yet although they built no ships and did not themselves buy and sell in far countries, it was inevitable that from great distances commodities of all sorts should flow toward the rich land of the Nile. In the story of Joseph we find "a company of Ishmeelites came from Gilead with their camels bearing spicery and balm and myrrh, going to carry it down to Egypt" (Gen. xxxvii. 25). This spice trade must have been a very great one, as enormous quantities would be used annually by the embalmers. In the time of Solomon horses and linen yarn were received "at a price" by the king's merchants (1 Kings x. 28). Wine was imported at first from Phoenicia and afterwards from Greece. In the description given of the treasure-house of "the Erpa Peta Ast" we have mention of gold and silver, lapis-lazuli, turquoises and precious stones" (Conquest of Egypt, *Annals of Nubian Kings*, pp. 110–111). When the Israelites spoiled the Egyptians they took from them "jewels of silver, and jewels of gold" (Exod. xi. 2). The precious metals were probably introduced into Egypt by way of Nubia, and also by the Phoenicians. From the crude materials the Egyptians manufactured bracelets, ornaments for the neck or breast, ornaments inlaid with precious stones, or amulets for any member of the body, or crowns for the head or rings for the ears or ornaments of any kind . . . (Conquest of Egypt, *Annals of Nubian Kings*, p. 112). The wine of the north and the spices of Arabia were, until well into the period of the Greek conquest, exchanged for this manufactured jewellery (often, no doubt, of the trinket variety), the linen yarn and the pedigree horses of the stud farms. The corn of Egypt, afterwards of such vital importance to the Mediterranean world, would not in the early period have any market beyond the borders of the country itself, as Palestine grew sufficient grain for its own consumption.

CHAPTER III

THE PHOENICIANS

The Phoenicians, a Semitic people, occupied from a very early period a strip of Syrian coastline stretching from the mouth of the Eleutherus in the north to Mount Carmel in the south—a total distance of about one hundred miles. They were hemmed in between the sea and the mountain ranges of the interior. The soil was fertile, although the acreage was small, and the harbours were excellent for the ships of the day. It is impossible to give any exact date of settlement, but it probably preceded the Jewish conquest of Palestine by several hundreds of years. Geographically, Phoenicia was placed in the very midst of the then known world, and at the most distinct meeting-place of land and water. The camel trains of Asia, with their bales of merchandise from the highly developed civilizations of the East, could proceed no farther than the Palestinian coast. The ships of the Mediterranean were stayed by the same line. The Phoenicians seized their opportunity and became the common carriers of the Mediterranean world. Their harbours were crowded with ships. With raw materials of every sort pouring into their midst they rapidly became not only traders but manufacturers on a great scale. An immense population crowded into the narrow area between the sea and the hills. For more than five hundred years Phoenicia was the most considerable influence in the economic system of antiquity. Although a cultured and luxurious people, they developed no literature. Of their written history we have a few fragments only preserved in Josephus's *Antiquities of the Jews.* Our main knowledge of them comes from scattered remarks in Herodotus and

Thucydides, from various references in the Old Testament and a description of what is probably one of their island colonies in the *Odyssey*.

At a time preceding the siege of Troy, many islands to the south of Greece had been colonized by "Carians and Phoenicians" (Thucydides, Bk. I, c. 1). In the *Odyssey* Ulysses is represented as being thrown up on the coast of a Phoenician settlement.

> "gallant barks,
> Line all the road, each stationed in her place."
> (Bk. VI, ll. 328-329)

In the great stone forum they keep:

> "... the rigging of their barks.
> Sailcloth and cordage and make smooth their oars;
> (For bow and quiver the Phaeacian race
> Heed not; but marts and oars and ships well poised,
> With which exulting they divide the flood.)"
> (Bk. VI, ll. 331-337)

If the men surpass all others in their knowledge of seamanship, the women are not less expert in the weaving of tissue "of richest fancy and superior skill." The queen herself

> "beside a column sits
> In the hearth's blaze, twirling her fleecy threads
> Tinged with sea-purple bright magnificent."
> (Bk. VI, ll. 378-380)

The utmost magnificence abounds everywhere throughout the city, and especially in the palace of the king. Ulysses paused

> "ere with his foot he pressed
> The brazen threshold; for a light he saw
> As of the sun or moon illuming clear
> The palace of Phaeacia's mighty king.
> Walls plated bright with brass, on either side
> Stretched from the portal to the interior house
> With azure cornice crowned; the doors were gold.

A STUDY IN CREATIVE HISTORY

> Which shut the palace fast: silver the posts
> Reared on a brazen threshold: and above
> The lintels, silver, architraved with gold.
> Mastiffs in gold and silver lined the approach.
>
> . . . . . .
>
> Sheer from the threshold to the inner house
> Fixt thrones the walls, through all their length, adorned
> With mantles overspread of subtlest warp
> Transparent, work of many a female hand.
> On these the princes of Phaeacia sat
> Holding perpetual feasts."
>
> (Bk. VII, ll. 99-118)

In the Book of Judges we have a reference to the people of Laish—evidently a Phoenician settlement at some distance inland from Sidon—who "dwelt careless, after the manner of the Sidonians, quiet and secure" (Judges xviii. 7). Unfortunately for them they had not the massive walls of the great sea city to justify their confidence, and so fell an easy prey to the fierce Danites. Joshua chased a great army of confederate kings "unto great Sidon" (Josh. xi. 8), but was obviously unable to make headway against the walls of the fortress. During the period of the Conquest the Israelites, fierce predatory invaders, were no doubt a thorn in the flesh of the great trading cities. There was continual fighting, in which the Phoenicians, either themselves or with the assistance of mercenary troops hired from the numerous petty principalities of the sea coast and the north, endeavoured to defend their own settled territories, and also to keep open great land trading routes, which the semi-barbarous invaders were threatening to cut. As time passed new borders became more or less firmly established. The invasion became a conquest, the conquest a settlement. Under Saul and David the Israelites became a fully conscious and thoroughly organized nation, with the result that the days of the marauder and the plunderer rapidly passed before the insistent need for economic development. The newly established people, quickly absorbing higher cultural standards, opened up for the Phoenicians a great and convenient market for manufactured goods, while they, on the other hand, an immense population crowded into a narrow space, required foodstuffs and raw materials, which the Israelites—agriculturists and pastoralists—could supply in great quantity. As soon as the monarchy was established we find that Hiram, King of Tyre, "sent messengers to David, and cedar trees, and carpenters, and masons: and they built David an house" (2 Sam. v. 11). The building of the king's house was no doubt followed by the building of many more—on terms which probably resulted in much gold won in the wars finding its way into Phoenician coffers. Solomon and Hiram made a league of peace, and considerable exchange of goods took place between the kingdoms. The servants of Hiram cut, dressed and rafted the great quantities of cedarwood required for the immense building programme of Solomon. In return, twenty thousand measures of wheat and twenty of pure oil were carried annually into Tyre (1 Kings v.). It is significant of the difference in the technical skill of the Israelite and the Phoenician that when the great Temple of Solomon was in course of construction that "builders"—probably architects of Hiram's—co-operated in the work, and that practically the whole of the decorative work, both for the interior and the exterior, was placed in the hands of a Phoenician artist—a man "filled with wisdom, and understanding, and cunning to work all works in brass" (1 Kings vii. 14). Peace with Solomon enabled Hiram to carry out, in concert with him, great trading ventures from Eziongeber, a port on the Red Sea, then controlled by the Israelites. "And king Solomon made a navy of ships. . . . And Hiram sent in the navy his servants, shipmen that had knowledge of the sea, with the servants of Solomon. And they came to Ophir, and fetched from thence gold, four hundred and twenty talents, and brought it to king Solomon" (1 Kings ix. 26–28). "And the navy . . . brought in from Ophir great plenty of almug trees, and precious stones" (1 Kings x. 11). "Once in three years came the navy of Tharshish, bringing gold, and silver, ivory, and apes, and peacocks" (1 Kings x. 22). The above quotations would make it appear that these ventures were undertaken primarily by the Israelites. This probably was not so. The league of friendship gave the Phoenicians access to the Red Sea, to India and to the eastern coast of Africa, and they immediately seized the opportunity, necessarily in collaboration with their friends, to reap the rich harvests of these wealthy seas. The "traffick of the spice merchants, and of all the kings of Arabia" (1 Kings x. 15), added considerably to the revenue of Solomon. This probably would accrue from duties levied upon the caravans as they came in from the desert and crossed through Israel and Judah on their way to the great trading centres of Tyre and Sidon. These enlightened economic relationships established at the very beginning of the monarchy do not seem to have persisted: Judah and Israel relapsed into a chronic state of civil war. This probably brought the great trading ventures in the Indian Ocean to an abrupt conclusion. The Phoenicians were traders and not conquerors, and when the path to the east was blocked, turned again to the west, and passing the Pillars of Hercules made Britain and the Gold Coasts their far goal.

About 1000 B.C. commenced the steady migratory movements which carried the Greeks to the south, to the east and ultimately to the west. At this time Phoenician influence was probably dominant amongst the Aegean Islands. Their trading relationships with the mainland extended far back into the past. Herodotus says, "Now the Phoenicians who came with Cadmus introduced into Greece upon their arrival a great variety of arts, among the rest that of writing" (Bk. V, c. 58). The Greek thrust southwards was steadily strengthening at about the same period that the internal commotions of Judæa made communication with Arabia difficult, and access to the Red Sea and the Indian Ocean impossible without the good will of Egypt. Apparently there was no struggle with the Greeks. The Phoenicians surrendered their settlements and factories in the Archipelago, retaining only the eastern shore of Cyprus, and concentrated their attention on the northern shore of Africa, the southern coast of Spain and those more distant ports which lay beyond the Straits of Gibraltar. How far they reached no one knows. Necho, the King of Egypt, sent certain Phoenicians in his employ to sail round Africa. "They took their departure from Egypt by way of the Erythraean Sea, and so sailed into the southern ocean. When autumn came they went ashore, wherever they might happen to be, and having sown a tract of land with corn, waited until the grain was fit to cut. Having reaped they again set sail, and thus it came to pass that two whole years went by, and it was not till the third year that they doubled the Pillars of Hercules and made good their voyage home" (Herodotus, Bk. IV, c. 42). The general result of the movement along the African coast was the establishment first of trading-posts and then, as the homeland became over-populated, of colonies. Gades (Cadiz) and Utica were founded as early as 1100 B.C.—Carthage 814 B.C. (*Ency. Brit.*, v. 18, p. 806). The attachment of the colonies to the great mother cities was probably of a very loosely defined nature. The Phoenicians could form a federation of city-states, bound together by common ties of blood and culture, but they had not the imperial instinct of the empire-builders. Tyre and Sidon maintained their prosperity until the days of the final Assyrian and Babylonian conquest of Palestine, drawing wealth from the ends of the earth. Their influence on the material and technical development of the peoples of the Mediterranean basin must have been enormous. Everywhere they went they took with them a system of weights and measures, the art of writing, some knowledge of architecture, astronomy, manufacturing methods generally, and all that was then to be known of seamanship. They had little originality, but were expert copyists. They were business men, not artists, and their endeavour was to meet the demand of widely varying markets. Where the demand could be met by the profitable exchange of the wares of Arabia for the products of the African coast they were satisfied. When, however, more was needed they copied and improved the best models available. So they lived "careless and secure," using mercenary troops—"they of Persia and of Lud and of Phut" (Ezek. xxvii. 10)—to guard against the possible incursions of the neighbouring petty kingdoms. When the Assyrian deluge swept down upon Palestine they paid tribute to various monarchs for as long a period as the invading armies remained in effective strength. This was a matter of business security, pure and simple. It was better to pay than to suffer the inevitable loss of trade brought about even by a successful war. Judging by the description given by Ezekiel, Tyre, at the time of Nebuchadrezzar, was still at the very height of its power. The builders had perfected its beauty. The very sails of the ships were of "fine linen with broidered work from Egypt." The masts were of cedar wood. All manner of riches poured in from the corners of the world: silver, iron, tin, vessels of brass, horns of ivory, ebony, emeralds, purple and fine linen, coral and agate; wheat, honey, oil and balm; wine and white wool, lambs, rams and goats, horses and mules; spices, precious stones, gold, and the bodies of men. Well might the prophet say: "When thy wares went forth out of the seas, thou filledst many people; thou didst enrich the kings of the earth with the multitude of thy riches and of thy merchandise" (Ezek. xxvii. 33). The wars of Nebuchadrezzar were enormously costly. With the short-sightedness that almost inevitably underlies all schemes of military conquest, this monarch no doubt desired the rich plunder of the merchant city to finance his grandiose schemes. The Phoenicians united could probably have maintained their strongholds against the whole power of Asia. Their incapacity for organization and united action, however, coupled with the long-standing jealousies which divided the principal cities one from another, brought about the downfall of Tyre after a siege of thirteen years (587–574 B.C.). The conditions of capitulation were not severe. The besiegers were themselves as exhausted as the besieged. "Nebuchadrezzar, king of Babylon caused his army to serve a great service against Tyrus: every head was made bald, and every shoulder was peeled: yet had he no wages, nor his army . . ." (Ezek. xxix. 18). Yet Tyre never fully recovered. The Phoenicians of Palestine were not again independent. Their decline, although gradual, was sure. During this period of disaster Carthage, which had maintained something more than a nominal touch with the mother city, finally became independent, and embarked upon the career of expansion which three centuries later was to lead to the most decisive clash in the history of the Old World.

CHAPTER IV

ASSYRIA AND BABYLON

The river basins of the Tigris and the Euphrates were densely populated in those ancient days of which our most authentic historical documents are the numerous ruins, which now lie hidden under drifting heaps of sand. These peoples, so numerous and apparently so prosperous, perhaps from pressure on the northern and eastern frontiers, more likely by reason of natural expansion from within, established great empires, and wave after wave poured into the surrounding countries, giving to history the first of the great succession of imperial powers which have for longer or shorter periods dominated great tracts of country and large populations. For a great period of time even the very memory of Assyria and Babylon almost completely faded from the mind of man. To Europe they were of incidental interest only in so far as they influenced for a century or so the history of the Hebrew people. To-day scientific excavation is slowly revealing to us the law, social and political organization, culture, learning and religion of these empires. Ancient libraries of great size have been unearthed, and scholars are slowly reducing and organizing this mass. In another generation or less we may be in possession of a literature tolerably complete. This, however interesting it may be, will be of real concern to the scholar and antiquarian alone, for the religion and thought of Babylonia has entered the life of the world at second-hand and through other living channels whose direct and intensive study belong to other sections of our research. Whatever secrets the deserts of Mesopotamia may still reveal will not alter the fact that for over two thousand years and more the once mighty and far-flung empires of Assyria and

Babylon have not been, and now never can be, a world influence. We shall consider their history in outline only, mainly to give us background for ideas and developments which have in the long run proved of more enduring importance than the glittering splendours of great military empires.

Ancient Babylonia about 3000 B.C. was divided into two main portions—Accad in the north and Sumer to the south. In the first dwelt the Chaldeans and in the second the Sumerians, people of somewhat indefinite Eastern extraction. The first imperial city was Ur, from which a Chaldean prince ruled a wide extent of territory. He was a great builder of enormous temples which showed a high degree of architectural skill. The supremacy of Ur was in time disputed, and several cities rose to power and again dwindled to comparative insignificance. During all this time there was strong and increasing pressure from Semitic tribes who continually pushed in from the Arabian deserts. These peoples—the Amorites of the Old Testament—gradually established an ascendancy over the native Sumerians, and raised their chief settlement of Babylon into prominence. They established dynasties under which a comparatively high level of civilization was reached. Hammurabi, the greatest of the Amorite kings, may have ruled as far west as the shores of the Mediterranean. He thoroughly organized the legal system. His famous code is the first recorded instance of the numerous codifications which from time to time have crystallized the instinctive desire of great peoples to move toward clearly defined and improved social organization. No doubt much that is subsequently familiar to us in the Pentateuch, and through the Pentateuch in our own laws, can be traced back to this ancient promulgation of a Babylonian king ruling some four thousand years ago.

Babylon was sacked by the Hittites and left so exhausted

that waves of Kassites—an Indo-European people—flowed in from the East, took possession of the country and ruled from about 1750 B.C. to 1204 B.C., during which time the power of the kingdom waned to some extent.

Semite tribes had conquered the hilly country to the north of Babylon and had completely mingled with the earlier Sumerian population, adopting to a very large extent the culture, language and religion of the conquered. Round the city-state of Asshur there gradually developed the strong kingdom of Assyria. To the north the Egyptians, the Syrians, the Hittites and the Aramaean states clashed heavily. These people either destroyed each other or fell into periods of lethargy, and the Assyrians were free to start on a career of conquest. In 1400 B.C. Tiglath-Adar had conquered the Chaldean kingdom. Shalmaneser (1300–1275 B.C.) advanced to the Euphrates. For a time, during a period of great unsettlement and movement of peoples, there was a set-back. Babylonia again won its freedom, other boundaries contracted, but Tiglath-Pileser I (1120–1100 B.C.) conquered toward the Mediterranean and established a wide sphere of influence. The gains, however, were unstable, and fresh hordes from the heart of Arabia overran many of the Assyrian territories. A fresh outburst of national energy saw Assur-natsi-pal (885–860 B.C.) and his successor, Shalmaneser III, carrying the Assyrian armies west, north and east. Shalmaneser struggled desperately for the prize of the Mediterranean coast, but met with a fierce resistance, and was not wholly successful in his plans. In fact, beyond the Euphrates he made no sure gains. Exhausted by such great efforts, Assyria fell again into a period of weakness. Under Tiglath-Pileser IV (745–727 B.C.) she made her fourth and greatest effort to attain Empire. This monarch, moving to the south, chastised the Arabian tribes. He conquered also toward India, but mainly concentrated on the rich and populous west. The great fortress of Damascus was taken. Hamath was overthrown and a puppet king placed on the throne of Samaria. Sargon II continued the movement through Palestine, and in a great battle at Raphia overthrew the Philistines and the Egyptians. He razed Ashdod and captured Cyprus. As crowned King of Assyria, Babylon, Sumer and Accad he was perhaps the most powerful monarch the world had yet known. He was far from being merely a conqueror. The legislative system was again codified, the great library of Calah was restored, astronomical researches were carried out. In the midst, however, of his work of organization Sargon was murdered and was succeeded by his son Sennacherib (705-681 B.C.). This ruler carried on in the steps of his father—conquering, building and organizing. He overthrew Tyre and Sidon, and Carchemish became the great trading centre of the time. Victorious on every side, he was in his turn murdered. Essarhaddon (681-668 B.C.) removed the Sidonese from the coast to the central region of the Empire. He invaded Arabia, penetrating a distance of 980 miles, reached the Caucasus, and in 672 B.C. conquered Egypt. The Assyrians were now in touch with Aryan peoples. Many kingdoms great and small had been broken down. Populations were removed from their ancient habitations. New trade routes were opened up. Over the whole area the soldier, the trader and the administrator helped to fuse conflicting cultures into something like a common level of civilization. Under Assurbanipal (Sardanapalus, 668-626 B.C.) Assyria reached its culminating point. The career of conquest was not stayed, although Egypt managed to secure her freedom. The Cimmeranians were defeated and deflected upon Asia Minor. Elam was utterly subdued and Susiana reduced to a wilderness. The wealth and power of the Assyrian kings were such, perhaps, as the world has seldom seen. The gold, silver and precious stones—the tribute of two-and-twenty kings—glittered on the roofs and walls of palace and temple.

An immense irrigation scheme made a rich garden of soil that is now an arid desert. The trader followed the army, and Nineveh became the clearing-house of the rich wares of East and West and South. Great libraries were founded. Scholars engaged in philological research, and the scientists of the day plotted the position of the stars. Art and architecture reached a level of distinction. But Assyria, powerful and prosperous though she might appear, was in reality weak. "Woe to the bloody city!" says Nahum; "it is all full of lies and robbery; the prey departeth not . . . that selleth nations through her whoredoms and families through her witchcrafts" (Nahum. iii. 1-4). Strong rulers and powerful armies can for a little while hold in subjection a diversity of unwilling peoples—but for a while only. Blood makes a poor cement for an enduring bond between nations. The Scythians swept southwards, and their pressure caused the loss of Syria and Palestine. Babylonia broke away. The Medes commenced their advance and Assyria fell. The organization of the Empire, however, must have remained almost intact, for Nebuchadrezzar (604-563 B.C.) quickly established a Babylonian Empire which covered almost, if not the whole, of the territory once swayed by the sceptre of the Assyrian monarchs. Under this ruler Jerusalem fell, and the people of Judah were carried into captivity. Nebuchadrezzar was a great and powerful ruler, but on his death the mushroom empire quickly fell before the Persians, and in 539 B.C. Cyrus entered Babylon as a conqueror.

CHAPTER V

THE ISRAELITES

About the year 1500 B.C. a small Hebrew tribe of Semite extraction left their habitat in the south of Canaan and settled in the north-east of Egypt in the land of Goshen. They were pastoralists, and in their new home continued to tend their flocks. For some considerable period they were probably practically independent. Time brought a considerable increase in their number and in their wealth. The rulers of Egypt came to regard them with feelings of mingled cupidity, anxiety and fear. The Israelites supplied a great part, if not the bulk, of the wool and meat for the Egyptian market, and in return would set up a steady demand for corn and manufactured goods. Being still largely nomad, there was no guarantee that they would not go as they had come and leave behind a very considerable state of economic dislocation. Their growing wealth was a source of continual temptation to Pharaohs, whose expenditure on building alone must have been enormous. More serious still was their fecundity. They were an intractable people, ready enough, no doubt, to fight on small provocation. Man for man they would be more than a match for the softer Egyptians. Far-seeing rulers saw that it was only a question of time until the shepherd clans would be sufficiently powerful to pillage and perhaps rule their neighbours. To guard against the danger of flight or of insurrection the Israelites were reduced to slavery. The process was no doubt a long one—a tightening of administrative control, a definite levying of taxes, a levy on the labour surplus that would automatically develop in a community wherein seasonal employments varied, the quartering of troops and the suppression of any political or religious organization likely to serve as a common rallying-point for the tribes of Israel. Severe as were the measures adopted, they were insufficient to check the growth or to break the spirit of the subject people. The labour levy was increased and the labourers harshly treated. "Therefore they did set over them taskmasters to afflict them with their burdens . . . and they made their lives bitter with hard bondage, in morter, and in brick, and in all manner of service in the field: all their service, wherein they made them serve, was with rigour" (Exod. i. 14).

The rapid increase of population still continued, and the Egyptian authorities attempted in some degree to exterminate the race by ordering the exposure of male infants. As the Israelites apparently lived in their own communities and were enslaved as a race rather than as individuals, this drastic step naturally broke down, although, if the measures taken by the mother of Moses to preserve her son be correct, it must have been enforced to some extent for a period. There is no reason to doubt the beautiful story of the babe taken from the river by the princess of Egypt. The child's education would be according to the rank of his adopted mother, and he may, as some legends indicate, have exercised large powers in the Egyptian State. As a grown man "he went out unto his brethren, and looked on their burdens" (Exod. ii. 11). Some especial act of brutality on the part of an overseer stirred his hot blood, and he slew the man out of hand. The mere slaying was in itself no great matter, especially when committed by one of such rank, but the circumstances aggravated the crime beyond all possibility of forgiveness. Such an action on the part of a man so notable could be explained only by his intention to lead the Hebrews either in flight or insurrection. Pharaoh sought to slay him, and Moses fled for his life to the land of Midian, where dwelt free Semite tribes, akin to the Israelites and very like to them in language, customs and religion. Here he married and remained for a period of some years. No doubt in the quietness he devoted much time to contemplation, and what previously had been but a half-formed idea hardened into a definite purpose. He determined to lead his people out of Egypt to freedom. This determination was strengthened by a profound religious experience. During the whole period of his exile he apparently maintained communication with the chieftains of Israel and was apparently regarded by them as their natural leader. Some crisis arose in Egypt—pestilence perhaps, or war on the southern border—and the central authority was weakened. The opportunity seemed heaven-sent. Moses returned to Egypt, assumed control of the tribes and ultimately, with or without the consent of Pharaoh, led the Israelites out into the desert. They were pursued, but escaped across an arm of the Red Sea into the safety of Arabia Petraea. After a heavy brush with the Amalekites the tribes plunged into the desert and encamped about Mount Sinai. Here a halt was made for some months while the mixed multitude was organized into a community. Sacrifices were offered. Their god El, now perhaps for the first time called Yahweh, was worshipped—for, indeed, had he not "triumphed gloriously"? A code of laws was promulgated. What these were we do not know. The whole of the legislation outlined in the Pentateuch obviously could not have been given at that time. Some nucleus was laid down, and on this foundation the later edifice of the Torah was built up. Again the march was continued through mountainous country and across desert, until a settlement which may have been intended as a permanent one was made in Kadesh. Here the tribes remained for a period of some years until increasing numbers set them once more in motion toward the fertile and spacious land of Canaan.

About this time Moses died and was succeeded by Joshua, under whose leadership the Israelites marched through

Edom and Moab, north past the Dead Sea, and then, facing west, crossed the Jordan and stormed Jericho. Debouching on the plains below, they commenced a war of conquest—and frequently of extermination—against the various peoples who were then in occupation. For two or three centuries this struggle continued. Fresh waves of the invaders came up out of the desert and spread north, west and south. Occasionally they were beaten back. Sometimes a section would be temporarily subjugated. At other times new territory was won. By the year 1170 B.C. they were firmly established throughout the greater part of Palestine. There was no regular central authority—"every man did that which was right in his own eyes" (Judges xxi. 25); but at Shiloh there was a yearly "feast of the Lord" (Judges xxi. 19). "A house of the Lord" (1 Sam. 1. 7) was established in this place, and it was apparently a yearly custom for men to make pilgrimage to the shrine and there "to sacrifice unto the Lord of hosts." In times of great stress some notable man came to the front and commanded the people in battle. Othniel beat back Chushanrishathaim (Judges iii. 8–10). Ehud delivered the people from the Moabites (Judges iii. 12–30). Gideon overthrew the tyranny of the Midianites (Judges vi–viii). Samson strove with the Philistines (Judges xiii–xvi). The continual struggle against these outside nations resulted ultimately in the establishment of a monarchy and some sense of political as well as religious unity. Saul, a Benjamite, was chosen as the first king. He maintained a constant and on the whole victorious struggle against a ring of enemies. He was succeeded by one of his captains, David Benjesse, one of those extraordinary personalities with a genius for capturing the imagination and winning the devotion and loyal service of great multitudes of men. Under this king, who was first and foremost a war chief, some real measure of political unity was achieved. The Israelites passed from the defensive to the offensive

THE ISRAELITES

and largely extended their borders. Jerusalem, a Jebusite stronghold, was stormed and became the capital of the kingdom (2 Sam. v. 6-9). The Philistines were smitten from "Geba to Gazer" (2 Sam. v. 25), and later lost Methegammah (2 Sam. viii. 1). David dedicated to the Lord the spoils "of Syria, and of Moab, and of the children of Ammon, and of the Philistines, and of Amalek, and of the spoil of Hadadezer, king of Zobah" (2 Sam. viii. 12). After a reign of some forty years he died, leaving the nation powerful, prosperous and free, and was succeeded by his son Solomon about the year 970 B.C.

The new monarch, having "peace on all sides around about him" (1 Kings iv. 24) and a people "as the sand which is by the sea shore in multitude" (1 Kings iv. 20), proceeded to organize the kingdom and to levy systematic taxation. He entered into close relationships with the great Phoenician city of Tyre (1 Kings v. 12). Common trading ventures and a great market for the wheat and the other products of an essentially agricultural and pastoral people led to a vast increase of wealth (1 Kings v. 11–ix. 26, 28). An alliance with a princess of Egypt marked the rising power of the kingdom and opened up trade in horses and linen yarn (1 Kings iii. 1–x. 28). The long peace after generations of war and the close economic relations with powerful and highly civilized peoples brought about an era of prosperity unknown before. "Judah and Israel" were "eating and drinking and making merry" (1 Kings iv. 20). Solomon was able to maintain a most luxurious Court (2 Chron. ix.) and to embark on vast building operations (2 Chron. viii.). The most notable of his many foundations was the first Temple—a building which, allowing for all errors and exaggerations, must have cost fabulous sums (1 Kings vi.–2 Chron. iii.–iv.). Toward the end of the great king's reign the taxation necessary to meet so tremendous an outlay was heavy, but apparently the people bore it without making any very determined protest.

Under the rule of David and Solomon the peoples of Israel were united, and attained to the greatest height of political power and military prestige that they ever reached. At a time when herdsmen wandered over the Seven Hills and the Greeks were without verifiable history the Israelites had established a kingdom that was no mean rival of ancient Egypt and splendid Assyria. For a brief space it seemed that all the kingdoms of the world lay before them. But the day of temporal glory quickly passed.

Rehoboam succeeded his father about the year 933 B.C. His refusal to lessen taxation broke the kingdom in two. Judah and Benjamin remained loyal, but the northern tribes broke away and established a separate government under the rule of Jeroboam—a certain "mighty man of valour" who had been exiled by Solomon (1 Kings xii. 2–2 Chron. x).

Jeroboam broke all possible connections with the southern capital, even to the setting up of "calves of gold" (1 Kings xii. 28) in Bethel and Dan, to check pilgrimages to Jerusalem. He maintained continual war with Rehoboam. His son Nadab (912 B.C.) continued in his father's policy until he was slain by Baasha, who then succeeded him and ruled for twenty-three years. His successor Elah (888 B.C.) was murdered by Zimri while "drinking himself drunk" (1 Kings xvi. 9). Omri, "captain of the host," was made king (1 Kings xvi. 16). He "did worse than all that were before him" (1 Kings xvi. 25). His son Ahab (876 B.C.) likewise "did evil in the sight of the Lord" (1 Kings xvi. 30). In his reign Elijah prophesied. Ahab was a powerful king and defeated the great host of Benhadad the Syrian in a bloody fight at Aphek (1 Kings xx. 26–34). Three years later, however, he was defeated and slain at Ramoth-Gilead (1 Kings xxii. 29–37). Ahaziah, his son, was succeeded by

Jehoram (853 B.C.) (2 Kings iii. 1). Through the advice of the prophet Elisha he ruinously defeated the Moabites (2 Kings iii. 5-27), but was severely checked by the Syrians under Hazael (2 Kings viii. 28). As the result of an intrigue backed by Elisha, Jehoram was murdered by Jehu, son of Nimshi, who seized the throne (2 Kings ix). During his long reign of twenty-eight years, commencing in 842 B.C., the Syrian pressure was maintained throughout and "in those days the Lord began to cut Israel short" (2 Kings x. 32). He was succeeded by his son Jehoahaz (2 Kings x. 35), who "did that which was evil in the sight of the Lord" (2 Kings xiii. 2). His son Jehoash (798 B.C.) "departed not from all the sins of Jereboam" (2 Kings xiii. 11). For a time he kept the Syrian power at bay and recovered lost ground (2 Kings xiii. 25). He warred against Judah and plundered Jerusalem (2 Kings xiv. 13-14). Jereboam II, his son, succeeded him in 783 B.C. and managed by hard fighting to still further restore "the coasts of Israel" (2 Kings xiv. 25). Zachariah (743 B.C.) was murdered by Shallum, who in his turn was slain by Menahem. This king bought off an Assyrian invasion by a payment of a thousand talents of silver (2 Kings xv. 25). His son Pekakiah was murdered and succeeded by Pekah (736 B.C.), in whose reign Tiglath-Pileser, king of Assyria, invaded the country, reduced several cities and carried the inhabitants of these into captivity (2 Kings xv. 29). Pekah was in his turn murdered by Hoshea, who seized the throne (2 Kings xv. 30). The Assyrians were continually pressing upon the border. Hoshea was reduced to the payment of a yearly tribute, but having leagued with the Egyptians against his overlord, was taken and cast into prison. After a three years' siege Samaria was taken and the people of Israel carried captive into Media (2 Kings xvii. 6).

The kingdom of Israel had endured from 975 B.C. to 721 B.C.—a space of two hundred and fifty years. During almost the whole of this time the Israelites were at war sometimes with Judah, sometimes with Syria, and finally with the great and growing power of Assyria. Civil war, too, must have been of frequent occurrence. The prosperity of the people must have been far below the level attained in the overflowing times of King Solomon. There was no longer the old security for the huge caravans, which in the days of the great king had poured in from Arabia. The trading ventures in which Solomon and Hiram had joined with such advantage to both were no longer possible across a country torn by war and distracted with civil strife. It was probably at this time that the Phoenicians turned their faces almost wholly to the West—the far limits of the Mediterranean Sea and beyond. The agriculturists who formed the backbone of the Israelitish community would be at the mercy of the military, and in the event of civil war would suffer from the chronic state of insecurity. General culture almost certainly declined. Idolatry and the basest superstitions prevailed. With the fall of Samaria, ten of the old Hebrew tribes passed out of history and their place was taken by colonists from Babylonia (2 Kings xvii. 2-24).

The history of the Southern Kingdom is very similar. Rehoboam, after the defection of Jereboam, organized his realm and fortified the borders of Judah and Benjamin (2 Chron. xi. 5-12). The priestly class of the Levites abandoned the newly established kingdom of the north and settled in and about Jerusalem. They were accompanied by all those who "set their hearts to seek the Lord God of Israel" (2 Chron. xi. 14, 16). In this reign Shishak of Egypt plundered Jerusalem, and there was continual war on the frontier between Israel and Judah (2 Chron. xii. 9, 15). Abijah succeeded his father in the year 916 B.C. He won a great victory over Jereboam, who did not "recover strength again in the days of Abijah" (2 Chron. xiii. 17-20). In the time of his successor Asa occurred a great religious revival. The people "entered into a covenant to seek the Lord God of their fathers with all their heart and with all their soul" (2 Chron. xv. 12). A great victory was gained over an invading host of Ethiopians (2 Chron. xiv. 12), and the policy of fortification was vigorously carried on during the intervals of peace (2 Chron. xiv. 7). Jehoshaphat (873 B.C.) reigned prosperously. He entered into alliance with Ahab (2 Chron. xviii. 1), "set judges in the land" (2 Chron. xix. 5) and received tribute from the Philistines and Arabians (2 Chron. xvii. 11). A great host of Ammonites, Moabites and the inhabitants of Mont Seir was broken before him (2 Chron. xx. 24). The comparative quietness of the times, the friendly relationships with Israel and the consequent increase in wealth revived memories of the rich trade of Tarshish, but an attempt to build a navy came to nothing (2 Chron. xx. 26-37). Jehoram, his son (849 B.C.), was a weakling who died miserably (2 Chron. xxi. 19). Ahaziah (842 B.C.) perished by the hand of Jehu (2 Chron. xxii. 9). For six years Athaliah, the queen mother, ruled over the land (2 Chron. xxii. 12) until Joash, a child of seven years, who had been hidden in the Temple, was crowned by the Levites and Athaliah herself slain (2 Chron. xxiii. 11). His reign was prosperous during the lifetime of Jehoiada the priest, but subsequently he perished miserably after having murdered Zechariah the prophet, the son of his benefactor (2 Chron. xxiv. 21-25). The league with the kingdom of Israel was broken during the reign of his son Amaziah, and the northern king plundered Jerusalem (2 Chron. xxv. 23). Amaziah was murdered. His son Uzziah (779 B.C.), a great and proud king, "strengthened himself exceedingly" (2 Chron. xxvi. 8). Jotham (740 B.C.) inherited his father's power, fortified the mountain and forest country and exacted tribute from the Ammonites (2 Chron. xxvii. 45). In the following reign, that of Ahaz, Judah was brought very low. There was war with Syria (2 Chron. xxviii. 5), with Israel, with the Edomites and with the Philistines

(2 Chron. xxviii. 17–18). The wretched king called in Tiglath-Pileser of Assyria to his assistance, but this ally "distressed him but strengthened him not" (2 Chron. xxviii. 20). In the time of Hezekiah (727 B.C.) a great religious revival broke out. Multitudes of people from both kingdoms kept the Passover in Jerusalem "with great gladness" (2 Chron. xxx. 21). Sennacherib of Assyria failed in an attempt to subjugate Judah, which continued in a state of great power and prosperity during the lifetime of Hezekiah (2 Chron. xxxii. 21, 27–30). The Assyrian pressure was maintained, and Manasseh (698 B.C.) was for a time captive to that power (2 Chron. xxxvi. 1). Amon, his son, was murdered, and Josiah, a child of eight years, was raised to the throne (2 Chron. xxxiv. 1). Again there was a period of religious revival and national stability, but it was not to last. There came at last the inevitable clash between the age-old power of Egypt and the ever-growing might of the Assyrian Empire. Between the two Judah was crushed. In the reign of Jehoahaz, Necho, king of Egypt, imposed tribute, and set a puppet of his own on the royal seat (2 Chron. xxxvi. 3–4). Eleven years later Nebuchadrezzar plundered Jerusalem and carried Jehoiakim captive to Babylon (2 Chron. xxxvi. 6). The shadow of a kingdom remained, but in the year 586 B.C. the Chaldeans slew without mercy and carried the wretched remnant to captivity in Babylon (2 Chron. xxxvi. 17–20).

The history of the kingdom of Judah, while following on somewhat similar lines, was on the whole more prosperous than that of Israel. Two main factors operated to bring this about. In the first place the geographical position of the two kingdoms made the northern one a buffer state. Israel lay right open to the infiltration of Syro-Phoenician ideas and idolatry. These must have had a tremendously disintegrating effect upon a nation whose main characteristic had been a peculiar and very exclusive religious belief.

On the northern kingdom, too, fell the first shocks of the Assyrian advance into Palestine. Secondly, the Temple was in Jerusalem, which in consequence became the religious, if not the political, metropolis for all devout worshippers of Jehovah. This no doubt attracted numbers of settlers from the north, especially during times of great religious revival. Judah, being less exposed and with a more distinctive culture, was enabled to endure longer, but after a little while the resistless tide of Assyrian invasion swept over it also. At this stage it would seem that the history of the Hebrew people had closed. Emerging from the desert, they had by degrees built up a powerful kingdom which, for a brief space, under three great kings—Saul, David and Solomon—had risen to great power and glory. Even when divided the fragments were considerable enough. From about 1000 B.C. to 586 B.C. some part at least of the Hebrew people had been free and independent. Now they were utterly crushed. Their cities were destroyed. The sacred Temple was in ruins. The people themselves—those who survived—were carried captive into a far country. One might well imagine that no nation could survive so terrible a destruction. And, indeed, they never again became a great people in the ordinary political sense. Nevertheless by the time of the Assyrian conquest they had developed such an idea of God and of God's relation to them that political extinction and captivity in an alien land utterly failed to break the national spirit. The rise and development of the Hebrew ideas concerning God is one of the most important facts of all history. The narrative so far outlined is in itself of small importance. Many a small people has raised itself to temporary greatness, fought valiantly to preserve its freedom, and in the end has fallen back into the obscurity from which it emerged without leaving a permanent mark of any kind on the life of the human race. The story of the Israelites is important only when we realize that under accounts of Egyptian bondage, desert wanderings, wars of conquest, extermination and defence, in the descriptions of Court intrigue and civil strife, in the legal codes of priests and the passionate outbursts of prophets, in the human interest of some of the most moving stories ever told, we have the steady growth of thinking and feeling about God, which finally, still further expanded and developed, has become of enormous importance not merely for the modern Jew but for all mankind.

THE IDEAS OF GOD IN PRE-EXILIC PERIOD

What, then, were the ideas of God before the captivity in Babylon? To be on sure ground we must consider in some detail such parts of the ancient Hebrew literature as were produced prior to 586 B.C. The Old Testament and the Apocryphal books as we have them are the remnant of a national literature produced over a period of nearly a thousand years. Many of the sources are irretrievably lost. The various books have been edited and re-edited with the utmost freedom, and there is the greatest difficulty in determining the date of many passages. For our purpose the method of study will be to commence with the oldest passages (in so far as these are reasonably ascertainable) and so work through to those produced just before the Exile. The order of reference will be:

1. Song of Lamech (Gen. iv. 23). Curse on Canaan and Blessing on Shem and Japhet (Gen. ix. 19-28). These fragments are probably pre-Mosaic.
2. Song of the Well (Num. xxi. 17). Miriam's Song (Exod. xv. 21). These are possibly contemporaneous with Moses.
3. Joshua's Speech to the Sun (Josh. x. 12).
4. Song of Deborah (Judges v.). Riddle of Samson (Judges xiv. 14). Samson's Boast (Judges xv. 1-16). Fable of Jotham (Judges ix. 8-15). These are probably of the period of the Judges (*circa* 1230 B.C.-1025 B.C.).
5. The couplet in 1 Samuel xviii. 17. David's Lament over Saul and Jonathan (2 Sam. i. 17-27). Elegy on Abner (2 Sam. iii. 33-34). These are of the Davidic period and the last two are possibly the work of David himself.
6. Oracles of Balaam (Num. xxiii-xxiv) Solomon's speech at opening of Temple (1 Kings. viii. 12-13). David's Court History (2 Sam. ix-xx) (1 Kings i-ii).
7. Old Records of Conquest—including the major parts of Joshua and Judges.
8. Primitive form of Documents J and E before 750 B.C.

9. Amos, Hosea, Micah, Isaiah, with the exception of certain portions in the period 800 B.C.–700 B.C.
10. Deuteronomy—the major part 640 B.C. (*circa*).
11. Nahum, Zephaniah, Jeremiah, Ezekiel about 607 B.C.

Peake's Commentary.
Introduction to the Literature of the Old Testament, Driver.

(a) THE EARLY FRAGMENTS

The song of Lamech (Gen. iv. 23) is the revengeful and bloodthirsty boasting of a barbarian in front of his women. Noah's curse and blessing on his sons (Gen. ix. 19–27) is the natural expression of the patriarchal head of a family. The sons who have done well are placed in the power of the family god. They especially possess him and will therefore flourish. The erring one has no part in the god. He is therefore weak and must fall into servitude.

Miriam's "Song of Triumph"—

"Sing ye to the Lord, for he hath triumphed gloriously;
The horse and his rider hath he thrown into the sea."
(EXOD. xv. 21)

is probably the fragment of an ecstatic victory paean chanted by Miriam as she danced by the seashore. The influence of this verse—sung as it was for centuries in every household—on the religious conceptions of the Israelites may have been very great. Their God was very powerful, stronger far than all the gods of mighty Egypt. Joshua's prayer to the sun and moon (Josh. x. 12) may reveal some conception of the God of Israel as a ruler of nature. The Song of Deborah (Judges v) "was written without doubt under the inspiration of the actual events" (Strahan, *Peake's Commentary*: Judges). The Lord God of Israel had brought such unity in Israel that the leaders were followed by a willing people. He—the Lord—was the same before whom the mountains had quailed—even Sinai. And now once more He has come down amongst His people. They had chosen new gods and there was war in the gates. But the spoilers of the land were the enemies of its God, and so He will show forth His righteous acts in the governance of Israel. There was a great victory, and the song closes with a verse characteristic of much of the Old Testament literature:

"So let all Thine enemies perish, O Lord,
 But let them that love him be as the sun when he goeth forth in his might."

The fable of Jotham (Judges ix. 7–20) may perhaps indicate an anthropomorphic conception of God—"the wine which cheereth God and man." David's lament over Saul and Jonathan (2 Sam. i. 19–27) "is almost universally accepted as the work of David." There is scarcely anything in it, however, that gives a hint of the writer's views concerning God. The rite of circumcision is clearly mentioned, and there may be just a hint at God's power in nature in the lines:

"Ye mountains of Gilboa,
 Let there be no dew, neither let there be rain upon you, nor fields of offerings."

The reign of Solomon was a time of profound peace. There was a high level of culture and considerable literary activity. Old songs, legends and stories of great events in history had no doubt passed from lip to lip and from generation to generation. Now they were collected and written down. Most of these early redactions—for instance, the Book of Jasher and the Book of the Wars of Yahweh—are irretrievably lost, or exist only in the merest fragments. There remain, however, some parts of Joshua, Judges, 1 and 2 Samuel and 1 Kings, together with the primitive form of the Hexateuchal documents known as J and E respectively. We can with every confidence assume that the books, or parts of books, referred to above were produced perhaps as early as the reign of Solomon, and certainly not later than 750 B.C.

A STUDY IN CREATIVE HISTORY

The four Oracles of Balaam (Num. xxiii. 7–10, xviii. 18–24, xxiv. 3–9 and xxiv. 15–24) are possibly older than the J E narrative in which they are set. They must have been written after the establishment of the monarchy, "the shout of a king is among them" (xxiii. 21), and before the numbering of the people by David, "who hath ever numbered the fourth part of Israel" (xxiii. 10). The oracles are the war songs of a fighting and a conquering people:

> "Behold, the people shall rise up as a great lion,
> And as a young lion shall he lift himself up" (xxiii. 24).

and

> "He shall eat up the nations his enemies,
> And their bones shall he break in pieces" (xxiv. 8).

and

> "There shall come a Star out of Jacob,
> And a Sceptre shall rise out of Israel,
> And shall smite through the temples of Moab
> .   .   .   .   .   .
> And Israel shall do valiantly" (xxiv. 17–18).

God is represented as other than man. He does not lie, nor does He act in such a way that afterwards He needs to repent of His deeds. He has authority:

> "Hath he said, and shall he not do it?
> Or hath he spoken, and shall he not make it good?"
> (xxiii. 19).

God blesses and curses. In Israel, whom He has brought forth from Egypt, He beholds neither iniquity nor perverseness and so—

> "The Lord his God is with him" (xxiii. 21).

protecting, strengthening and blessing, and in consequence destroying His enemies before Him. It would be too much to say that God in these passages is merely the local God of Israel, but He is at any rate a very partial Being who actually

THE ISRAELITES

works with the people for the destruction or subjugation of hostile races.

We have so far studied fragments of verse which lived in some cases for many generations without ever being reduced to written form. Our next study is a narrative which is probably the oldest portion of the ancient Hebrew literature to be first written and then published—the Court History of David (2 Sam. ix-xx and 1 Kings i-ii), Driver says: "The abundance and particularity of detail show that the narrative must date from a period very little later than the events related" (*Introduction to the Literature of the Old Testament*, p. 183). The history deals exclusively with the Court life and the internal affairs of the kingdom. Other peoples are barely mentioned—and their gods not at all. Only by inference from such passages as:

"Be of good courage, and let us play the men for our people, and for the cities of our God" (2 Sam. x. 12).

and

"Thus saith the Lord God of Israel, I anointed thee king over Israel" (2 Sam. xii. 7).

and

"Wherefore then hast thou thought such a thing against the people of God?" (2 Sam. xiv. 13).

do we gain the idea that God was in a particular sense their God and not also the God of all nations. God is active in times of crisis. Joab exhorts his men to be of good courage, but when all is done the Lord will "do that which seemeth him good" (2 Sam. x. 12). During the rebellion of Absolom, at the most critical moment Ahitophel gives sound and excellent advice, which acted upon would have meant the certain ruin of David, but

"the Lord had appointed to defeat the good counsel of Ahitophel, to the intent that the Lord might being evil upon Absolom" (2 Sam. xvii. 14).

The final victory and the defeat of the pretender is the work of God:

"Then said Ahimaaz the son of Zadok, Let me now run, and bear the king tidings, how that the Lord hath avenged him of his enemies" (2 Sam. xviii. 19).

God is not only the Lord God of Israel, the Ruler of the nation and the Arbiter of its fate, but He is concerned with the actions of men as individuals:

"Wherefore hast thou despised the commandment of the Lord, to do evil in His sight? Thou hast killed Uriah the Hittite with the sword" (2 Sam. xii. 9).

Judgment is denounced against him, but David repents and makes confession of his sin. His accuser Nathan the prophet then speaks more comfortable words:

"The Lord also hath put away thy sin; thou shalt not die." "Howbeit ... the child ... shall surely die" (2 Sam. xii. 13-14).

Nathan's reference to the commandment of the Lord is of the greatest interest. There was evidently in the time of David a moral code which was regarded as the Law of God. Religion and morality were even at that early date identified one with the other, and he who would serve the God of Israel must be mindful of his conduct towards his fellowmen. In the passage "as the Lord liveth, that hath redeemed my soul out of distress" (1 Kings i. 29) we may have another reference to spiritual religion and the experience of a sinful man once more unified and happy as the result of a right relationship with God. There are two passages which may refer to a future life. After the death of Bathsheeba's child David says:

"But now he is dead, wherefore should I fast? can I bring him back again? I shall go to him, but he shall not return to me" (2 Sam. xii. 23).

THE ISRAELITES

The woman of Tekoah in her speech to the king says:

"For we must needs die, and are as water spilt on the ground, which cannot be gathered up again; neither doth God respect any person: yet doth he devise means, that his banished be not expelled from him" (2 Sam. xiv. 14).

Neither of these passages can be strained too far, but in both there seems to be a distinct hint of a life beyond the grave. David will go to where his son is, and God, although the life has been spilt like water on the ground, will devise means whereby the banished once more stand before Him. While there is mention of priests and Levites, of the Ark of the Covenant (2 Sam. xv. 24) and of the altar (1 Kings i. 50), the only definite reference to ritual is in the account of the coronation of Solomon. The ceremony was carried out by Zadok the priest in collaboration with Nathan the prophet—a personage evidently of great consideration in the kingdom. It is noteworthy that David and the other persons mentioned at the moment of their need cry out to God direct without help of priest and without ceremonial offerings. No doubt these all had their place, but ecclesiastical organization was rudimentary.

If we regard the Court History of David as the earliest piece of historical writing in the Old Testament, we can hardly fail to suppose that its production, probably in the long peace of Solomon's reign, gave a strong impulse to the reduction into literary form of the old stories of the Patriarchs, the Captivity, the Exodus and the Conquest that had passed orally from generation to generation. The result of this period of literary activity was to give us, at a time not later than 750 B.C., a large portion of the books known to us as Genesis, Exodus and Numbers; a small portion of Deuteronomy and the greater part of the books of Joshua, Judges and 1 and 2 Samuel. From these books we have already extracted those portions which seem on examination to be much older than the surrounding narratives.

At this stage it will be convenient to take the books in order, select the passages which in the main are clearly within our period, and deal with them along the lines of our preceding analyses.

(b) GENESIS

The book of Genesis is composed of three documents somewhat loosely woven together:

1. Document J, so called because God is designated as Yahweh—YHWH—or, as it is more commonly written in English, Jehovah. This document was produced in Judah (Peake).
2. Document E, so called because God is designated as Elohim. This document was produced in the Northern Kingdom before 750 B.C. (Peake).
3. Document P, or the Priestly Code, which is very much later and which does not at present concern us.

For our present purpose we shall consider J and E separately, and then sum up along the line of contrast and agreement.

I. DOCUMENT J

The author is unknown. The portions of Genesis as assigned to this writer by Driver (*Introduction to the Literature of the Old Testament*, pp. 5–21) are:

1. The Account of the Creation, Fall and Early Development of Man (ii. 4b–25; iii; iv).
2. The Flood, Resettlement and Babel (v. 29; vi. 1–8; vii. 1–4, 7–10, 12, 17b, 22–23; viii. 2b–3a, 6–12, 13c, 20–22; ix. 18–27; x. 8–19, 21, 25–30; xi. 1–9).
3. The Story of Abraham, Isaac and Jacob (xi. 28–30; xii. 1–4a, 6–20; xiii. 1–5, 7–18; xvi. 1–2, 4–14; xviii; xix. 1–28, 30–38; xxi. 1a–2b, 32b–33; xxii. 15–18, 20–24; xxiv; xxv. 1–6, 11, 18, 21–26a, 27–34; xxvi. 1–33; xxvii. 1–45; xxviii. 10, 13–16, 19; xxix. 2–14, 31–35; xxx. 9–16, 20b,

22, 24–43; xxxi. 1, 3, 46, 48–50; xxxii. 3–13a, 22, 24–32; xxxiii. 1–17; xxxiv. 2b–3, 5, 7, 11–12, 19, 25b–26, 30–31; xxxv. 14, 21–22; xxxvii. 12–18, 21, 25–28a, 31–35; xxxviii; xxxix; xlii. 38; xliii; xliv; xlvi. 29–34; xlvii. 1–4, 6c, 12–27a, 29–31; xlix. 1b–28; l. 1–11, 14).

(1) *The Account of the Creation, Fall and Early Development of Man*

In this section God is conceived as the creator of the heavens and of the earth. He makes a man from the dust of the earth and in like manner forms the beasts. He causes beautiful and pleasant trees to grow, and finally makes a woman to be the companion of the man. One thing only was forbidden—that they should eat of the Tree of Knowledge of Good and Evil. The forbidden fruit was plucked. Their eyes were opened and God—now that they had become "even as one of us"—drove them from the garden, fearing that they might eat of the Tree of Life also, and so live for ever. On the man was laid the curse of a hard struggle with the soil and on the woman a burden of suffering. In the end, too, they must die and return to the soil from which they had sprung. Yet even so God does not utterly leave them, although we infer that the old friendly intimacy was not renewed. Sacrifice is mentioned in the narrative of Cain and Abel. God rejects the fruit offering of Cain, but accepts the blood sacrifice of Abel. Cain murders his brother, and the Lord is shown as a righteous Judge tempering justice with mercy. Throughout this section there are elements of a distinctly anthropomorphic nature. God makes beasts and brings them to Adam to be named. He walks in the garden in the cool of the evening. He makes coats of skins and carries out conversations face to face. We must not, of course, press these passages too far. The narrative is poetic, and a certain amount of apparent anthropomorphism may have been introduced to give dramatic effect. The general tone is monotheistic. One sentence only "the man has become as one of us" (iii. 22) might be construed into an indication of polytheism. God is shown as the sole creator of the universe and of man. He is the Judge of all men, and lays down rules that none may break under pain of heavy penalty: "Therefore whosoever slayeth Cain, vengeance shall be taken on him sevenfold" (iv. 15).

2. *The Flood, Resettlement and Babel*

In this narrative we come in touch with history. The story is too deeply rooted in the folklore of many races to be wholly imaginary. Some considerable natural disturbance occurring in the neighbourhood of the centre from which many of the early races of mankind spread abroad impressed itself with great clearness on the oral tradition from which our history grew. God is shown at first relenting from the harshness with which He has visited fallen man. "My spirit shall not always strive with man, for that he also is flesh" (vi. 3). The wickedness of man, however, has become appalling—"every imagination of the thoughts of his heart was only evil continually" (vi. 5). At length God repented of having made man and proposed to destroy him. Noah, however, found grace—"for thee have I seen righteous before me in this generation" (vii. 1). He entered the ark and with the members of his family escaped destruction. When at length the floods subsided he built an altar and sacrificed. From the somewhat obscure passage that follows God seems to have regretted His action in so terribly destroying mankind, and to have determined that in the future He would not again "smite any more everything living" (viii. 21). In the story of the Tower of Babel there is again a hint of fear on the part of the Lord. He goes down to see the building and exclaims "now nothing will be restrained from them which they imagine to do" (xi. 6). To restrain and hinder men He introduces confusion of speech. In this section anthropomorphism is much more distinct than in the preceding one. God is represented as acting like a passionate man and then afterwards regretting the results of hasty action. In the Babel story He has a certain veiled fear of men and is apparently antagonistic to the carrying out of such works as would be calculated to make them too powerful. He is still, however, the God of all the earth, the Judge of all men, who saves alive or destroys as seems good to Him. No other is mentioned to compare with Him.

(3) *The Story of Abraham, Isaac and Jacob*

There is no reason to doubt that the accounts given of the life and wanderings of Abraham, Isaac and Jacob are in the main quite historical. The conception of God is high, except for occasional touches of anthropomorphism, as when in the visitation at Mamre He eats, and a little later determines to visit Sodom and Gomorrah to see "whether they have done altogether according to the cry of it" (xviii. 21). He is "the Lord, the God of Heaven and the God of the earth" (xxiv. 3). He is powerful in action—"Is anything too hard for the Lord?" (xviii. 14). He plagues Pharaoh (xii. 17) and destroys Sodom and Gomorrah (xix. 24–25). Sarah bears a child, though long past the age when that seemed a possibility. Men are called to do His will, and Abraham, in response to such a call, leaves home and kindred to adventure everything on the faithfulness of God. The Lord is "the Judge of all the earth" (xviii. 25) and in this capacity is associated with "justice" and "judgment" (xviii. 19). Angels attend Him and do His bidding (xviii). Men worship with bowed head (xxiv. 26) and with sacrificial offerings (xii. 8). Other gods are not mentioned. God blesses and curses, and the most remarkable idea running through the whole section is that of the potency and desirability of God's blessing. While it certainly seems to result in material prosperity—Jacob goes over the Jordan with his staff and returns at the head of two bands (xxxii. 10) —yet there is more in the blessing of God than this. We can best liken it, perhaps, to what nowadays might be called "a state of grace." The blessing is given either as the result of a direct visitation of God, or it is passed from father to son, or from brother to brother by the laying-on of hands. Jacob obtains the blessing by a mean subterfuge and Isaac is unable to recall it. At Padan-aram it is confirmed by God himself (xxviii). Esau, however, still remains the elder and more powerful of the two, while Jacob inherits nothing from his father except the blessing, the loss of which causes Esau to weep and to lament "with a great and exceeding bitter cry" (xxvii. 34). Later, on the return of Jacob, the brothers are reconciled. Esau consents, after some urging, to receive the blessing from his brother. No doubt in doing so the natural order of things was reversed, and he humbled himself exceedingly, but the blessing was so greatly to be desired that he was willing to do even this (xxxiii. 11). "The Lord said unto Abram... I will make of thee a great nation, and I will bless thee, and make thy name great; and thou shalt be a blessing: and I will bless them that bless thee, and curse him that curseth thee: and in thee shall all families of the earth be blessed" (xii. 1-3). Here we have one of the first hints in Hebrew literature of God as the Father of all nations. It is the dawn of an international idea.

II. Document E

This document contains no account of the Creation, the Fall, the Flood or the Resettlement of the earth. The author is unknown. The passages assigned to E by Driver (*Introduction to the Literature of the Old Testament*, pp. 5-21) are:

xv; xx. 1-17; xxi. 6-32; xxii. 1-14; xxviii. 11-12, 17-18, 20-22; xxix. 1, 15-23, 25-28, 30; xxx. 1-3, 6, 8, 17-20a, 21-22a, 23;

xxxi. 2, 4–45, 47, 51–55; xxxii. 2, 13–21, 23; xxxiii. 19–20; xxxv. 1–8, 15–20; xxxvii. 2c–11, 19–20, 22–24, 28c–36; xl; xli. 1–45, 47–57; xlii. 1–37; xlv; xlvi. 1–5; xlviii. 1–2, 8–22; l. 15–26.

They refer to the story of Abraham, Isaac and Jacob only. "E first appears in the history of Abraham (xv or xx)" (Driver: *Introduction to the Literature of the Old Testament*).

The traces of anthropomorphism are very slight. God never appears in the form of a man. While He repeatedly makes communications to men He appears "in a vision" (xv. 1): "God came to Abimelech in a dream by night" (xx. 3). While God is represented as the Judge of nations and the Shaper of history (xv. 13–21) there is a faint trace of polytheism—"Rachel had stolen the images that were her father's" (xxxi. 19). Apart from this one vague and indefinite reference God is consistently represented as the one Lord and Ruler of men. He heals (xx. 17). He is the Witness of oaths (xxi. 22). He overrules evil actions and brings good from them (xlv. 5). Joseph is definitely sent into Egypt "to preserve life" and "to save . . . lives by a great deliverance" (xlv. 5). God is all-powerful in His dealings with Abimelech, King of the Philistines, and with Pharaoh of Egypt, while His promise is sufficient to guarantee to Israel a great empire. He is served by sacrifice (xv. 9) and burnt offering. Men are able to approach Him in prayer (xx. 17). He is the Vindicator of a moral code, a breach of which is sin that will certainly be followed by retribution. Abimelech is to be struck dead for taking to himself the wife of another man. The wrong in this instance is directed not so much as we might suppose against Sarah herself or Abraham, but against God Himself. He demands the whole obedience of man, and tests Abraham by commanding him to sacrifice his son. In Jacob's Covenant (xxviii. 20–22) we have a definite bargain made with God. Jacob requires bread, raiment and safety. In return for these he will make the Lord his God, and he will offer a tenth of whatsoever he may become possessed. In the story of Rachel there is a hint, but no more, of a life beyond: "as her soul was in departing" (xxxv. 18).

Contrast and Agreement of J and E in Genesis

E is less anthropomorphic than J, but otherwise both documents agree in regarding God as the Supreme Ruler of the universe, the Judge of individual men and of nations. He is strong to initiate action, powerful to perform His promises or to execute His threats. God works throughout history, moving events toward His desired ends. He can be approached by men in prayer, and manifests Himself to individuals. In both documents men are sure of the Real Presence and of a living experience. There is a moral code, very indistinctly outlined, of which God is the Source and the Guardian. Throughout the whole of the J and E narratives in Genesis the material dealt with is practically non-national and is, indeed, the common possession of non-Israelitish peoples of Semitic race. The history and religion of the patriarchs have, it is true, a strong formative influence upon the development of Israel, but the patriarchs themselves are shown as being generally in harmonious touch with a somewhat cosmopolitan society of various nationalities. There is consequently an absence of any strong colouring of racial antipathy. The religion of Genesis is a high form of monotheism. Such a representation is only possible, dealing as it does with an age that was unquestionably polytheistic, because of the absence of conflict. Abimelech, Pharaoh and other persons mentioned were almost certainly worshippers of many gods, but as they were prepared to respect and worship Yahweh or Elohim, and even, perhaps, to identify Him with the chief god of their pantheon—the writers of J and E being interested only in the God of Abraham, Isaac and Jacob, who was to them the only true and universal Lord, fail to mention beliefs of an inferior nature.

(c) BOOK OF EXODUS

The Book of Exodus is similar in structure to Genesis. Selections from the narratives of J and E are again loosely interwoven and combined with the narrative of P.

I. Document J

The portions assigned by Driver (*Introduction to the Literature of the Old Testament*, pp. 22-42) are as follows:

i. 6, 8-12, 20b; ii. 15-23a; iii. 2-4a, 5, 7-8, 16-18; iv. 1-16, 19-20a, 22-26, 29-31; v. 3, 5-23; vi. 1; vii. 14-15a, 16-18(?), 20c-21a, 23-25; viii. 1-4, 8-15, 20-32; ix. 1-7, 13-21, 23b, 24b, 25b-34; x. 1-11, 13b, 14b-15a, 15c-19, 24-26, 28-29; xi. 4-8; xii. 21-27, 29-30; xiii. 3-16(?), 21-22; xiv. 5-7, 10a, 11-14, 19b-20, 21b, 24-25, 27c, 30-31; xv. 22-27; xvi. 4-5, 25-30; xvii. 1b-2, 7; xix. 3, 20-25; xxiv. 1-2, 9-11, 18b(?); xxxii. 25-34; xxxiii. 1-4, 12-23; xxxiv. 1-2.

The Book of Genesis dealt with the traditional history of the human race and with the lives of certain extremely important individuals. The whole book is a prologue to the national history of the Israelites which commences in the first chapter of Exodus. The individual ceases to be of primary importance. Even such a colossal and towering figure as that of Moses is of interest only in so far as he is the leader and inspirer of the nation which has now come into existence. Its religion, culture and even its self-consciousness are rudimentary, but nevertheless sufficient, taken into account with the misery of bondage, to place the Hebrew people in conflict with the rulers of Egypt. Their religious ideas were affected by their circumstances. The people in the wretchedness of their slavery turned anew to the God of the patriarchs. He became their own God—a possession which of all others they were the least disposed to share with the haughty oppressor. He is now "the Lord God of the Hebrews" (iii. 18), "there is none like unto the Lord our God" (viii. 10). God acts throughout on behalf of Israel and ruthlessly breaks all opposition. "Knowest thou not yet that Egypt is destroyed?" (x. 7). Pharaoh's servants ask their king after the plague of "mighty thunderings and hail." The vast destruction in Egypt stirs no pity in Yahweh. He is bent only on saving His own people. So the plagues ravage and the host of Egypt is destroyed in the Red Sea. Other gods are mentioned, and the Israelites are strictly warned lest "thou make a covenant with the inhabitants of the land, and they go a whoring after their gods, and do sacrifice unto their gods, and one call thee, and thou eat of his sacrifice; And thou take of their daughters unto thy sons, and their daughters go a whoring after their gods, and make thy sons go a whoring after their gods" (xxxiv. 15–16). The altars and images of other gods are to be destroyed and cut down. "For the Lord, whose name is Jealous, is a jealous God" (xxxiv. 14). Traces of anthropomorphism are very distinct. "I come unto thee in a thick cloud, that the people may hear when I speak unto thee" (xix. 9). "For the third day the Lord will come down in the sight of all the people" (xix. 11). After the descent of God on to the top of Sinai, Moses is commanded to "charge the people, lest they break through unto the Lord to gaze" (xix. 21). Moses and Aaron, with the elders of the people, "saw the God of Israel. . . . And upon the nobles of the children of Israel He laid not His hand: also they saw God, and did eat and drink" (xxiv. 10, 11). On another occasion the Lord said to Moses: "Thou shalt stand upon a rock: and it shall come to pass, while my glory passeth by . . . that thou shalt see my back parts" (xxxiii. 21–23). God is represented as being all-powerful in nature.

He sends plague after plague upon the Egyptians. The winds are controlled, and the strong East wind blowing all night makes the sea as dry land (xiv. 21). A pillar of cloud leads the march by day and at night changes to flaming fire to give them light (xiii. 21). Bitter waters are made sweet (xv. 25). In His relations with the Israelites God is revealed as "merciful and gracious, longsuffering, and abundant in goodness and truth, keeping mercy for thousands, forgiving iniquity and transgression and sin" (xxxiv. 6–7), and again as "visiting the iniquity of the fathers upon the children unto the third and fourth generation." Whatever comfortable words are admitted as belonging to our period apply only to Israel. There is a deepening sense of the isolation and peculiar position of the nation in so far as the presence of God is with them in so marked a fashion. If the Lord is really with them, "so shall we be separated, I and thy people, from all the people that are upon the face of the earth" (xxxiii. 16). Sin and the necessity of atonement are stressed. "Ye have sinned a great sin: and now I will go up unto the Lord; peradventure I shall make an atonement for your sin" (xxxii. 30). This is accounted for by the development of the moral code into a definite system and the association of moral ideas with God. While the J document does not actually give a text of the Ten Commandments, it is distinctly stated that Moses wrote upon the tables the words of the covenants, the Ten Commandments (xxxiv. 28). The observance of certain religious feasts—those of Unleavened Bread (xxxiv. 18) of Weeks, of the First Fruits of Wheat Harvest, of Ingathering (xxxiv. 22)—is made obligatory. Thrice a year all males had to appear before God (xxxiv. 33). Certain offerings are also prescribed. The ideas of God outlined are in the main those of a people already in settled occupation and engaged in agricultural and pastoral pursuits.

II. Document E

The portions assigned by Driver (*Introduction to the Literature of the Old Testament*, pp. 22-42) are as follows:

i. 15-20a, 21-22, ii. 1-14; iii. 1, 4b, 6, 9-15, 19-22; iv. 17-18. 20b-21, 27-28; v. 1-2, 4; vii. 15, 16-18(?), 20b; ix. 22-23a, 24a, 25a, 35a; x. 12-13a, 14a, 15b, 20-23, 27; xi. 1-3; xii. 21-27(?), 31-36, 42a; xiii. 3-16(?), 17-19; xiv. 10b, 19a; xv. 1-18, 20-21; xvii. 3-6, 8-16; xviii; xix. 2b, 14-17, 19; xx; xxi; xxii; xxiii; xxiv. 3-8, 12-14, 18b.

There are traces of anthropomorphism in this document. Moses is afraid "to look upon God" (iii. 6). Mount Sinai was altogether on a smoke because the Lord descended upon it in fire (xix. 18). He is a national God, Israel is His people—"thou mayest bring forth my people, the children of Israel, out of Egypt" (iii. 10). He is not known or reverenced by Pharaoh, "Who is the Lord that I should obey His voice . . .? I know not the Lord" (v. 2). He is mighty in His control of nature and sends dreadful plagues upon the Egyptians. When the horse and rider are thrown into the sea it is the Lord's doing (xv. 21). At His first command the rock is smitten and the people have water to drink (xvii. 6). The most important and interesting part of the E section of Exodus is contained in xx-xxiii, which contains the Decalogue and a considerable number of other laws. In all probability the base of this legislation was laid down by Moses during the wilderness period and expanded as need arose. The Decalogue itself (xx. 1-17) is most likely to be the original, somewhat enlarged—the following section (xx. 23-xxiii. 33) is either case law explanatory of the commandments or points not clearly covered by them, which became increasingly important as the people commenced to lead a settled agricultural life. The complete code would represent, no doubt, the legislation actually observed during the later period of Solomon's reign when the nation was free, safe and settled. The enormous importance of the code as a whole depends upon the identification of a lofty conception of God with personal and social morality. Religion is no longer a question of sacrifices only, but of a definite kind of life. The first four commandments (xx. 1-11), while not definitely declaring a theoretical monotheism, certainly establish a very practical one for the Israelites. God is exalted above all other gods and definitely shown as the creator of heaven and earth. The fifth commandment is designed to strengthen those family ties on which the strength of a nation must so largely depend. The five remaining ones tend to make sacred and inviolable the life and honour of the individual or to secure property. Slavery is clearly indicated in xxi. 2-11, and the regulations laid down tend to mitigate any intolerable severity toward such Hebrews as were reduced to a slave condition. A general principle of retributive justice is outlined: "life for life, eye for eye, tooth for tooth, hand for hand, burning for burning, stripe for stripe" (xxi. 23-25). Adequate penalties are provided for all breaches of the law and a suitable scale of damages to cover civil cases. Witches, and those convicted of horribly unnatural offences, were to be slain without mercy (xxii. 18, 19). The murderer (xxi. 12), the smiter of father or mother (xxi. 15), the man-stealer (xxi. 16) and the sacrificer to strange gods were all condemned to die (xxii. 20). The widow, the fatherless (xxii. 22), the stranger (xxiii. 9) and the poor (xxiii. 3, 6, 11) are under the care of God. Usury is strictly forbidden (xxii. 25). If all these laws are kept the blessing of God will follow. Other nations will be cut off and destroyed, but as for Israel "the Lord your God ... shall bless thy bread, and thy water; and I will take sickness away from the midst of thee. There shall nothing cast their young, nor be barren, in thy land: the number of thy days I will fullfil. I will send my fear before thee" (xxiii. 25-27).

CONTRAST AND AGREEMENT OF J AND E IN EXODUS

The documents are agreed in exalting God above all gods and making Him all-powerful in nature and history. Both exhibit traces of anthropomorphism and polytheism. Monolatry, at any rate, is urged upon Israel. With the rise of national consciousness God comes to be the possessor and the possession of Israel. He is the most powerful of all gods, perhaps the sole Creator of heaven and earth and man. He is all-powerful in history and sways the destinies of nations. Yet His only delight is in Israel. Despite the narrow nationalism of the setting, the narratives in Exodus in delineating the God of power as being also moral, and demanding a high moral standard from His servants, make an imperishable contribution to the stock of ideas which have made world history. The influence of the Ten Commandments on the development of mankind simply cannot be over-estimated.

(d) NUMBERS—DEUTERONOMY—JOSHUA

BOOK OF NUMBERS

The Book of Numbers does not show clear division between the J and E documents. They are closely combined—"as is often the case in J E the data do not exist for separating the sources employed with confidence" (Driver: *Introduction to the Literature of the Old Testament*, p. 62). The passages assigned to J E by Driver are:

x. 29–33, 35–36; xi; xii; xiii. 17b–20, 22–24, 26b–31, 32b–33; xiv. 3–4, 8–9, 11–25, 31–33, 39–45; xvi. 1b–2a, 12–15, 25–26, 27b–35; xx. 3a, 5, 14–21; xxi. 1–9, 12–35; xxii; xxiii; xxiv; xxv. 1–6; xxxii. 1–17; 20–27, 34–42 (pp. 60–69).

The conception of God in this book reaches almost the lowest level in the whole of the Old Testament. He is now altogether a national deity. His power is in no sense diminished, but the estimate of His character is affected by the changing fortunes of the people who for a considerable period were compelled to endure all the hardship, discomfort and danger inseparable from a long-continued trek across an inhospitable desert. Food was either short or greatly lacking in variety. Manna they came to loathe, and so "the mixt multitude . . . fell a lusting . . . and said, Who shall give us flesh to eat . . . our soul is dried away" (xi. 4-6). For this very natural murmuring the Lord was displeased. His anger was kindled, "and the fire of the Lord burnt among them, and consumed them that were in the uttermost parts of the camp" (xi. 1). Again, "while the flesh was yet between their teeth . . . the wrath of the Lord was kindled against the people, and the Lord smote the people with a very great plague" (xi. 33). There was a scarcity of water—"neither is there any water to drink" (xx. 5). "And the people spoke against God and against Moses, Wherefore have ye brought us up out of Egypt to die in the wilderness? for there is no bread, neither is there any water; and our soul loatheth this light bread" (xxi. 5). This murmuring again stirred the anger of the Lord, and the people were punished by a plague of poisonous serpents, by which means many of them perished (xxi. 6). At one time the Lord is represented as being so utterly provoked by the people that He proposes to destroy them altogether and to fulfil His covenant by bringing forth from Moses an even greater and mightier nation. Moses is hardly able to persuade Him from this determination by representing that such action would be regarded by the Egyptians as a confession of weakness, "Because the Lord was not able to bring this people into the land which he sware unto them, therefore he hath slain them in the wilderness" (xiv. 16). The argument is sufficient. God pardons the nation as such, but condemns all the adult males to die in the wilderness, "Your children shall wander in the wilderness forty years, and bear your whoredoms, until your carcases be wasted in the wilderness" (xiv. 33). Throughout the book the people are dissatisfied with their God, to whom they attribute their hardships, while God is angry and dissatisfied with His people for their murmurings and faintness of heart. God approves of the ruthless destruction of the southern Canaanites. When Og, King of Bashan, went out in battle array against them the Lord said unto Moses, "Fear him not . . . thou shalt do to him as thou didst unto Sihon king of the Amorites. . . . So they smote him, and his sons, and all his people until there was none left them alive" (xxi. 34–35). The low ideas concerning God are due to His complete appropriation by the Israelites as their God and to the further fact that the narrative records a period of national suffering.

Book of Deuteronomy

This book contains small sections only taken from the J E narratives. These are:

xxvii. 5–7; xxxi. 14a, 15; xxxi. 23; xxxiii; xxxiv. 1a; xxxiv. 1b–5a, 6, 10 (p. 72).

The general influence of J E on the completed book is very great. But this will be dealt with in a later section.

Joshua is called by God to succeed Moses, and receives a personal blessing (xxxi. 33). God is the God of Israel, "Happy art thou, O Israel: who is like unto thee, O people saved by the Lord, the shield of thy help, and who is the sword of thy excellency! and thy enemies shall be found liars unto thee; and thou shalt tread upon their high places" (xxxiii. 29).

Book of Joshua

This book is largely composed from the J E documents with notes and additions by D (the Deuteronomic writer) and P. The J E sections, according to Driver, are:

ii. 1–9, 12–24; iii. 1, 5, 10–17; iv. 1–11a, 14, 18, 20; v. 2–3, 8–9,

13-15; vi; vii. 2-26; viii. 1-29; ix. 3-9a, 11-15a, 16, 22-23, 26-27a; x. 1-7, 9-11, 12b-14a, 15-24, 26-27; xi. 1-9; xiii. 13; xiv. 6-15; xv. 14-19, 63; xvi. 1-3, 9-10; xvii. 1b-2, 5-6, 8, 9b, 10b-18; xviii. 2-6, 8-10; xix. 9, 47 (pp. 103-116).

God is powerful in nature and in history. He makes a dry crossing for the army to go over Jordan (iii. 16). The walls of Jericho fall flat (vi. 20). Great hailstones fall on the army of the Five Kings (x. 11). Later the very sun stands still in the heavens so that the rout may become a massacre (x. 13). Everywhere through His agency the Israelites are victorious, except in one case where the sin of Achan causes them to forfeit the Divine favour (vii). The conquered populations are for the most part ruthlessly exterminated at the command of God. "The Lord hath given you the city. And the city shall be accursed, even it, and all that are therein, to the Lord" (vi. 16-17). Joshua is commanded to do unto Ai and her king "as thou didst unto Jericho" (viii. 2). A league of kings with a mighty host were smitten at Merom. "And the Lord delivered them into the hand of Israel, who smote them . . . until they left them none remaining . . . And Joshua did unto them as the Lord bade him" (xi. 8-9). While God is "the living God" (iii. 10) and "the Lord of all the earth" (iii. 13). He is practically the God of Israel alone—and is absolutely merciless to their enemies.

(e) I AND II SAMUEL

1 and 2 Samuel (exclusive of Court History of David) is composed of:

1. A Document similar to the Hexateuchal J.
2. A Document similar to the Hexateuchal E.
3. A Document similar to the Hexateuchal E, but later.
4. Deuteronomic material, D.
5. Remarks added by a Post-Exilic Editor, R.

The J material is given by W. H. Bennett (*Peake's Commentary*: 1 and 2 Samuel) as:

1 Sam. ix; x. 1-16; xi; xiii. 1-7a, 15b-23; xiv; xvi. 14-23;

xviii. 6–16; xx; xxi; xxii; xxiii; xxv; xxvi; xxvii; xxviii; xxix; xxx; xxxi.

2 Sam. i. 1–5, 11–12, 17–27; ii; iii; iv; v. This is, of course, exclusive of the Court History which has already been dealt with.

There are traces of polytheism. Outside certain territorial limits it is apparently not possible to serve the God of Israel, "for they have driven me out this day from abiding in the inheritance of the Lord, saying, Go, serve other gods" (1 Sam. xxvi. 19). Within these bounds, however, He is the mighty leader and Saviour of Israel. Saul's most solemn oath is: "For, as the Lord liveth, which saveth Israel" (1 Sam. xiv. 39). At Gibeah in Benjamin "The Lord saved Israel that day" (1 Sam. xiv. 23). He gives counsel for the conduct of battle: "And when David enquired of the Lord, he said, Thou shalt not go up; but fetch a compass behind them . . . and let it be, when thou hearest the sound of a going in the tops of the mulberry trees, that then thou shalt bestir thyself: for then shall the Lord go out before thee, to smite the host of the Philistines" (2 Sam. v. 23–25). The theocracy is now definitely established under a form slightly different from that of the desert wanderings and the conquest. The rise of national self-consciousness and the decreased importance of tribal chiefs made possible a central governing executive vested in the person of a reigning king. Saul was selected for this office by God Himself. "Behold the man, this same shall rule over my people" (1 Sam. ix. 17). Samuel, the "man of God," anoints him, "The Lord hath anointed thee to be captain over his inheritance" (1 Sam. x. 1). There was apparently some resentment at this appointment, but this was quickly dispelled by the subsequent victory. There was a threat from Nahash the Ammonite. "The Spirit of God came upon Saul . . . and the fear of the Lord fell on the people" (1 Sam. xi. 6–7). A great deliverance was wrought, and the new king was firmly established. His office was regarded with reverence. Even when David was fleeing for his very life from before the face of Saul he refused to take advantage of a sudden turn of fortune to slay the king—"for who can stretch forth his hand against the Lord's anointed, and be guiltless?" (1 Sam. xxvi. 9). With the king there are also associated, as representatives of God, priests and prophets. The former are apparently mainly concerned with the ritual of worship and with divination. They have charge of the sacred symbols: "the ark of God" (1 Sam. xiv. 18), "the showbread" (1 Sam. xxi. 6) and "the ephod" (1 Sam. xxi. 9). The persons of the priesthood were sacred. Even at the command of Saul himself the soldiers refused to kill any of them. Only Doeg, an Edomite, could be prevailed upon to destroy them (1 Sam. xxii. 17–18). The prophets were less directly part of the ecclesiastical and political system. God frequently spoke through them. When prayer was made by the king, as representative of the people, a reply might be made in three ways, by vision, on the Urim (an oracular response) or through the prophets (1 Sam. xxviii. 6). God is concerned not only with the nation as a whole, but with the individual. One such as Nabal He destroys (1 Sam. xxv. 38). His anger slays Uzzah for presuming to touch the sacred Ark (2 Sam. vi. 7). He troubles Saul with an evil spirit (1 Sam. xvi. 14). We read that Jonathan "wrought with God this day" (1 Sam. xiv. 45). He cuts off the enemies of David, blesses him and appoints him a sure house (1 Sam. xxv. 28). There are definite references to low forms of spiritism. Although by his own orders witches were condemned to death, we find Saul in an hour of extremity visiting the witch of Endor. This incident also shows that there was some sort of belief in a continued existence after death. Samuel is not only conscious and able to give a reply —and that a terrible one—but his message is still, as aforetime, from God. Moreover, he asserts that after the battle Saul and his sons shall be with him (1 Sam. xxviii. 3–20).

A STUDY IN CREATIVE HISTORY

The E material is given by the same authority as:

1 Sam. iv. 1b–22; v; vi; vii. 1; xvii; xviii. 1–5, 17–19; xix. 1–17; xxiv.
2 Sam. i. 6–10, 13–16.

The Lord of Hosts is the very mighty God of Israel. Calamity is regarded as His judgment (1 Sam. iv. 3). Victory is His salvation (1 Sam. xix. 5). He is recognized and feared even by the Philistines. . . . "God is come into the camp. . . . Woe unto us! who shall deliver us out of the hand of these mighty gods? . . . that smote the Egyptians" (1 Sam. iv. 7–9). Even after their victory they were terrified at the strange plagues that fell upon them, apparently as the result of their possession of the sacred Ark. "The Ark of the God of Israel shall not abide with us: for his hand is sore upon us, and upon Dagon our God" (1 Sam. v. 7). Hebrew and Philistine alike evidently regarded the Ark as being in some sort a "Real Presence." While it was held by strangers the God of Israel was in some measure a captive. The Philistines found Him, however, too terrible a One to hold, and the Ark was in consequence sent back with rich presents to propitiate His wrath. Powerful as they recognized the God of Israel to be—more powerful than their own gods—there could be no possibility of their turning to Him. He belonged to the Hebrews by history, covenant and the whole nature of things. The Philistines were plainly polytheists—Goliath "cursed David by his gods" (1 Sam. xvii. 43). There are slight traces of this amongst the Israelites also. Michal saves David by placing an "image" in the bed (1 Sam. xix. 13). God is conceived as being very merciless. Not only are the Philistines destroyed, but on the return of the Ark the men of Bathshemesh met it with joy and offered burnt offerings, but because "they had looked into the ark . . . the Lord, even he smote of the people fifty thousand and three score and ten men" (1 Sam. vi. 19).

THE ISRAELITES

While no account is given of the establishment of the monarchy the person of the king is regarded as sacred. When David in the cave of En-gedi has Saul at his mercy he refuses to use his advantage—"The Lord forbid that I should do this thing unto my master, the Lord's anointed, to stretch forth my hand against . . . the anointed of the Lord" (1 Sam. xxiv. 6). Saul's madness is attributed to an evil spirit from the Lord (1 Sam. xix. 9).

The E_2 passages are given as:

1 Sam. i; ii. 11–16; iii; iv. 1a; xiii. 7b–15a?; xv; xvi. 1–13(?); xviii. 10–11; xix. 18–24(?); xxi. 10–15.

There are traces of anthropomorphism. God calls Samuel with a human voice (1 Sam. iii. 4–5). After Saul has been anointed king and well established he is ordered to—"Go, and utterly destroy the sinners the Amalekites" (1 Sam. xv. 18). This command is only partially obeyed, for Agag, the Amalekite king, is saved alive. This "rebellion" and "stubbornness" so stirs the anger of God that Saul is rejected "and the Lord repented that he had made Saul king over Israel" (1 Sam. i. 35). The interest of E_2 is in the accounts given of the experience of individuals with God. Hannah pours out her soul in silent prayer before God in the sanctuary at Shiloh. Eli blesses her and prays for her, but knows nothing of the nature of her prayer. Later the Lord remembered her (1 Sam. i. 9–19). Samuel is represented as being continually in close communion with God, who makes constant revelations to him from the time he was a little lad serving in the Temple until as a very old man he executed his last commission and anointed David as the future king. When David had been anointed "the Spirit of the Lord came upon David from that time forward" (1 Sam. xvi. 13). Shiloh was evidently the established centre of the national religion. The Temple had been established in that place, and in it was the Ark of the Covenant in the custody of priests who were evidently maintained by tithes levied on sacrificial offerings. The sons of Eli were evil men who greatly abused their privileges (1 Sam. ii. 12–16). The Ark being the dwelling-place of God, devout families such as that of Elkanah were in the habit of making pilgrimage to Shiloh once yearly—"to worship and to sacrifice unto the Lord of Hosts" (1 Sam. i. 3). Sacrifices were offered in many places, and prayers made, but nowhere would the worshippers feel themselves so near to the God of Abraham, Isaac and Jacob as at Shiloh. The priests, besides carrying out in a proper fashion the ceremonial of sacrifice and the ritual of worship, no doubt enquired of God and gave oracular responses. If 1 Samuel xix. 18–24 actually forms part of the E_2 Document, we have a most interesting account of an outburst of ecstatic religion presided over by Samuel himself. This orgy was no doubt similar to those conducted in our own times by members of the Pentecostal Church and similar bodies. Whether or not these orgies were primitive remnants in Israel or had been introduced by contact with the peoples of Palestine, it is impossible to say. While there is evidently a developed ritual, religion is represented as being primarily a matter of obedience to God. "And Samuel said, Hath the Lord as great delight in burnt offerings and sacrifices, as in obeying the voice of the Lord?" (1 Sam. xv. 22.)

Contrast and Agreement of J, E and E_2 in I and II Samuel

There is general agreement between the three documents. The prevailing polytheism of the Palestinian peoples is more clearly shown than in any passages previously considered. God is the Divine Ruler of Israel, who blesses them and leads them to victory against all their enemies. He is quite ruthless to other peoples and is in no sense the Father of all men. Even His own people suffer very terribly if they are in any way disobedient, or even if they show insufficient regard for ceremonial obligations. There is much of the power of God—very little of the love of God. Religious organization has proceeded to a considerable extent, and there is an established centre of worship with a regular priesthood. Prophets are also mentioned. The monarchy, the establishment of which is described, is assigned to God. Religion has become not only the national worship of a national God, but individuals are able to approach Him directly and to experience His Presence and blessing. No definite moral codes are indicated. Traces of witchcraft and low forms of spiritism are observable.

(f) AMOS

Amos, an herdman and fruit-gatherer of Tekoa, felt the call of God, and leaving his flock went into the kingdom of Israel and there prophesied (i. 1 and vii. 15). It was a time of great victory. Jeroboam II was a powerful and able ruler "who restored the coast of Israel." His reign was a long one, and for the greater part of it the general security of the country induced an era of great prosperity. The mass of the people were agriculturists—hardy peasants able both to dig and to fight. Over them and living on their labour would be some sort of feudal aristocracy such as is almost inevitable in a country whose very existence depends upon its power to quickly and vigorously take the field. Close proximity to the Phoenician and Syrian peoples brought strong outside religious and cultural influences to bear upon Israel. The constantly repeated references in Kings to idolatrous practices of one sort or another show how effective these influences were in undermining the old established worship of Yahweh. There was then abundant prosperity and power on the one hand, and on the other materialism, idolatry and oppression.

Amos preached publicly for some period—the length of which we do not know. At a time probably subsequent to his public mission he placed the gist of his teaching in written form. The document has been edited to some extent, and the following sections iv. 13, v. 8-9, ix. 5-6, and the comfortable words which close the book in its present form, were probably added by some later hand. With the exception of these verses, however, there is little question that the remainder was actually written practically as it stands by the prophet himself. The main features of his teaching are:

1. A passionate conviction of the power, might and majesty of God—the Ruler of nature and the Judge of nations. God causes it to rain upon one city and not upon another (iv. 7). He smites with blasting and mildew (iv. 9). He overthrows Sodom and Gomorrah (iv. 11). God has power over all nations. The terrible "Thus saith the Lord" is addressed to all peoples of whose prevailing conditions Amos could possess accurate knowledge: Syria (i. 3-5), Philistia (i. 6-8), Moab (ii. 1-3), Tyre (i. 9-10), Edom (i. 11), Ammon (i. 13-15), as well as Judah (ii. 4-5) and Israel (ii. 6 *et seq.*). God is no longer the God of the Hebrews only—He is the God of all nations. The scornful reference to Moloch and Chiun "your images the star of your god, which ye made to yourselves" (v. 26) may possibly admit the existence of other gods, but even if this be so "Yahweh" is supreme over all.

2. A proclamation of a moral law which is the law of God —"the Law of the Lord and . . . his commandments" (ii. 4).

3. An impatience with ritual divorced from morality: "I hate, I despise your feast days. . . . Though ye offer me burnt offerings . . . I will not accept them. . . . Take thou away from me the noise of thy songs" (v. 21-23).

4. Fiery denunciation of breaches of the moral law accompanied by threats of terrible judgment. There is strong condemnation of the sins of the flesh—unnatural relationships (ii. 7) and drunkenness (ii. 12 and vi. 6). Judgment is pronounced against Edom "because he did pursue his brother with the sword, and did cast off all pity, and his anger did tear perpetually" (i. 11), and against the barbarous atrocities of Ammon (i. 13). The prevailing idolatry, though indicated, is not stressed (ii. 8 and v. 26). The wrath of God will fall because of the unsocial conduct of the strong. They have introduced false weights (viii. 5), afflicted the just (v. 2), accepted bribes and turned "judgments into wormwood" (v. 7). By violence they stored up spoil in the palaces (iii. 10). They sold the righteous for silver and the poor for a pair of shoes. They panted after the very dust of the earth on the head of a poor man (ii. 6–7).

5. An appeal for righteousness: "but let judgment run down as waters, and righteousness as a mighty stream" (v. 24).

The official Church, even if not hopelessly corrupt and idolatrous, had evidently become a mere department of State. The ritual observances of religion were carried out with something approaching to enthusiasm, but real observance of the moral law which lay behind all forms and symbols had vanished. There was no doubt a splendid ceremonial, but righteousness as a living thing had disappeared. A military and priestly aristocracy lived on the very life's blood of the poor. Into this corrupt and rotten society came the herdman of Tekoa—no professional prophet, but a plain, poor man to whom God had spoken. He condemned the rich and powerful and pronounced terrible judgments on merciless and violent men. God was not with the violent and the strong, He was with the poor man and the meek. Let the oppressors of the needy tremble, for God said: "I will turn your feasts into mourning, and all your songs into lamentation ... and the end thereof as a bitter day" (viii. 10). The social gospel of Amos must have caused something like a revolution. "The land is not able to bear all his words," complained Amaziah, priest of Bethel. In his conception of God there is little of love or tenderness, except in so far as we may infer that the stern and terrible Judge had pity for the sufferings of the poor. Men must be righteous or they would bring upon themselves terrible judgments. There is scarcely a word to indicate a personal relationship between the individual and God. Amos deals with the sins of society as they are displayed in the wrong-doings of social classes. In world history he holds a unique position as the first working man to champion the poor against the rich and to question the structure of society in which the fruits of the common labour are exploited by the strong and violent, the greedy and cunning.

(g) HOSEA

Hosea was contemporary with Amos, but from the list of monarchs in i. 1 probably flourished a few years later. The same general conditions prevailed. "There is no truth, nor mercy, nor knowledge of God in the land. By swearing, and lying, and killing, and stealing, and committing adultery, they break out and blood toucheth blood" (iv. 1-2). "And as troops of robbers wait for a man, so the company of priests murder in the way by consent: for they commit lewdness" (vi. 9). "Ephraim is joined to idols" (iv. 17). "O Israel ... thou hast gone a whoring from thy God" (ix. 1).

The prophet faced with so fearful a breakdown of all true religion and sound morality could at first see no escape from the judgment of God. "My God will cast them away, because they did not hearken to him: and they shall be wanderers among the nations" (ix. 17). "The Assyrian shall be his king . . . and the sword shall abide on his cities" (xi. 5-6). God will "be unto Ephraim as a moth, and to the house of Judah as a rottenness" (v. 12). But in the happenings of his own life he saw how God must feel for his people Israel. Hosea's wife was unfaithful to him. She deserted him for wealthy lovers, but in the end fell into misery and was sold into slavery. Though she had wrecked his home and broken his heart, Hosea loved her through it all, redeemed her, took her back, and in the end love prevailed and she sang again as in the days of her youth. In some such way can we reconstruct the moving story that lies half revealed and half concealed in the first three chapters. And now the prophet had in his own experience the key to God's dealing with His erring people. Sin inevitably brought misery and judgment. God was pleading for "mercy and judgment" (xii. 6), for "mercy and not sacrifice" (vi. 6), speaking to His people "in multiplied visions" and "similitudes" and "by the ministry of the prophets" (xi. 10). If they were deaf to His voice disaster must needs come, but through the disaster and beyond it God would never cease to care for His people. For their ultimate good He may in the day of luxury and pride humble and chasten them by the removal of His good gifts, but when adversity has come He will speak "comfortably," and in that day "I will break the bow and the sword and the battle out of the earth . . . and I will betroth thee unto me for ever; yea, I will betroth thee unto me in righteousness, and in judgment, and in lovingkindness, and mercies" (ii. 18-19).

Hosea has no message for the individual. He is concerned with the nation as a whole. There is no conception of God as the Father of all nations, but to His own people, if they will abandon their fearful sins, He will be most gracious, very near and intimate and—"I will say to them. . . . Thou art my people; and they shall say, Thou art my God" (ii. 23).

(h) MICAH

Micah wrote in the reigns of Jotham, Ahaz and Ahaziah, Kings of Judah, that is to say between the years 740 B.C.-693 B.C. Chapters i–iii, except for ii. 11–12, are the "undoubted work of the prophet" (H. Wheeler Robinson, *Peake's Commentary*: Micah). Chapters v. 10–15, vi. 1–16, vii. 1–6, although not certainly the work of Micah, are similar in tone and probably very little if any later than the earlier portions. God is represented from the outset as being of mighty power, the great Lord of Nature, before whom the mountains are molten, and "the valleys cleft as wax before the fire" (i. 4–5). He comes from His Holy Temple—His own place, because of the prevailing wickedness. His Spirit comes upon Micah (iii. 8), who becomes thereby "full of power . . . and of judgment, and of might, to declare unto Jacob his transgression, and to Israel his sin" (iii. 8). Micah is apparently a man of no particular account, a dweller in an unimportant country town to whom the word of God has come because the apostasy and lying of the regular prophets make it impossible for them to have "visions." They "make my people to err . . . and he that putteth not into their mouths, they even prepare war against him" (iii. 5). There is hot condemnation of prevailing idolatry—"all the graven images thereof shall be beaten to pieces . . . and all the idols thereof will I lay desolate" (i. 7). "Thy graven images also will I cut off . . . and thou shalt no longer worship the works of thine hands" (v. 13). Hand in hand with the idol worship there has been an outbreak of degrading spiritism: "And I will cut off witchcrafts out of thy hand; and thou shalt have no more soothsayers" (v. 12). Drunkenness may have become a serious evil in the national life, for if a lying prophet should prophesy "of wine and strong drink," his popularity is assured. Above all, however, Micah is the champion of the poor and thunders against their violent oppressors: the "heads of Jacob," the "princes of the house of Israel" (iii. 1); the "rich men who are full of violence" (vi. 12); the judges who ask for "reward" (vii. 3). A terrible picture it is that he draws of social wrong and injustice. Evil men "covet fields and take them by violence" (ii. 2). Women of the people are cast out from their pleasant homes (ii. 9). There is the robbery of the merchant in the market, his "scant measure," "wicked balances" and "bag of deceitful weights" (vi. 10–11). To such a pass have things come that "the good man is perished out of the earth: and there is none upright among men: they all lie in wait for blood; they hunt every man his brother with a net" (vii. 2). All this is abomination in the sight of God, and only fearful judgment can be the result. Samaria will become "as an heap of the field" (i. 6). Evil must come down "from the Lord unto Jerusalem" (i. 6). For God is righteous. He hides His face from the cry of them who, hating good and loving evil, have destroyed their brethren (iii. 2–4). There has apparently been no lack of ceremonial religion. In an imaginary conversation between God and the nation there is mention of burnt offerings, of yearling calves, of thousands of rams, of ten thousand rivers of oil—even of the sacrifice of a man's first-born for the sin of his soul (vi. 6–7). Will not all these things be pleasing to God? The reply comes in one of the greatest verses of religious literature. "He hath shewed thee, O man, what is good; and what doth the Lord require of thee, but to do justly, and to love mercy, and to walk humbly with thy God?" (vi. 8). The word as it came to Micah was a stern word spoken to the men of an evil generation. He did not see, as Hosea saw, the redeeming love of God following His people through all their sin and misery, but he did see God as righteous and moral—a God who stood for the poor and the oppressed and against the violent, greedy and proud.

A STUDY IN CREATIVE HISTORY

(i) I ISAIAH

Isaiah apparently prophesied in Judah from the year of Uzziah's death, 740 B.C., to a period possibly subsequent to 701 B.C., the year of Sennacherib's invasion. The first thirty-nine chapters only of the book which bears his name can be assigned to him, and in all probability the following passages must be regarded as additions by other hands:

xi. 10–16; xii; xiii; xiv. 1–23; xv; xvi; xxi. 1–17; xxiii; xxiv; xxv; xxvi; xxvii; xxxiii; xxxiv; xxxv (A. S. Peake, *Peake's Commentary*: Isaiah).

The prophet was a man of the highest culture, and was for lengthy periods, at any rate, the counsellor of kings and reckoned amongst the great and influential of the land. While there is little that is new or original in his message as compared with his predecessors Amos, Hosea and Micah, his social passion is none the less. The burden of his prophecy is uttered with great power, sublimity and beauty of expression.

God is Holy—the Holy One of Israel. In the hour of his vision Isaiah sees the Lord of Hosts "high and lifted up." He has all the retinue and trappings of a temporal king. The temple was shaken and the whole house was full of smoke. The Seraphim proclaimed His glory that filled the whole earth. Yet all these things are the non-essentials. The prophet sees this Mighty One, not as a potentate so much, not as a manifestation of material force or even as a mysteriously untouchable One, but as a vision of absolute purity and righteousness. Before such a One his feelings are not primarily those of wonder or fear, but of a profound sense of sin. He is a man of unclean lips. His iniquity is heavy upon him. He is undone. And yet not so! The presence of the Living Passion of Goodness burns into his very being and purifies him. His iniquity is purged, and through him the message of the Lord of Hosts—the Holy! Holy! Holy!—can be spoken to the nations. So far it is the greatest proclamation in history of the righteousness of God.

Because God is so utterly righteous He is the Judge of men and nations. The prophecy is largely one of the judgment of God. Sin everywhere abounds. There is evidently much ritual observance and costly ceremonial. The people drew near to God with their mouth (xxix. 13) and honoured Him with their lips. There is a multitude of sacrifices, vain oblations, solemn meetings, feasts of the new moon and of the Sabbath (i. 11-14). And yet underneath all outward appearance there was the most frightful corruption, the most unrestrained wickedness. Men made for themselves idols of gold and idols of silver (ii. 20). The land was full of them (ii. 7). Material prosperity swelled men's hearts with pride and vain glory. Strange superstitions, mystery religions from the East, had crept in, and the house of Jacob had become soothsayers even as the Philistines (ii. 6). Men rose up early and continued until night—inflamed with strong drink (v. 11). The drunkards of Ephraim were a byword (xxviii. 1). The daughters of Zion were wanton (iii. 16). The luxury and pride of the rich is made possible only by the oppression and degradation of the poor. The princes rebelling from the law of God have become the companions of thieves. Their thirst for wealth makes them open to bribery, and as a result the cause of the fatherless and the widow comes not to them (i. 23). Once the Holy City was full of righteousness and judgment, but now of murderers (i. 23). The princes eat up the vineyards. The spoil of the poor is in their houses. They beat the people to pieces and grind the faces of the poor (iii. 14-15). They join house to house and field to field (v. 8). Against all this sum of wickedness Isaiah denounces the wrath and judgment of God. "They that forsake the Lord shall be consumed." Men shall be slain by the sword in war (iii. 25).

Again and again comes the terrible Woe! Woe! of denunciation. "Woe unto them that call evil good, and good evil" (v. 20). "Woe unto them that draw iniquity with cords of vanity, and sin as it were with a cart rope" (v. 18). "Woe to them that go down to Egypt for help" (xxxi. 1). "Woe to the rebellious children" (xxx. 1). "Woe to Ariel, to Ariel, the city where David dwelt" (xxix. 1). And so the prophet goes on with the recital of the terrible judgment of the wrath of the Holy God falling on the sinful peoples. For it is not only Israel and Judah with whom the Lord of Hosts has a controversy but also Damascus (xvii), Ethiopia (xviii), and Egypt (xix). God is represented as having power over all these nations and as working out His mighty purpose through and by them as He pleases. While Israel may still be in a sense His peculiar people, He is the God of all nations, as powerful with one as with another.

But Isaiah does not stop with denouncing the wickedness of the times, and prophesying of just and terrible punishment. He can see beyond punishment to redemption. Though the sins of the people be as scarlet they shall be white as snow (i. 18). The mountain of the Lord's house shall be established in the top of the mountains, and many people shall go and say: "Come ye, and let us go up to the mountain of the Lord . . . and he will teach us of his ways" (ii. 2-3). "When the Lord shall have washed away the filth of the daughters of Zion . . . by the spirit of judgment, and by the spirit of burning" (iv. 4). "The covenant with death shall be disannulled" (xxviii. 18).

How is the transformation to be worked? Perhaps the prophet means that his own vision is to be regarded as a parable of the cleansing of the nation. In some profound experience of God—"the spirit poured upon us from on high" (xxxii. 15)—the nation will be purified. Three times, however, occur great passages in which he looks forward to the coming of a great king—a rod out of the stem of Jesse on whom the spirit of the Lord shall rest (xi. 1-2). Usually the prophet in his dreams of the great age for which he hoped probably did not go farther than picturing a ruler such as David, only even more after God's heart. But on one occasion, at least, he went far beyond. Agonizing over the tragedy of the present, profoundly conscious of the reality and holiness of God, comprehending something of His nature, and in that comprehension finding grounds for a passionate hope, Isaiah, in a great moment of exalted vision, wrote words which were to be as a beacon light to the race: "For unto us a child is born, unto us a son is given: and the government shall be upon his shoulder: and his name shall be called Wonderful, Counsellor, the Mighty God, the Everlasting Father, the Prince of Peace. Of the increase of his government and peace there shall be no end, upon the throne of David, and upon his kingdom, to order it, and to establish it with judgment and with justice from henceforth even for ever" (ix. 6-7).

Isaiah drew a definite picture of an ideal future for Israel and, indeed, for all the nations of the earth. In various ways sinners will be destroyed by the action of God. The way being thus prepared, Zion will become the centre of the world. God's house being established there on the mountains, "All nations shall flow into it" (ii. 2). Of their own desire they will come to learn the law. In the good society thus established there will be social righteousness: "With righteousness shall he judge the poor, and reprove with equity for the meek of the earth" (xi. 4). The very beasts even will lie down together, and a "little child shall lead them" (xi. 6). For: "They shall not hurt nor destroy in all my holy mountain: for the earth shall be full of the knowledge of the Lord, as the waters cover the sea" (xi. 9). In those great days—"they shall beat their swords into plough-shares, and their spears into pruninghooks: nation shall not lift up sword against nation, neither shall they learn war any more" (ii. 4). Through all the ages men had fought with hate and fury. The earth had been dyed with unavailing slaughter. Men appealed to all their gods to strengthen their hands to fight. Isaiah was the first great seer to proclaim that war was not inevitable and that in the Kingdom of God—universal and Holy—there could be no place for the hideous curse of the ages. A time was coming when there would be no more war. International peace would prevail. "In that day there shall be a highway out of Egypt to Assyria, and the Assyrian shall come into Egypt, and the Egyptian into Assyria, and the Egyptians shall serve with the Assyrians. In that day shall Israel be the third with Egypt and with Assyria, even a blessing in the midst of the land: whom the Lord of Hosts shall bless, saying, Blessed be Egypt my people, and Assyria the work of my hands, and Israel mine inheritance" (xix. 23–25). Such, then, is Isaiah's vision of the good time coming when "The meek also shall increase their joy in the Lord, and the poor among men shall rejoice in the Holy One of Israel" (xxix. 19).

(j) DEUTERONOMY

The Book of Deuteronomy is usually identified with the book of the Law discovered in the Temple during the eighteenth year of King Josiah (621 B.C.). How much earlier it was actually produced cannot be stated with any definiteness. Critics vary in assigning it to a date falling between the last years of Hezekiah and some time in the period of the heathen reaction in the reign of Mannasseh. Internal evidence makes it abundantly clear that Mosaic authorship is impossible, and, indeed, that the major portion of the book as it stands could not have been written so very many years before the date at which it became an effective influence in the life of the people. "The main part of the book is pervaded throughout by a single purpose and bears the marks of being the work of a single writer" (*Introduction to the Literature of the Old Testament*, p. 71, Driver). The following portions only need be assigned to a later date than 621 B.C. (*Introduction to the Literature of the Old Testament*, Driver):

i. 2; xxxii. 48-52; xxxiv. 1a, 5b, 7-9.

There is nothing more natural than to suppose that Moses actually did make certain discourses of an exhortatory and valedictory nature. The traditional account of these addresses would be passed down through the generations. To the reformer of, say, the period of Mannesseh, surrounded on all sides by the influences and even the visible signs of pagan idolatry, the breakdown of the national faith, social injustice and personal immorality, the natural desire would be to direct the attention of the backsliding people to the great days of old and to the giant figure of the mighty lawgiver, the hero of every generation. Taking, then, the existing legendary account of a great Mosaic discourse, the writer of Deuteronomy used it as the framework of an appeal for national revival. The speeches are attributed to the lawgiver himself. In the main, no doubt, they are what the writer thought Moses either actually did say or would have said under the circumstances of the day.

Throughout the book there are many references to God of a distinctly anthropomorphic nature. Little attention need be paid to these, however, as they are probably merely incidental to the historical setting. The need of the age is a tremendous proclamation of the fact of God—and so He is proclaimed with all the intensity of conviction. Throughout the history of the nation God has been their helper and preserver. "The Lord your God . . . he shall fight for you, according to all that he did for you in Egypt before your eyes; and in the wilderness, where thou hast seen how that the Lord thy God bare thee as a man doth bear his son in all the way that ye went" (i. 30–31). God is all-powerful. He disposes of the destinies of nations. Israel is bidden to spare the children of Esau, the Moabites and the Ammonites, but the Amorites are to be utterly destroyed (ii). "This day will I begin to put the dread of thee and the fear of thee upon all nations that are under the whole heaven" (ii. 25). God is jealous. There are fearful condemnations of idolatry. Should any incite to "serve other gods . . . thou shalt not consent unto him, or hearken unto him, neither shalt thine eye pity him, neither shalt thou spare . . . thou shalt surely kill him . . . and thou shalt stone him with stones that he die." No tie of kinship or of friendship is to prevent the rooting out of the idolatrous persons. The altars, the pillars, the groves, the graven images are to be utterly destroyed. "Ye shall destroy the names of them out of that place" (xii. 3). The idolatrous nations themselves are to be exterminated. "The Lord thy God shall deliver them unto thee, and shall destroy them with a mighty destruction . . . and thou shalt destroy their name from under heaven" (vii. 23–24). The sternness of God, His anger against the worship of other gods, is explained by the conception of Him as being essentially moral and the author of the moral law. The Decalogue is repeated. The preamble is concerned with the relationships of men one to another. Yet the connection is plain. The great and mighty God, Ruler of all men and nations, is vitally concerned, not only that men should love, honour and obey Him, but that they should treat one another with justice and righteousness. Israel is a peculiar people. Yet they have not been chosen because of their righteousness, but rather as a scourge to drive forth other peoples whose idolatry has stirred the wrath of God. The international outlook is indeed terrible. With the exception of an admonition to love the stranger—"for ye were strangers in the land of Egypt" (x. 19)—there is little but the wrath of God upon all the surrounding nations. No doubt, from the viewpoint of the writer, these peoples were so idolatrous as to be beyond the pale of God's mercy. Even with Israel the case was desperate enough. The whole book is an almost ceaseless "choose ye"—God or the idols. If Israel choose to "fear the Lord thy God, to walk in all his ways, and to love him, and to serve the Lord thy God with all thy heart and with all thy soul" (x. 12), then there would follow blessing upon blessing: blessing of material prosperity, blessings of children, victory in war; the fear of all nations and world supremacy (xxviii. 1-11). "The Lord shall open unto thee his good treasure, the heaven to give the rain unto thy land in his season, and to bless all the work of thy hand and thou shalt lend unto many nations, and thou shalt not borrow. And the Lord shalt make thee the head, and not the tail" (xxviii. 12-13). But if the choice went against God—"the Lord of Lords, a great God, a mighty and a terrible" (x. 17)—the result would be curse on curse through all the possible gamut of human misery until—"The tender and delicate woman among you . . . her eye shall be evil . . . toward the children which she shall bear: for she shall eat them for want of all things secretly in the siege and straitness, wherewith thine enemy shall distress thee in thy gates" (xxviii. 56-57). If Israel chose once more the God of their fathers, worship was to be centralized. "In the place which the Lord shall choose in one of thy tribes, there shalt thou offer thy burnt offerings" (xii. 14). The Levites were to be a special priestly class without any special inheritance in the land. "The Lord is their inheritance" (xviii. 2) Their living was to consist in tithes of the Temple offerings.

(k) NAHUM

The prophecy of Nahum could not have been written later than the year 607 B.C. Before this time the kingdom of Israel had been swept away. Wave after wave of Assyrian invasion had swept down upon the southern kingdom, which was now become but a shadow of its former self. In the hour of the last extremity Nineveh, the Assyrian capital itself, was in its turn threatened by the mighty power of Media. Nahum denounces its doom as an act of God. In our consideration of the brief but brilliantly written prophecy we must omit Chapter i. 2-10 (Professor A. B. Gordon, *Peake's Commentary*: Nahum). The remainder is substantially the work of the prophet of whose personal history nothing is known.

The Assyrians have been the scourge of God, and through them "the Lord hath turned away the excellency of Jacob, as the excellency of Israel: for the emptiers have emptied them out" (ii. 2). But now the wrath of God is about to fall upon Nineveh. She has multiplied her merchants "above the stars of heaven" (iii. 16). Her crowned ones are "as the great grasshoppers which camp in the hedges" (iii. 17). Despite all her power and wealth, her strong fortifications and her military preparations, the day of her doom is at hand. "Behold, I am against thee, saith the Lord of Hosts; and I will discover thy skirts upon thy face, and I will shew the nations thy nakedness, and the kingdoms thy shame ... and it shall come to pass that all they that look upon thee shall flee from thee, and say, Nineveh is laid waste" (iii. 5-7). The anger of God has been stirred by "the multitude of whoredoms of the well-favoured harlot" (iii. 4). She is "a bloody city full of lies and robbery" (iii. 4). Nations are sold "through her whoredoms, and families through her witchcrafts" (iii. 4).

From the prophecy we can draw two conclusions only

with regard to the nature of God. He is powerful in the affairs of the nations, and He can indeed cast down the mighty from their seats: Bloodshed and robbery, the oppression of nations and the spoiling of families excites His wrath.

(*l*) ZEPHANIAH

Zephaniah prophesied in the days of Josiah, King of Judah (640–608 B.C.). His prophecy was uttered during a period of years commencing about the year 627 B.C. (Professor A. B. Gordon, *Peake's Commentary*: Zephaniah). During his lifetime the kingdom of Judah, despite the Deuteronomic revival, was obviously tottering to its fall before the tremendous world movements of the time. Zephaniah is a prophet of doom. The following passages are probably later additions: ii. 8–11 and iii. 14–20. The prophet denounces the shameful sins of the people; idolatry is rampant. The host of heaven is worshipped upon the housetops (i. 5). The priests have polluted the sanctuary and done violence to the law (iii. 4). Deceit and violence abound (i. 9). Oppression is rife (iii. 1). The princes of Jerusalem are roaring lions and the judges ravening wolves (iii. 3). Even the prophets are light and treacherous persons (iii. 4). In the midst of corruption and wickedness there is One whom men have forgotten—"the Just Lord," who "will not do iniquity" (iii. 5). His word comes to Zephaniah: "I will utterly consume all things from off the Land" (i. 2). Nothing can deliver the wicked from the great and terrible day of an angry God whose determination is "to gather the nations, that I may assemble the kingdoms, to pour upon them my indignation, even all my fierce anger: for all the earth shall be devoured with the flame of my jealousy" (iii. 8). Only those who seek meekness and righteousness may perchance be hid in the day of wrath (ii. 3). But after the tempest of destruction suppliants shall come from beyond the rivers of Ethiopia (iii. 10). Judah shall no more be haughty (iii. 11). An afflicted and poor people shall trust in the name of the Lord (iii. 12). The remnant of Israel shall not do iniquity or speak lies.

God is the righteous judge of the earth. By terror and judgment, a fearful outpouring of wrath, all sin and iniquity will be purged away. And in the end men will "serve him with one consent" (iii. 9).

(*m*) JEREMIAH

Jeremiah, the descendant of an old priestly family, prophesied during the last stormy years of the kingdom of Judah. He taught from the year 626 B.C., five years before the publication of Deuteronomy, until 586 B.C., the year in which Nebuchadrezzar captured Jerusalem and carried the Jews away into captivity. Chapters l–li are almost certainly not the work of Jeremiah, and Chapter lii, an historical Appendix, is taken word for word from 2 Kings. The remainder is either the work of the prophet himself or of men closely in touch with his time and spirit. Although the book is a long one, the leading ideas are relatively simple, and for the most part do not introduce anything especially new into the general content of prophetic teaching.

1. God is all-powerful in nature and history. "But the Lord is the true God, he is the Living God, and an everlasting king: at his wrath the earth shall tremble, and the nations shall not be able to abide his indignation . . . he hath made the earth by his power, he hath established the world by his wisdom, and hath stretched out the heavens by his discretion" (x. 10, 12). Geographical barriers and distance make no difference to the God of Jeremiah. Nebuchadrezzar—"My servant" from distant Babylon—will be brought against this land and the inhabitants thereof (xxv. 9). In the last section of the prophecy the wrath of

God is pronounced, not against backsliding Israel only, but against Egypt, Philistia, Moab, Ammon, Edom, Damascus, Kedar and the kingdoms of Hazar and Elam (xlvi–xlix).

2. There is no other God beside the true God. The idols so commonly worshipped "have not made the heavens and the earth" (x. 11). The "molten image is falsehood; and there is no breath in them" (x. 14). They are not inferior beings to the Lord of Hosts—perhaps less just and certainly less powerful—but are, indeed, mere nothings, figments of the imagination, just "stones" and "stocks"— that and nothing else. Jeremiah is uncompromisingly monotheistic.

3. God has revealed Himself in a special manner to Israel and Judah. Through His servants the prophets He has given them a code of law. In the past He brought them "up out of the land of Egypt ... through the wilderness, through a land of deserts and of pits, through a land of drought, and of the shadow of death ... into a plentiful country" (ii. 6, 7). When they had come up unto the good country there were no commands given as to burnt offerings and sacrifices, only: "Obey my voice, and I will be your God, and ye shall be my people: and walk ye in all the ways I have commanded you" (vii. 23). From those first days of their settled national life: "I have even sent unto you all my servants, the prophets, daily rising up early and sending them" (vii. 25).

4. There were good times when Israel and Judah remembered God and obeyed His law. When the people walked in the "old ways" in the "good paths." "Thus said the Lord; I remember thee, the kindness of thy youth, the love of thine espousals, when thou wentest after me in the wilderness.... Israel was holiness unto the Lord" (ii. 2, 3).

5. Now, however, a wicked generation has forgotten God and gone a whoring after all manner of idols and false

gods. "They have forsaken me . . . and have estranged this place, and have burned incense in it unto other gods . . . they have built also the high places of Baal" (xix. 4, 5). "The children gather wood, and the fathers kindle the fire, and the women knead their dough, to make cakes to the queen of heaven, and to pour out drink offerings to the other gods" (vii. 18).

6. Idolatry has brought in its train moral degradation and social wrong. "Also in thy skirts is found the blood of the souls of the poor innocents" (ii. 34). "Will ye steal, murder, and commit adultery, and swear falsely, and burn incense to Baal . . .?" (vii. 9). "They be all adulterers, an assembly of treacherous men" (ix. 2). So thoroughly has lying become a part of them that in the midst of all their evil they trust by lying words to deceive even God and to cloak their oppression of the stranger, the fatherless and the widow by the repetition of vain and meaningless ceremonial, saying: "The Temple of the Lord! The Temple of the Lord! The Temple of the Lord are these!" (vii. 6).

7. Because of their idolatry and moral corruption the wrath of God is about to fall. He has been present with them throughout their history. The prophets have spoken in entreaty and warning. Last of all came the fall of the Northern Kingdom—a flaming sign of the inevitable ruin that national apostasy brings in its train. And yet the people persist in all their unrighteous doings. They will not turn to the Lord their God. The cup is full. God will no longer forbear. "Behold! mine anger and my fury shall be poured out upon this place, upon man, and upon beast, and upon the trees of the field, and upon the fruit of the ground; and it shall burn, and shall not be quenched" (vii. 20). Nebuchadrezzar, King of Babylon, is to be the instrument of the wrath of God. "I will deliver Zedekiah king of Judah, and his servants, and the people, and such as are left in this city, from the pestilence, from the sword, and from the

famine into the hand of Nebuchadrezzar king of Babylon ... and he shall smite them with the edge of the sword" (xxi. 7). Even, however, in this last desperate hour they may still be saved from catastrophe if they will turn again to the Lord, the hope of Israel. "Therefore now amend your ways and your doings, and obey the voice of the Lord your God; and the Lord will repent him of the evil that he hath pronounced against you" (xxvi. 13).

8. The Kingdom will fall. The people will suffer the extremity of famine, pestilence and the sword. The survivors will be carried away into captivity and for seventy years will dwell in Babylon. Yet this is not the end. God will punish His people, but He will not utterly destroy them for ever. Backsliding and evil though they may be, they are still His people. He loves them, and in the end they will repent, and He will bring them back rejoicing. "For thus saith the Lord, That after seventy years be accomplished at Babylon I will visit you, and perform my good word toward you, in causing you to return to this place. For I know the thoughts that I think toward you, saith the Lord, thoughts of peace, and not of evil, to give you 'a future and a hope.' Then shall ye call upon me, and I will hearken unto you. And ye shall seek me, and find me, when ye shall search for me with all your heart. And I will be found of you, saith the Lord: and I will turn away your captivity" (xxix. 10-14). God will make a new Covenant with His people. "Behold, the days come, saith the Lord, that I will raise unto David a righteous Branch, and a King shall reign and prosper, and shall execute judgment and justice ... and His name shall be called, The Lord our Righteousness" (xxiii 5-6).

The life and character of Jeremiah as revealed to us in the course of the book is almost, if not quite, as of much abiding importance as the actual matter of his prophecies. The word of God came to him when he was still a very young man—so young that he could exclaim: "Ah! Lord God! Behold, I cannot speak, for I am a child." He was a man of the most acute sensibilities, capable of the most profound emotions, capable above all else of entering into the most lofty of all experiences—that close communion with God in which men feel the certainty of the Living Presence—and receive a message which must at all costs be delivered. This young man, at the age, perhaps, of twenty-five, felt called to deliver a message of doom to his people. He shrank appalled from the prospect. He was, no doubt, a man of books, a quiet student by choice and a lover of his kind, and yet feeling the word of God like a fire in his bones—and that word one of terror and wrath to come. "Woe is me, my mother, that thou hast borne me a man of strife and a man of contention to the whole earth! I have neither lent on usury, nor men have lent to me on usury; yet every one of them doth curse me" (xv. 10). Yet he does not falter, but proclaims his message in Jerusalem and through the cities of Judah, in the courts of the Temple and from a prison cell, to a king in secret, and to the nobles, the priests and people in the full light of day. God's word was unto him "the joy and rejoicing of mine own heart" (xv. 16), but, nevertheless, it spelt for him loneliness: "I sat alone because of thy hand" (xv. 17). There is for him no joy of wife or child—only Baruch and some few faithful friends who help hold up his hands. He is mocked daily, defamed of many. His enemies lie in wait for his halting. He calls curses on the day of his birth, but yet must on, "for the word is in my heart as a burning fire" (xx. 10). In the midst of tribulations he can "Sing unto the Lord . . . for he hath delivered the soul of the poor from the hand of evil doers" (xx. 13). At one time the priests and prophets hale him before an assemblage of the princes and the people and demand his death. In this hour he calls upon his judges to repent. Awed by this accused who so completely

THE ISRAELITES

turns the tables, and speaks as the direct representative of the Great Accuser, they let him go. During the siege of Jerusalem he is a close prisoner in constant peril of his life. On one occasion he is flung into a horrible pit without light or food, his feet sunk in the horrible mire. He is saved by an Ethiopian captain. Traitor, betrayer of his country, as he seems to the fierce soldiers, his life is again in danger. "We beseech thee, let this man be put to death: for thus he weakeneth the hands of the men of war that remain in this city . . . for this man seeketh not the welfare of this people, but the hurt" (xxxviii. 4). At the very end, when Jerusalem has fallen, and the people are carried captive, the Chaldeans release him and treat him with kindness, but the remnant of his own people carry him away with them against his will to Tahpanhes in Egypt. According to legend, he was stoned to death. For something like forty years Jeremiah faced detraction, prison, hatred and death itself. "It will be seen that the life of Jeremiah was one of suffering and apparent failure; with perfect truth he compares himself with 'a lamb that is led to the slaughter.' But like Him of whom Jeremiah is the truest and most impressive Old Testament type, Jeremiah wins his victory through defeat. The influence of his life on posterity is a striking example of the power of great ideas, once they have entered the world by the conquest of a human soul" (H. Wheeler Robinson, *Peake's Commentary*, p. 475).

(n) SUMMARY OF PRE-EXILIC IDEAS CONCERNING GOD

The Old Testament books whose contents we have examined were produced between the years 1000 B.C. and 586 B.C.—a total of about four hundred years. Very little was written prior to 800 B.C., and consequently we are reviewing a literature which came into existence in a period of a little more than two hundred years. From the viewpoint of the men of God it was a black period. The world, including Israel and Judah, was no worse than it had ever been, indeed the bloodthirsty savagery of earlier times was mellowing somewhat before the rising tide of knowledge, the development of a rudimentary international economic organization and some slow but sure developments in religion. But there had risen in the south-western corner of Asia, among the people of the Hebrews, a school of men who by whatever process of history and of revelation had developed a conception of God of the most advanced sort. They were men who had had such an experience of the living God that they saw men and society, not with the eyes of the historian, but with the eyes of God. What they felt burned within them like fire until it burst forth in some of the most impressive and passionate utterances in all literature. These men—the prophets of Israel—are one of those pivotal groups who have swung humanity into new paths of progress. Their books are as important as any in history, and their ultimate influence on the subsequent development of humanity is beyond all calculation.

The age was, of course, a non-critical one, and even in the works of a single writer we find divergencies. The writers of the J E narratives maintain a high monotheism throughout Genesis, but sink to much lower levels in subsequent books as the influence of nationalism becomes stronger in the actual narrative. Old sources beyond our knowledge, obscure influences, difference in cultural levels, the personality and surroundings of the writers, give sufficient reason for numerous contradictions and for considerable difference in level of inspiration; nevertheless, the final impression is not one of conflict and divergence, but of clear and distinct agreements concerning the nature, character and operations of God.

With a startling emphasis they proclaim the fact of a living God who is One God. On every hand polytheism was rampant and scarcely questioned. There were gods in trees and rivers and mountains, nature gods of seedtime and harvest, gods personifying all human attributes, gods of the nations, gods conceived in the most anthropomorphic fashion, and gods that were the merest abstractions of natural phenomena; gods of gold, silver, wood, brass, iron and stone; and gods who were spiritualized and removed somewhat from the immediate gaze of men; gods of laughter and song, of wine and love, of hunting and war; gods of the heaven above, of the earth, and of the circling seas, and gods in unfathomed abysses beneath the earth. The worship of these gods, fatally attractive because of the low standard of demand on moral endeavour or the satisfaction of fleshly lust which so often attended their ritual, was a strong and evil lure to the Hebrews as to the other nations of the time. To the prophets whose souls were full of the great vision of the living God, these were utterly abhorrent. Against the pantheons of paganism they place one only—Yahweh of Hosts. In some of the earlier portions it would seem that He is perhaps limited within the borders of Israel—that there are other gods even if they are not so powerful—but as we get into the full stream of the prophecies the majestic conception grows until we are face to face with One God, exalted above every name in heaven and earth.

Yahweh of Hosts is the creator of the world and the maker of man. The whole conception of God operative in nature is one of majestic, unfaltering power. As He is the source of all things in the heavens and in the earth, so also is He the Orderer and Maintainer of them. Immanent in His world and yet not of it, He speaks in the thunderstorm, in the lightning and again in the still small voice. He is revealed and yet concealed in a pillar of fire and a pillar of cloud. The winds are at His command. The Red Sea divides. Jordan leaves a passage for the multitude of Israel. The walls of Jericho fall flat. In the day of His anger every resource of nature is at His disposal, and He rains down every manner of plague. Material blessings are in His hand also. Corn and wine and oil, lands flowing with milk and honey, cattle and sheep and beasts of burden, the sunshine and the rain are the gifts He showers upon favoured peoples. God in nature is supreme power working towards His own desired ends.

No conception before the exile, except, perhaps, the fact of the unity of the Living God, is quite so clear-cut and definite as the idea of Almighty God—the Judge of all men. Occasional fragments may perhaps give an idea of limitation to the power of God, but the general idea throughout is of God who judges with equal authority the near and remote nations, kings and common men. The idea of judgment carries with it the idea of law. A definite and detailed code is laid down which men transgress at their peril. This code is in no sense one of ceremonial obligations—sacrifices and washings and fastings—but a series of commandments concerned altogether with men's actions toward God and their fellows. Idolatry is a breach of the law as concerns God. Various unsocial acts are breaches which concern not only the men who are hurt thereby but God also. The Great Judge is concerned not merely with an insistence upon due rights payable to Himself, but on the right conduct of men to each other. The frightful punishments denounced against those who worship idols is not mere senseless jealousy —it goes much deeper than that. The choice of God or the idols is a choice not of ceremonials but of conduct. The prophets see conduct as being intimately connected with men's idea of God. If there is a wrong choice of the divine object of worship, then everything is wrong. The law of the Living God is broken, social relationships are degraded, oppression and injustice, famine and the sword desolate the earth. Misery and unhappiness everywhere prevail. In the imagination of the stern preachers, who denounced in blazing terms the corruption of their times, there was then nothing but for the wrath of the righteous Judge to fall upon the wicked until they were broken in fragments, their wickedness rooted out, and the remnants of an idolatrous generation humbled and penitent before the judgment-seat of God.

The identification of the Living God of Power, the Judge of all men with morality and right living, is one of the great achievements of history. The assertion of the holiness of God—in Whom there is no uncleanness—no moral fault of any sort, means ultimately that men must likewise become holy and consciously right in all their relationships. The prophetic conception of morality, and therefore of the God whom they believed to be completely moral, may have been—and indeed was—inadequate; but the contact of ideas was made, and the conception could grow as it spread abroad and entered into the consciousness of succeeding generations.

Throughout the whole history of the race God is shown ceaselessly active, working with men to bring them into a right relationship with their environment. The will of God is that men should live in prosperity, in happiness, and in unity with Himself. This is one clear meaning of the story of Eden. Adam and Eve break the conditions which make this possible, and there is progressive wickedness until God is represented as making a fresh start with Noah. Again there is a relapse. This time there is no immediate catastrophe, but God makes another beginning, choosing out for Himself a man in whom all the nations of the world are to be blessed. On this foundation He will build a nation—a peculiar people—a chosen instrument for the transmission of blessing. This people is guided and sustained by God through every vicissitude of fortune—captivity, desert wandering and warfare—until, established in Palestine, they become a powerful and well-organized kingdom. Then, just as we would imagine that the time was ripe for the next step in the unfolding purpose of God, there supervenes another terrible period of apostasy. The prophets denounce this wickedness of the times. Desolation will fall upon the nation. There will come—after devastating wars—a second period of captivity. Yet this is by no means the end. God's plan is checked for the time only. A remnant will be saved and the Chosen People will yet fulfil their destiny. The pre-exilic writers were so concerned with the state of Israel that we might almost suppose that the nation was the end and not the instrument. Nevertheless, in stray gleams here and there we see the greater whole. They are naturally concerned with their own people—with immediate problems —but God is in the long run working, not merely for the supremacy and prosperity of Israel, but the establishment of His Holy Mountain, the centre to which all nations shall come and from whence peace and concord shall go out to all the earth, so that war shall be no more.

God is in an amazing fashion represented as the champion of the widow and the fatherless, of the toiling masses, of the humble and defenceless poor. He is not so much the God of kings and priests as the God of poor men who do the useful work of the world. The wrath of God blazes upon those who violate the principles of social righteousness and who act with violence for the sake of gain. In all literature there is to be found no more violent and uncompromising denunciation of the common action of the rich against the poor than is to be found in the writings of these ancient seers.

We have noted the proclamation of the unity of God, the power of God in Nature, God living in History as the Lawgiver and Judge of men at whose inspiration and command the race moves toward the good goal of social righteousness and international peace. But there are other sides to this lofty presentation. These might be passed over almost without mention as the inevitable deposit of inferior material found in any given historical complex, but for their enormous influence on subsequent events, not only in the history of Israel, but in that of the most modern European nations. At times God is so intimately connected with the fortunes of the Chosen People that all sense of His responsibility or care for other peoples is completely lost sight of. With a jealous intensity the Hebrews claim Him as absolutely their own, and refuse to recognize any other nation as having any claim on His benefits. For their sake God vexes Egypt with every manner of plague, in their defence He overthrows the armies of the aliens. To make them an habitation and an abiding home, He sanctions the extirpation of populous cities and the ruin of pleasant countrysides. This identification of the One Universal and All-Powerful God with the life and fortunes of a single nation is an idea that, under the direct influence of a partial and insufficient interpretation of Old Testament scriptures, has recurred many times in the development of European nationalities. This idea of the partiality of God to an isolated fragment of the race is accompanied by a belief in the frightful ruthlessness of the All-Powerful in His dealings with those who oppose Him, or who, even accidentally, come between Him and the workings of His purpose. The old stories of the Conquest represent God as being almost incredibly brutal. When Israel enters the Promised Land neither age, rank, nor sex is spared. The fierce conquerors destroy all before them in the fanatical belief that the occupants of the soil are cursed of God and that their destruction is as the savour of a sweet and acceptable sacrifice before the Lord. The prophets denounced judgments on the people which, well deserved as they may be from the legal point of view, are almost unthinkably severe. Famine, pestilence and war in their utmost frightfulness may be the accumulated inevitable result of human folly and sin, but it is hard to think that a God—not only Powerful but also Holy and Moral—should directly cause such tribulation as a direct retribution, even for the most degraded idolatry or the cruellest outbursts of social injustice. The belief in the hardness, severity and even cruelty of God is another survival of a more barbarous day that still influences the lives of men and nations.

What we to-day would speak of as personal religion—the experience of God in the individual life of the believer—holds no prominent place in the pre-exilic idea. It is certainly true that individuals can and do approach God in prayer and that prayer is directly answered. It is also true that nearly every communication of God is made through men who become conscious in some form of the Divine Presence. Yet the writers are more concerned with national or social righteousness than with holiness in the individual. Good living is expected from every man. The Decalogue is a sure indication of that. But such living was the rightful contribution of the individual to the life of the nation, and therefore to the purpose of God. That a man was an end in himself and that the Creator of life was interested in every human life seems hardly to have dawned on the minds of even the best men of the age. There is, as we should therefore expect, scarcely a hint of any firm or widespread belief in the possibility of life beyond the grave.

(*o*) THE EXILE

Nebuchadrezzar in person first appeared before Jerusalem in 597 B.C. The city was taken, and the king, the household, the nobility and some thousands of picked soldiers and craftsmen were carried captive to Babylon. Zedekiah was placed on the vacant throne by the conqueror, but after a reign of ten years this puppet committed the suicidal folly of rebelling against his overlord. Nebuchadrezzar again besieged Jerusalem and took it after a prolonged and desperate resistance in the year 586 B.C. This time a very large part of the population was transferred to Babylon. Only the poorest labourers were left behind to till the vineyards of the new rulers. These remnants, and also a considerable body of fugitives who reached Egypt, were probably completely absorbed by surrounding populations. Few, if any, of their descendants ever came back into the stream of the national life.

The captives in Babylonia were not reduced to chattel slavery, and, indeed, seem within limits to have been allowed great freedom. They were permitted to live in communities, to engage in agriculture and in trade. Many, no doubt, became prosperous and powerful members of the community. From the purely material point of view their sufferings, beyond those incidental to the violent dislocation and the necessity of establishing themselves under new conditions, were not great. As time went on great numbers were probably absorbed in the increasingly cosmopolitan population of the great capital. To the considerable remnant who remained true to the worship of the One God, or who in the hour of desolation returned to the old faith of their fathers, no material prosperity could atone for the deprivation they suffered in the forcible removal from the one land and the one city in which all the rites, ceremonials and feasts of their religion could be observed. The nation as such was under an interdict. Much was impossible, but there was undoubtedly concentration on what was still possible. The rite of circumcision, the observance of the Sabbath and certain feasts were rigidly observed. The books of the prophets whose warnings had been so neglected were studied with a new earnestness. Amongst this section of the people there was without doubt a reformation both true and lasting, and with repentance came aspiration and hope, a sense of pardon, a realization of God as their refuge and strength, a present Comforter and the Hope of the future.

During the seventy years of the captivity we have no certain knowledge of events. There may have been, and probably were, religious persecutions, such as those described in the story of Shadrach, Meshach and Abednego (Dan. iii) in the reign of Nebuchadrezzar himself, and the story of Daniel in the den of lions after the Median conquest. The result of these would be to make a clear-cut division between the faithful and those who through fear, the prospect of material gain or the sensuous lure of paganism became apostate. Individual Jews—Daniel possibly—Nehemiah certainly—attained great power under the various rulers, but the main fact of historical importance was the steady development, under adversity, of their ideas concerning God.

In 538 B.C. Babylon fell to Cyrus the Persian. No doubt his rapid success was largely possible owing to assistance from within the crumbling Empire. The Jews, whose importance was considerable, and who hated the idolatrous Babylonians, may have intrigued with the Persians—monotheists like themselves—especially if in the process of bargaining a hope was held forth of a return to Palestine. Whatever negotiations may have taken place, it is certain that in the first year of the Persian king a written proclamation was circulated throughout the whole kingdom authorizing any Hebrew, who was willing, to return and assist in the rebuilding of the Temple. A great thank-offering was made throughout the Empire, and Cyrus added the sacred vessels which Nebuchadrezzar had carried away from the first Temple (Ezra i). Some fifty thousand of the exiles returned. For a year they were busied with the re-establishment of their homes, but in the second year they "set forward the work of the house of the Lord" (Ezra iii. 8). Many who "were ancient men, that had seen the first house . . . wept with a loud voice; and many shouted aloud for joy" (Ezra iii. 12). The work went but slowly. A mixed multitude of the dwellers in the land, who probably held some sort of debased faith acquired from the absorbed remnants of the poor, who had never been carried away, were anxious to amalgamate with the returned exiles. Their advances were repulsed with austerity. Exasperated at this treatment they did all in their power to hamper the work, and in the reign of Artaxerxes (Cambyses), secured an injunction from the king which suspended operations until the second year of Darius, 523 B.C. An appeal to State records brought to light the decree of Cyrus. Again the work went forward. There was no further interruption, and the task was finished in 516 B.C. The priests were sanctified. The passover was killed and "the children of Israel, which were come again out of captivity, and all such as had separated themselves from the filthiness of the heathen of the land . . . did eat, and kept the feast of unleavened bread seven days with joy: for the Lord had made them joyful" (Ezra vi. 21-22). There was much still to be done. Many difficulties to be met, but Israel had returned to the ancient home. The altar of Jehovah was again established on Mount Sion.

Such a profound disturbance of national life as that of the exile was bound to leave deep and lasting traces on religious ideas. Three men—the writer of Lamentations, Ezekiel and the writer of 2 Isaiah—produced complete works; while there were also additions made to existing books.

(*p*) LAMENTATIONS

Peake, in the Century Bible, considers that Chapters ii and iv were the work of an eye-witness of the siege and capture of Jerusalem by Nebuchadrezzar, and that Chapters iii and v were produced later, while Chapter i is probably post-Exilic.

Chapters iii and iv contain vivid descriptions of the destruction of the city. It was the Lord's doing in judgment against the iniquity of His people. The kings of the earth stand amazed at the fearful outpouring of wrath. Even the writer can hardly believe that the sin of the people could have brought in its train so terrible a chastisement as this, that "The hands of the pitiful women have sodden their own children" (iv. 10).

Chapters iii and v show a development. The stroke of doom so long dreaded has fallen with utter completeness. The Lord has dealt very heavily with His people, but after all the humbling, the wormwood and the gall, the great discovery is made that despite the failure of every material hope, the loss of freedom, the extinction of the people as a political entity, that in a great mysterious fashion "It is of the Lord's mercies that we are not consumed, because his compassions fail not. They are new every morning . . . The Lord is my portion. . . . The Lord is good unto them that wait for him, to the soul that seeketh him" (iii. 22–25). In the time of trouble there is a turning towards the Most High: "Let us search and try our ways, and turn again unto the Lord. Let us lift up our heart with our hands unto God in the heavens. We have transgressed and have rebelled: thou hast not pardoned" (iii. 40–42). And yet the anger of God will not last for ever: "For the Lord will not cast off

THE ISRAELITES

for ever: but though he cause grief, yet will he have compassion according to the multitude of his mercies" (iii. 31-32). Although the writer has gained an insight into the mercifulness of God, he has still only thoughts of vengeance for the oppressor. "Give them sorrow of heart, thy curse unto them. Persecute and destroy them in anger" (iii. 65-66).

(*q*) EZEKIEL

Ezekiel was the son of a priest. As he was a grown man in the "fifth year of King Jehoiachim's captivity" (i. 2), it is obvious that he must have spent his youth and early manhood in the kingdom of Judah, under the strong influence of the Deuteronomic revival. He had seen the bright promise of better times fade in another outburst of apostasy. He was probably in Jerusalem at the time of the siege, and was then carried captive to Babylonia, where he dwelt "among the captives by the river of Chebar" (i. 1).

A large part of the book is taken up in the denunciation of immorality and idolatry. There seems to have been some questioning amongst the captives as to the justice of God in inflicting so fearful a punishment. The prophet vindicates Jehovah. Israel is likened to an infant child exposed by its parents. The Lord in passing saw its misery and took it up and gave it life. The child grew and waxed beautiful. The Lord entered into a covenant with her and lavished upon her every gift and favour. But the proud beauty forgot her Benefactor, abused His gifts and favours, engaged in fearful idolatries and played the harlot with many strange loves (xvi). Such, in parable, is the history of Israel. God brings a fearful judgment on the backsliding people. The robbers, the shedders of blood, the adulterers, the oppressors of the poor and needy, the violent, the idolaters and the usurers shall surely die (xviii. 10-13). "The soul that sinneth it shall surely die" (xviii. 20). Yet

God has no pleasure in these punishments. The moral order must be maintained, "but if the wicked will turn from all his sins that he hath committed, and keep all my statutes, and do that which is lawful and right, he shall surely live, he shall not die" (xviii. 21).

While Ezekiel justifies the action of God in the fearful punishment meted out to the idolatrous and wicked nation, yet it would seem that the chastisement altogether failed in its purpose. Far from displaying penitence the people even in the very period of captivity profaned "my holy name" (xxxvi. 20). So far the almost inevitable idea in Hebrew thinking has been that of God the stern Lawgiver and Judge, demanding absolute obedience to a code which is enforced by means of drastic and terrible punishments. Whenever there has been a breach of the law there has followed in due time repentance induced by present suffering and the fear of worse to come. This idea is present in Ezekiel and continues indeed throughout the whole of the Old Testament, and even, indeed, in the New. And yet in Ezekiel we find definitely the commencement of another very different train of thought. Punishment does not work. So God will take His people from among the heathen and bring them again to their own land. "Then will I sprinkle clean water upon you and ye shall be clean. . . . A new heart also will I give you, and a new spirit will I put within you: and I will take away the stony heart out of your flesh . . . and I will put my spirit within you . . . and ye shall dwell in the land that I gave to your fathers; and I will be your God" (xxxvi. 25–28). The meaning here can be nothing else than that God will enter the life of the people as a spiritual force, and so work a revolution in conduct which punishments, however drastic, have failed to bring about. The idea is reinforced in the vision of the valley of dry bones (xxxvii). They were very dry, utterly lifeless and incapable of any volition, until the breath of God breathed into them and they lived again. In the good providence of God there will be complete restoration. The Temple will be rebuilt and sacrifice again offered on the great altar. Ezekiel lingers very lovingly over all the details of the restored and purified worship. One united nation will take the place of the two warring kingdoms. "And I will set up one shepherd over them, and he shall feed them, even my servant David" (xxxiv. 23). Peace and prosperity will everywhere abound. Evil beasts will cease in the land. Even the wilderness and the woods will be safe. "And the tree of the field shall yield her fruit, and the earth shall yield her increase, and they shall be safe in their land, and shall know that I am the Lord, when I have broken the bands of their yoke" (xxxiv. 27).

While the mercy and love of God are to be thus shown forth to Israel there is a prophecy of doom only for every other nation. The Ammonites are to be delivered "to the men of the East for a possession" (xxv. 4). God will "execute judgments upon Moab" (xxv. 11), and "lay vengeance upon Edom" (xxv. 14). His hand will be stretched out against Philistine and Cherithim and the remnant of the sea coast upon whom will be executed "great vengeance ... with furious rebukes" (xxv. 15–17). The very isles shall "shake at the sound" of the fall of Tyre, and its place shall be known "never any more" (xxvii. 36). The streets of Sidon shall run with blood (xxviii. 23). Egypt will become the basest of kingdoms (xxix. 15). Upon the ruin of Assyria "shall all the fowls of the heaven remain" (xxxi. 13). In the latter days a vast assemblage of the nations will make "a great shaking in the land of Israel" (xxxviii. 19). Fearful destruction will fall upon them and Israel "shall spoil those that robbed them" (xxxix. 10). The nationalism of Ezekiel is as exclusive as that of any of his predecessors.

The prophet lays direct emphasis upon the responsibility of the individual. Every man must stand or fall upon his own works. The good man can become bad. The wicked can turn from his wickedness and live. "The soul that sinneth, it shall die" (xviii. 4). In this last pronouncement there may well be some conception of life beyond death. Beyond all question Ezekiel must have observed the apparent immunity of the violent transgressors from judgment in this world. If his statement is meaningful at all it must refer to the final action of God in a state of being certainly beyond present experience. Throughout the whole prophecy Ezekiel is himself peculiarly conscious of the dealings of God with himself as an individual. The word of the Lord comes to him. He is set "a watchman unto the house of Israel" (xxxiii. 7). His duty is to warn wicked men from their ways. If he fails in his duty the wicked man shall die in his iniquity, "but his blood shall I require at thy hand" (xxxiii. 8). Ezekiel "knows himself to have the 'cure of souls'; he is the first Hebrew Pastor" (Professor J. E. McFadyen, *Peake's Commentary*: Ezekiel).

(*r*) II ISAIAH

The second part of the Book of Isaiah, Chapters xl–lxvi, divides naturally into two parts. In the first we have Chapters xl–lv. This section is apparently the work of one man—although a tremendous controversy has raged round the inclusion of the four Servant Songs (xlii. 1–4; xlix. 1–6; l. 4–9; lii. 13; liii. 12). Of the author we know nothing except that in all probability he wrote some little time before and some little time after the victory of Cyrus and the fall of Babylon. The actual date of the work will on this understanding be about 540 B.C. and the years following. The concluding chapters of the book, Chapters lvi–lxvi, were probably added later, perhaps during the period of Ezra, and may therefore be regarded as falling in the post-Exilic period (see Isaiah xl–lxvi, Professor Wardle, *Peake's*

Commentary). The aim of the prophecy "is to arouse the indifferent, to reassure the wavering, to expostulate with the doubting, to announce with triumphant confidence the certainty of the approaching restoration" (Driver: *Introduction to the Literature of the Old Testament*, p. 231).

The Unknown Prophet, speaking with an intensity of conviction unsurpassed by any of his predecessors, proclaims God as the Creator of the heavens and the earth: "Who hath measured the waters in the hollow of his hand, and meted out heaven with the span, and comprehended the dust of the earth in a measure, and weighed the mountains in the scales, and the hills in a balance?" (xl. 12); He is the inspirer of History, judging the actions of men and determining world movements. The virgin daughter of Babylon is brought to the dust because of His vengeance on her for the cruel treatment of captive Israel (xlvii). Cyrus, though he knows it not, is the Lord's anointed for the deliverance of Israel (lxv. 1-5). All history, too, moves majestically toward the goal of God's purpose. The conception of God is purely monotheistic. He is not merely supreme, but "there is no God else beside me" (xlv. 21)—"unto me every knee shall bow, every tongue shall swear" (xlv. 23). So far there is a reproduction in very striking and distinctive language of ideas that had no doubt become familiar to the thinking of the best minds in Israel. At this point the great Prophet of the Exile commences to leave the beaten paths and steps out as the boldest pioneer of History.

Ardent nationalist as he is, looking forward as he does to the triumphant restoration and the glorious future in store for his people, writing as he does for their comfort, he sees with unerring vision that the future belongs not to Israel alone, or indeed to any Chosen Race, but to all men and nations equally. The purpose of God is a great society and holy brotherhood of peoples in which good will and peace shall prevail. His Servant shall be "a light to the Gentiles . . . .

salvation unto the end of the earth" (xlix. 6). He "shall sprinkle many nations" (lii. 15). "Behold, these shall come from afar: and, lo, these from the north and from the west; and these from the land of Sinim" (xlix. 12). This great idea is not in itself absolutely original, but it had been anticipated in occasional passages only by earlier writers.

We are given a new insight into the character of God. The attributes of power and judgment have grown familiar. We have seen a stern Judge fencing the moral law with terrible punishment. A man of unclean lips has been awed by His holiness. One in his own sorrow saw something of the tenderness of God for a people stricken for their sin. Here in 2 Isaiah God is above everything else the Saviour, One whose nature it is to raise up and restore again. "I have blotted out, as a thick cloud, thy transgressions, and, as a cloud, thy sins: return unto me; for I have redeemed thee" (xliv. 22). "I will help thee, saith the Lord, and thy redeemer, the Holy One of Israel" (xli. 14). "I, even I, am the Lord; and beside me there is no Saviour" (xliii. 11). God can indeed take up the isles as a very little thing (xl. 15), but the Old Testament has no higher conception of Him than when it is written: "He shall feed his flock like a shepherd: he shall gather the lambs with his arm, and carry them in his bosom, and shall gently lead those that are with young" (xl. 11).

If we take the Suffering Servant to represent a saved and purified Israel working out God's plan of redemption for all peoples, we get a still further vision of His nature and method. The servant is upheld by God. "I have put my Spirit upon him" (xlii. 1). His ideal action, therefore, will be like that of God. He is to set judgment in the earth. The isles shall wait for his law. But how is this transformation to be brought about? By signs and wonders and fiery judgments? Not so! The tides of the spirit will flow in a great quietness. "He shall not cry, nor lift up, nor cause his voice to be heard in the streets." "A bruised reed shall he not break, and the smoking flax shall he not quench" (xlii. 2, 3). He gives his back to the smiters. His face is not hid from shame and spitting (l. 6). "He is despised and rejected of men; a man of sorrows, and acquainted with grief . . . surely he hath borne our griefs, and carried our sorrows. . . . He was wounded for our transgressions, he was bruised for our iniquities: the chastisement of our peace was upon him; and with his stripes we are healed . . . by his knowledge shall my righteous servant justify many; for he shall bear their iniquities" (liii). So through suffering the Servant wins his victory, and overcomes the evil of the world. He sees the travail of his soul and is satisfied. The whole conception only becomes fully meaningful when we consider the Servant is like God—and God like His servant. God is not, then, merely a potentate intolerably just and armed with terror, but a Being who feels the agony of men, and who identifies Himself with the race in suffering. His spirit moves across the chaos of human sin, bringing light and life, opening the blind eyes, bringing out the prisoners, and those who dwell in the houses of darkness (xlii. 7), giving water to the thirsty and food to the hungry (lv. 1). His salvation shall be to the ends of the earth (xlix. 6).

(s) SUMMARY OF EXILIC IDEAS

The exile intensified the best in the older beliefs concerning God, and also introduced fresh elements. Many of the exiles were, no doubt, absorbed into the mixed multitude. Those who retained their identity did so by concentrating on the national heritage of religious belief. The existing conceptions were insufficient to satisfy the needs of a community reduced to such sore straits. They needed comfort, hope and salvation. Adversity tests the foundations of belief to the uttermost. Men must have a philosophy adequate to the strain of life or they break, and they must have an experience adequate to the philosophy. The idea of God was put to the supreme test—and stood. Not only did it stand, but the content deepened. The old ideas were not supplanted, but new ones appeared, growing side by side with them. God still remains a stern and ruthless Judge. His actions, indeed, are vindicated, but at the same time the futility of mere punishment is developed. Another way is shown. God's spirit will move amongst men giving a new life in the soul. God in love and suffering works for salvation. The reality and the unity of God had become axiomatic, but the idea of His passion for men had penetrated in flashes only through thick clouds of primitive error. At last we commence to see that "the heart of the Eternal is most wonderfully kind." God is not only the Saviour of fallen Israel, but of all men. History is the record of His steady progress toward a good goal. At the darkest hour of the national fortunes the greatest prophet of Israel sets his face strongly towards the dawn of an international future of righteousness and peace.

CHAPTER VI

THE MEDES AND PERSIANS

Certain tribes of Aryan race settled at some indefinite period in Media and Persia. They were for many hundreds of years subject to the mighty power of Assyria. During this period they probably developed some sort of national consciousness, and at the same time absorbed religion from Bactria, and some amount of culture from Nineveh and Babylon. About the middle of the seventh century B.C. the power of Assyria was definitely declining. Seizing the opportunity—"the Medes set the example of revolt from their authority. They took arms for the recovery of their freedom ... and fought ... with such gallantry as to shake off the yoke of servitude and to become a free people" (Herodotus, Bk. I, c. 95). The new freedom quickly relapsed for a time into anarchy, easily accounted for by the total collapse of the whole machinery of Assyrian government. Order gradually emerged from the chaos, and, according to Herodotus, Deioces, a wise, just and virtuous man was raised to sovereign power. He organized the tribes into a strong kingdom and built fortified cities, of which Ecbatana was the chief. His successor, Phraortes, brought the Persians under his sway, and at the head of the united peoples commenced the conquest of Asia. For a while he met with considerable success, but in an attempt on Nineveh was defeated and slain. His son, Cyaxares, "still more warlike" than any of his ancestors, reorganized and rendered still more formidable the arms of the Perso-Median Confederacy. He conquered beyond the Halys, commenced the siege of Nineveh, but was then overwhelmed by a Scythian horde which poured in from central Asia. For a period of twenty-eight years the barbarians plundered rather than ruled.

In the end "Cyaxares and the Medes invited the greater part of them to a banquet and made them drunk with wine, after which they were all massacred" (Herodotus, Bk. I, c. 106). The Median Empire was revived at once. Nineveh was again attacked and fell in the year 607 B.C. The fall of Assyria gave the Babylonians opportunity for domination. They swept to the west and then to the south, and, under Nebuchadrezzar, finally conquered the whole of Palestine. At the same time the Medes, moving in a line roughly parallel, but more to the north, had advanced well into Asia Minor, where they came into contact with the growing power of the Lydian kings. The first clash occurred toward the end of the reign of Cyaxares. Fighting went on for five years without any decisive result. In the sixth year, when an engagement was at its height, a sudden eclipse of the sun terminated the battle. So impressed were the combatants by this—to them—utterly miraculous happening, that peace was speedily restored. Astyages, the son of Cyaxares, was dethroned by the Persian Cyrus. In the meanwhile Croesus, the rich and able ruler of Lydia, became increasingly powerful. . . . "he made himself master of all the Greek cities in Asia and forced them to become his tributaries" (Herodotus, Bk. I, c. 4, 27). Croesus, "in the course of many years, brought under his sway all the nations to the west of the Halys" (Herodotus, Bk. I, c. 28). Crossing the river he commenced to ravage the peaceful fields of the Cappadocians. Cyrus, with a great, but probably badly balanced army, marched against him. A furious battle was fought in the district of Pterir. The result was indecisive. Croesus, never imagining for a moment that the Persians would dare to penetrate his territory—especially in the winter season—disbanded his troops, returned home and commenced to form a coalition with which to overwhelm his rival in the following spring. Cyrus, however, did not pause. Meeting with no opposition, he reached Sardis before the Lydian king could be warned of his coming. He was victorious in a battle fought beneath the walls of the city itself. Siege lines were formed, but on the fourteenth day the precipitous walls were scaled and Sardis was given up to pillage. With scarcely another struggle the whole of Asia Minor came under the sway of the Persian. His empire was now a great and powerful one, but it lacked its natural capital—Babylon. Cyrus marched upon this city in the year 539 B.C. The Babylonians were quickly driven within their walls. They shut themselves in behind apparently impregnable fortifications and "made light of his siege, having laid in a store of provisions for many years in preparation against this attack; for when they saw Cyrus conquering nation after nation they were convinced that he would never stop and that their turn would come at last" (Herodotus, Bk. I, c. 190). With the fall of Babylon fell the Babylonian Empire. Cyrus was the supreme ruler of a vast territory stretching from Bactria to the Aegean, and from the Black Sea to the deserts of Egypt.

The Persians had risen above barbarism, but were definitely inferior to the conquered races in general culture and economic development. Their religion was, however, of the first importance.

At some period probably not later than 1000 B.C. there arose in Iran a great teacher named Zoroaster (Zarathustra). We have no sure details of his life, but the Gâthas (Zend Avesta sect. Yasna) are very generally assigned to him. These hymns are the foundation of the religion variously known as Zoroastrianism and Mazdaism.

CHAPTER VII

MAZDAISM

The Gâthas

The Gâthas consist of five fragments of great antiquity. There are, no doubt, some interpolations, but such is the unity of tone running through them that it is highly probable that the changes are minor ones only, which leave all essential meanings unchanged. While the mass is not large, the material is more important than that of any other ancient religious literature, except that of Israel. We will consider each fragment separately and then summarize the general position. In the Zend Avesta the Gâthas are included in the Yasna.

(a) THE GÂTHA AHUNÂVÂITI

YASNA XXVIII. This section is a prayer of Zarathustra to Ahura Mazda—"the Great Creator," "the Living Lord" (par. 3), who is "Righteousness" (par. 4). The attributes of God are the "Benevolent mind" (par. 2), the "Good Mind" (par. 6), the "Kindly Mind" (par. 10). This good and gracious Deity is the Lord of good life amongst men. He has prescribed "(ceremonial and moral) actions" (par. 5). He can be approached in prayer (par. 2). The "Obedience (of our lives . . . constitutes) the way to the most beneficent Ahura Mazda" (par. 6). Zarathustra is consecrated to the service of God and of the people: "our herds and folk which cry so bitterly to Thee" (par. 2). The task is beyond human strength. Yet he can cry to God, and there will be bestowed upon him "that sacred blessing which is constituted by the attainments of the

Good Mind (within my soul)" (par. 8). Righteousness is a growing cause. The Spirit of Ahura Mazda within the minds of men "is causing the imperishable Kingdom to advance" (par. 4). The righteousness of God entering the souls of men "may introduce those who are its recipients into beatitude and glory" (par. 3). Zarathustra is sure of "that heavenly Mount (whither all the redeemed at last must pass)" (par. 5).

YASNA XXIX. The people cry out in agony to Ahura and to "Asha (the personification of the righteous order in creation)." "For whom did ye create me, and by whom did ye fashion me? On me comes the assault of wrath and of violent power, the blow of desolation, audacious insolence and thievish might. None other pasture giver have I than you, therefore do ye teach me good (tillage) for the fields (my only) hope of welfare" (par. 1). Ahura then questions Asha as to whom he had appointed guardian of the Cattle-People. He can make no satisfactory reply. Zarathustra, who is represented as being present, again "with hands outstretched in entreaty," presented the prayer of the believing faithful: "Not for the righteous liver, not for the thrifty (tiller of the earth) shall there be destruction together with the wicked" (par. 5). Ahura then speaks and appoints Zarathustra "a spiritual master"—"a chieftain moved by righteousness" for the toiling husbandmen (par. 6). The Ameshospends, a company of the saints, question Ahura, doubting whether they can have heard aright that a mortal man should be found endowed with the Good Mind. The appointment is authoritatively reaffirmed. The people lament that they have obtained "a lord who is powerless to obtain (his) wish, the (mere) voice of a feeble and pusillanimous man," whereas they had desired one "of royal state to bring what he desires to effect" (par. 9). The Gâtha closes with the prayer of Zarathustra that the "(Divine) Righteousness, the Good Mind (of the Lord and

His) Sovereign Power (come) hastening to me (to give me strength for my task and mission)." The Kingdom of God will bestow upon believing men "gladness" and "the peaceful amenities of home and quiet happiness" (par. 10–11).

YASNA XXX. Represents Zarathustra as an established teacher to whom men draw near "seeking to be taught" (par. 1). He expounds to them the doctrine of dualism—challenging them as individuals to make a "decision as to religions" (par. 2). From of old two "primeval spirits," "each independent in his action ... a better thing ... and a worse, as to thought, as to word, and as to deed" (par. 3), have striven together for men's souls and the ruling of the Universe. Each chose for himself a separate realm. That of Ahura Mazda was Divine Righteousness. With Him stood the personifications of Piety, Sovereign Power, the Good Mind and the Righteous Order. He chose for himself those "who content Ahura with actions which (are performed) in accordance with faith" (par. 5). As time goes on the Kingdom comes in the minds of men. The indwelling of a living God is within men, "the Kingdom shall have been gained for Thee by (Thy) Good Mind (within Thy folk)" (par. 8). The good are to pray: "may we be such as those who bring on this great renovation and make this world progressive (till its perfection shall have been reached). . . . May we be (yea like Thyself) in helpful readiness to meet (Thy people) presenting benefits . . ." (par. 9). At the end of their travail "in the happy abode of the Good Mind and of Ahura the righteous saints shall gather, they who proceed in their walk (on the earth in good repute and honour)" (par. 10). Such was the realm of Ahura Mazda and His ever-growing Kingdom of Righteousness culminating in "the Holy (Heaven) the Best Mental State" (par. 4). The Evil Spirit chose that which was evil. He worked "for the worst of possible results" (par. 5). His personification of the

Worst Mind won over to him the Demon gods "who thereupon rushed together unto the demon of Fury that they might pollute the lives of mortals" (par. 6). Between the Evil One, with the Daêvas and all the powers of wickedness at command, and Ahura, the soul of the Righteous Order, there is age-long conflict. But in the end comes the victory of Good. The Demon of the Lie is delivered "into the two hands of the Righteous Order (as a captive to a destroyer)" (par. 8). "(And when perfection shall have been attained) then shall the blow of destruction fall upon the Demon of Falsehood (and her adherents shall perish with her)" (par. 10).

YASNA XXXI. Zarathustra declares with certainty that good will triumph. "And to the Great Creator (shall there be) a realm such as that (whose strength I asked for victory), and which (at the last) shall flourish in its holiness to His glory" (par. 6). He declares the unchangeableness of God. "Thou who art for every hour the same" (par. 7). Ahura Mazda is the source and the upholder of good life—"the one to be adored with the mind in the creation as the Father of the Good Mind within us, when I beheld Thee with my (enlightened) eyes as the veritable maker of our Righteousness, as the Lord of the actions of life" (par. 8). In a series of rhetorical questions to which answers are not given, but which suggest plainly their own answers, Ahura Mazda is described as the Creator of men and the Giver of laws (par. 11). He is the All-seeing One (par. 13). He is claimed as the guardian of the tiller's herd, of "the pious husbandman's flock" of all those "who abjure the Lie-Demon's faith" (par. 15). It is suggested that the good man "who with wise action has striven to promote (Thy Holy) Rule over house, and region and province in the Righteous Order and in truth" (par. 16) becomes like the Living Lord. The listening throngs are warned against the teachings of sinners. They must not be listened to but "(fly ye to arms without hearing), and hew ye them all with a halberd" (par. 18). The deceivers of the saints shall be destroyed. The wicked through their own evil deeds will receive "long life ... in the darkness" (par. 20). To the good Ahura Mazda will give both "Universal Weal and Immortality in the fulness of His Righteous Order" (par. 21).

YASNA XXXII. The conflict between Good and Evil is strong. The Daêvas "seed from the Evil mind" (par. 3) are confronting the followers of Ahura. They confuse the thoughts of man and thus, leading them out of the mind of God, cause them to bring forth "the worst deeds" (par. 4). Their leader, "full of crime ... has desired to destroy us" (par. 6). He is a blasphemer (par. 10). He endeavours "to destroy the meadows with drought" (par. 10). Zarathustra is even threatened with physical violence. The Evil One "will hurl his mace at Thy saint (who may fall before his arms)" (par. 10). The enemy and his confederates rob and despoil "seizing away the gifts of inherited treasures from both household lord, and housewife" (par. 11). They are "the destroyers of life" (par. 13). "They have come as an aid to the wicked" (par. 14). And yet though wickedness may rage and for a while seem victorious the prophet has sure faith. The sword of the wicked may be far-famed, but "the utter destruction of those things Thou, O Ahura Mazda! knowest most surely!" (par. 7). By the word of His mouth He will avenge and defend His saints (par. 16), and at the end of the conflict righteousness shall prevail: "And in Thy Kingdom and Thy Righteous Order I will establish Thy precepts (in Thy Name)" (par. 6).

YASNA XXXIII. Zarathustra offers the "life of his very body" and "his Obedience in deed and in speech" (par. 14) to the Sovereign Power of Ahura. He prays for himself beseeching "for a sight of Thee and for consultation with Thee" (par. 6) that he may be shown "the worthy aims of our faith" (par. 8). He prays "for all prosperous states in being" that Ahura will "cause our bodily and personal life to be blest with salvation" (par. 10): "O Ahura! do thou Thyself arise to me! . . . Grant me mighty strength. . . . Reveal to me thy nature" (par. 12, 13). He prays for himself and yet not for himself. In his mind all the time are all sorts and conditions of men: "lord's kinsmen" and "village labourer," "the sacred Kine," his people to whom he has given laws. "Come to my men, and my laws, my very own, O Mazda" (par. 7).

YASNA XXXIV. Zarathustra gives thanks for the three great blessings that Ahura has bestowed upon men: "Immortality, the Righteous Order and the established Kingdom of Welfare" (par. 1). He shows how "those gifts of the Good Spirit" are given back again in gratitude "by the mind and the deed of the bountiful man whose soul goes hand in hand with the Righteous Order" (par. 2). The goodness of God calls out the best in man. He inquires what is the nature of the Kingdom of Mazda, in order that he may "care for Your poor in their suffering" (par. 5). In all the world he can find none other than Mazda on whom to stay himself: "I know none other than You: then do Ye save us through Your righteousness" (par. 7). Men can become good and life really progressive only as the Spirit of God enters into the human soul and strengthens it to all good works: "Teach Thou us the paths through righteousness, those verily trod by (Thy) Good Mind as He lives within Thy Saints" (par. 12). "Yea (show me, O Mazda, that path and its reward): tell me the best (of truths): reveal the best words and the best actions and the confessing prayer of the praiser through Thy Good Mind (living within us)" (par. 15).

(b) THE GÂTHA USTÂVÂITI

YASNA XLIII. Zarathustra will devote himself to the preparations for the coming of Ahura's Kingdom. He stresses the idea of the differing rewards of the evil and of the good. For the evil there will be evil only, but "happy blessings for the good . . . (to be adjudged to each) in the creations final change" (par. 5). Zarathustra desires that he himself might be "To the wicked (would that I could be) in very truth a strong tormenter and avenger, but to the righteous may I be a mighty help and joy. . . ." (par. 8). Again he prays for the indwelling righteousness of God. Amongst men he had sorrows, but will persevere in doing those things "which Thou didst say was best" (par. 11). Before he goes out to his hard task he prays that the Spirit of Obedience be granted him "to go on hand in hand with me with holy recompense and mighty splendour, whereby to give the contending throngs as a blessing (Your) spiritual gifts (of certainty and peace)" (par. 12). He prays for long life that he may spend himself making known to men "the true and sacred aims" (par. 13). If the followers of Ahura have the "(quiet mind of faith)" then "full many a sinner" will be brought "unto Thee (as convert and in penitence)" (par. 15).

YASNA XLIV. Again he addresses a long list of questions to Ahura which in most cases suggest their own answers. The deity is represented as "the first father of the Righteous Order. The One "Who gave the recurring sun and stars their (undeviating) way; who established that whereby the moon waxes and whereby she wanes" (par. 3). He sustains the earth and the clouds, and has made the water and the plants, the nights and darkness. But marvellous as is the handiwork of God in the material things of nature, Zarathustra lifts the idea to a yet higher plane. The Creator of the heavens and the earth is the source of spiritual goodness, "the inspirer of the good thoughts within our souls" (par. 4). Only through the indwelling of Mazda can men attain "to this life's perfection," and their souls "with joyfulness increase in goodness" (par. 8). Zarathustra displays strong hatred of the wicked—the polluted worshippers—upon whom he looks "with (my) spirit's hate" (par. 11). He would banish the Demon of the Lie to the underworld "filled with rebellion" (par. 13). He prays for a mighty destruction "on the evil believers ... those deceitful and harsh oppressors" (par. 14). The Daêva-worshippers are anathema. They have never reigned as worthy kings—never been the givers of tribal wealth or blessings, nor have they brought water to the fields for the Kine (par. 20). In this Yasna Zarathustra displays a self-seeking spirit. He desires to be "in the chieftainship" (par. 17), to receive "signs of honour and blessing" (par. 18)—and even, apparently, material reward: "ten (costly) mares male-mated and with them the camel" (par. 18).

Yasna XLV. Zarathustra stresses the dualism of the Universe. Between the bountiful and the harmful spirits there is nothing in common. "Neither our thoughts, nor commands, nor our understandings, nor our beliefs, nor our deeds, nor our consciences, nor our souls, are at one" (par. 2). Again he proclaims God as the source of all goodness. His blessing is upon His followers both in this life and in the "eternal Immortality" (par. 7). Not here alone "but (in His home of song) His praise we shall bear" (par. 8). Ahura is "the Lord of Saving Power; a friend, a brother or a father to us" (par. 11). Men must choose between the good and the evil, and hard is the lot of those who make the wrong choice: "to these shall the end of life (issue) in woe" (par. 3).

Yasna XLVI. The times are evil. Zarathustra is faced with strong opposition and knows not where to turn for help. His following is scant and no one will give him offerings for the work. How can he establish the Faith? In his extremity he turns to Ahura Mazda: "Therefore I cry to Thee; behold it Lord; desiring helpful grace for me, as friend bestows on friend. (Therefore to meet my spirit's need and this as well) declare and teach to me the Good Mind's wealth" (par. 2). Then he apparently turns to the chiefs of the people assembled and shows how triumphant evil is ravaging amongst the people and holding back the progress of the Kingdom. Inspired by "vengeful hate" (par. 8), he appeals to the chiefs to rise and throw off the tyranny of "Karpan and the Kavu," who join "in governments to slay the life of man with evil deeds" (par. 11). In the parable of the Judge's Bridge he shows how they who follow him will at the last pass safely to the "prospered life," but the wicked shall "miss their path and fall, and in the Lie's abode for ever shall their habitation be" (par. 11). A voice from amongst the assembled chiefs asked where a leader could be found. Zarathustra immediately named "Vistapa the Heroic." This seems to show with considerable clearness the actual historical position of Zarathustra in the national life. His faith was a national one. He was the accepted chief of the national Church. In time of defeat—probably at the hands of marauding tribes—he rallies the broken nation and supplies every incentive of patriotism, backed by religious devotion, to establish the Cattle People in the security of their ancient settlements.

(c) THE GÂTHA SPENTÂ MAINYÛ

YASNA XLVII is a song of the indwelling of Ahura in the righteous and of His blessings and rewards. Yet bounteous as He is to those who maintain the Righteous Moral Order, His face is turned from the wicked: "far from Thy Love the wicked has his portion abiding in the actions of the Evil mind."

YASNA XLVIII. The nation is still afflicted. At times Zarathustra is not sure of the outcome of it all. A decisive struggle is at hand. He does not know the issue. He can but hope and pray that the good shall in the end prevail and that the "evil heretic" shall be smitten. The followers of the Good Mind must hold their refuge fast. The struggling saint toils with changing lot, believing where he cannot see, praying for the hour "when faith shall be changed to sight" (par. 9).

YASNA XLIX. The struggle is still doubtful. There has been disaffection in the host. Bendva, a brutal chieftain, has defeated the followers of Mazda. Zarathustra prays that the Good Mind may obtain for him "that (Bendva's) death" (par. 1). They have lost a battle, but Mazda still remains "our abundance and our fatness" (par. 5). To Frashaostra is entrusted the leadership of a new campaign. The faithless reprobates are cursed. "The souls (of the evil dead) shall meet these evil men who serve their evil rulers, who speak with evil words, and harbour evil consciences, these souls (in Hell) shall come with evil food (to welcome them) and in the Lie's abode their dwelling verily shall be" (par. 11).

YASNA L. The gloom has lifted and the Gâtha ends with a hymn of praise. "Your praiser then by eminence would I be named, and (more) would be it so long as by (Thine inspiring) Righteousness I am thus able and may have the power. And may the maker of the world give help through (His implanted) Good Mind (in my fellow-servants). And may that (all) be done (to further us) which through His veritable grace is most promotive (for the Cause)" (par. 11).

(d) THE GÂTHA VOHÛ KHSHATHREN

YASNA LI. The rule of Ahura is to be desired above everything. It is "that lot which most of all brings on (our happiness)" (par. 1). He grants material wealth and, better still, spiritual blessings. He is "the guide and light" of men (par. 3). They seek Him for a "ruler and defence" (par. 4). Zarathustra reaffirms his own calling "as a just controlling guide for those whom He has made" (par. 5). The world is full of conflict between good and evil, but Ahura Mazda has a "sword of justice . . . for the wounding of the wicked with its blade" (par. 9). Zarathustra himself will "wound the wicked to the quick" (par. 10). From the general sense of the Gâtha it would seem that the long struggle has turned in favour of the loyal. In the great council Zarathustra turns from one to another of the chiefs with gracious words of praise for their loyalty and steadfastness. There may still be dangers, but the fearful hour of doubt has passed, and the section closes with a great prayer of thankfulness. "For Ahura Mazda knows the man whose best gift for the sacrifices is given unto me, and from the motive of Righteousness (and in thankfulness for all, and in prayer for yet still further grace) I will worship (the eternal ones): yea, I will worship those who have ever lived and who still live, and by their own (holy) names, and to their (thrones) will I draw near with my praise!" (par. 22).

(*e*) GÂTHA VAHISTÂ ÎSTIS

YASNA LIII. The tone is one of victory. It is evidently a period of peace and prosperity. The occasion is the marriage of Zarathustra's daughter. Bride and bridegroom are urged to seek first after Righteousness, for only so can home life be happy. Falsehood brings death. Evil is in the long run overthrown. "Mazda, Thine is that power (which will banish and conquer). And thine is the Kingdom: and by it thou bestowest the highest (of blessings) on the right living poor" (par. 9).

(f) THE YASNA

In his introduction to the Yasna, L. H. Mills says: "It is now hardly necessary to say that the Yasna is the chief liturgy of the Zarathustrians, in which invocation, prayer, exhortation and praise are all combined as in other liturgies" (*Sacred Books of East*, Vol. XXXI, Introduction). In the Yasna the Gâthas are recited in much the same way that the Gospels are used in the Prayer Book services. Round these as a centre are gathered suitable responses, prayers and hymns and other expressions of religious feeling. A stately and elaborate ritual is of slow growth. In its completed form it bears the impress of many men and of long centuries. Process and development can sometimes be traced, but in the case of the Yasna, where all contemporary literature is lost, and in which there is no certain date from beginning to end, it is hardly possible to trace the progression of ideas with any degree of accuracy. We must be content, then, to take the Yasna as a whole—apart from the Gâthas—and reach if we can a general result. With regard to date, Mills says: "Placing, then, the oldest portions of the later Avesta somewhat earlier than Darius, we are obliged to extend the period during which its several parts were composed so far as perhaps to the third or fourth century before Christ, the half spurious matter contained in them being regarded as indefinitely later" (*S.B.E.*, Vol. XXXI, Introduction, p. 36). Probably we would make little error in suggesting that the Yasna was in all essentials complete by the time of the Persian conquest of the Assyrian and Babylonian Empires.

The Yasna opens with invocation and prayer to all good things in the Universe. The worshippers express their desire to approach. They name the objects of propitiation and make the due offerings. After a further act of worship the priest presents the offerings and makes the ritual sacrifice of which the congregation partakes. "Eat, ye men of this Myazda, the meat offering, ye who have deserved it by your righteousness and correctness" (Yasna VIII, p. 2). Then follow prayers for the rule of Ahura Mazda, for the blessing of the good, and the overthrow of the wicked.

Certain sections embedded in or attached to the Yasna are of great importance and interest.

I. The Mazdayasnian Confession (Yasna XII)

In this the believer, as a follower of Zarathustra, attributes all good things to the Lord: "the Holy One, the Resplendent, the Glorious" (par. 1). He is the ruler of "Asha (the righteous order pervading all things pure), whose are the stars, in whose lights the glorious beings and objects are clothed" (par. 1). Then follow patriotic sentiments. The believer will refrain from "robbery and violence against the (sacred) Kine" (par. 2). Moreover, he will not indulge in "wandering at will," rather will he "abide in steadfastness upon this land" (par. 3). He abjures the Daêvas "evil as they are; aye, utterly bereft of good and void of virtue" (par. 4), and all sorcerers who are possessed by them. In a final summary the believer proclaims himself "A Mazda worshipper . . . of Zarathustra's order. . . . I therefore praise aloud the well-thought thought, the word well spoken and the deed well done. Yea! I praise at once the creed of Mazda, the faith which has no faltering utterance, the faith that wields the felling halberd, the faith of kindred marriage, the holy (Creed) which is the most imposing, best, and most beautiful of all religions which exist, and of all that shall in future come to knowledge, Ahura's faith, the Zarathustrian creed. Yea, to Ahura Mazda do I ascribe all good, and such shall be the worship of the Mazdayasnian belief" (pars. 8 and 9).

II. Haoma Worship (Yasna IX, X and XI)

The worship of Haoma is not known in the Gâthas. It is probably the revival of the cult of a very ancient god of wine which was, at some time subsequent to Zarathustra, incorporated into the Mazdean Faith. Haoma is represented as appearing in the guise of a glorious immortal to Zarathustra, who sang aloud the Gâthas before the sacred Flame. He represented himself as "the Holy One that driveth death afar" (par. 2). He is besought for all manner of blessings, spiritual and material—the health of the body, victory in battle, long life and power. He grants speed to horse-racers, brilliant offspring to women, wisdom to the patient student and husbands to unwed maidens. Haoma hampers the wicked in all their evil deeds and hurls his mace at the fearful Dragon. He sanctifies the home. The tasting of his juice strengthens the faithful in their struggle against the Daêvas and brings health. Drunkenness caused through the drinking of his liquor is mild. So powerful is the hold which was obtained by the cult of Haoma that the special ritual prescribed for his worship forms part of the great Zarathustrian service of invocation, praise and sacrifice. The believer offers his own person "to Haoma, the effective . . . and to the sacred exhilaration which he bestows" (Yasna XI, par. 10). After considering this strange grafting on to the creed of Zarathustra, the remark of Herodotus: "It is also their general practice to deliberate upon affairs of weight when they are drunk . . ." (Bk. I, c: 133) becomes credible.

III. The Yasna Concluding (Yasna LXXI)

This is a summary of the whole Yasna, "the memorized recital of the rites" (par. 1), probably used by individuals for private devotions. Worship and sacrifice are offered to

Ahura Mazda, the Bountiful Immortals, the saints on earth and the saints in heaven, the entire system of the Mazdean faith, the holy creatures, the five Gâthas, the sacred words, the springs of waters, the streams, the growing plants and forest trees; the entire land and the heavens, the stars, the moon and the sun, and the lights without beginning; cattle and aquatic beasts, the holy male and female creatures, the mountains and the lakes; active men and those of good intent; health and healing; the Fire Ahura Mazda's son. The soul of the man who recites these words at the ending of his life shall be kept by Ahura far from Hell. His soul shall pass in safety across Kinvat Bridge and in Heaven he shall intone the "salvation hail."

IV. The Worship of Mithra

Mithra is mentioned several times in the invocations which introduce the Yasna. The usual formula is "Mithra of the wide pastures, of the thousand ears and of the myriad eyes, the Yazad of the spoken name" (Yasna II, par. 3).

The Visparads, Âfrînagên and Gâhs do not introduce any really new material.

(g) THE VENDÎDÂD

The Vendîdâd contains accounts of the creation; civil, ceremonial and moral law; and the codes of purification.

Fargard I. Ahura Mazda is represented as creating sixteen "good lands and countries." Angra Mainyu, "who is all death," endeavoured to counteract this by bringing forth disease and sin and various plagues—lust, unbelief, pride, unnatural sin, the burying and burning of the dead, evil wizards, abnormal issues in women, oppression by foreign rulers and the cold sharpness of winter.

Fargard II. Contains a description of an ideal society

in which "there were no hump-backed, none bulged forward . . . no impotent, no lunatic; no poverty, no lying, no meanness, no jealousy, no decayed tooth, no leprous to be confined, nor any of the brands wherewith Angra Mainyu stamps the bodies of mortals" (v. 37). Men and women share equally the delights of the good enclosure.

FARGARD III. Ahura Mazda declares that there is joy whenever worship is offered with the right ritual, wherever there is established a house in which "every blessing of life is thriving," wherever the earth is cultivated and there is increase of flocks and herds. The earth is rejoiced by those men who dig out the buried corpses of men and dogs, who pull down Dakhmas, who fill up the burrows of the creatures of Angra Mainyu, who cultivate the soil and who give alms in kindly and pious fashion to the faithful believers. The "Earth feels sorest grief" at that place, "the neck of Arezura, whereon the hosts of fiends rush forth from the burrow of the Drug." In those places where the corpses of men and dogs are buried, where the Dakhmas stand and where there are the burrows of the creatures of Angra Mainyu. There is sore grief also when "the wife and child of one of the faithful . . . are driven along the way of captivity, the dry, the dusty way, and lift up a voice of wailing." In a digression is described the terrible fate of the man who has allowed himself to become hopelessly defiled by carrying a corpse in his arms. He is kept close prisoner until he has become a Pairista-khshudra, "one whose seed is dried up," and then after the skin has been flayed from the body and the head cut from the neck the corpse is delivered to greedy beasts of prey. The blessings that follow the cultivation of the soil are set forth in a further digression. Abundance of corn is death to the Daêvas: "It is as though red-hot iron were turned about in their throats when there is plenty of corn."

FARGARD IV contains moral and civil law together with

penalties. Failure to restore a borrowed article is theft. The breaking of a contract is to be punished by stripes. Assault is followed by a like retribution. But this is not all, for the sinner will be plagued in hell for his evil doings: "Down there the pains for that deed shall be as hard as any in this world."

FARGARDS V–XII deal with the defiling power of the Drug Nasu and with the various means by which the pollution can be removed. Immediately after death this fiend, "in the shape of a raging fly, with knees and tail sticking out, all stained with stains and like unto the foulest Krafstras" (Fargard VII, v. 2), rushes upon the corpse which becomes a fearfully contagious centre of defilement. Evil is victorious and enthroned in the dead threatens all on every side. Whatever clothes touch the body are rendered unclean. Whosoever touches the clothing or the corpse becomes no less polluted than they. Immediate steps are necessary to confine the fiend within as narrow a limit as possible. The greatest precautions must be observed against contact. One man must not endeavour to handle the body, which must be removed from the house of the living and as soon as possible placed on the Dakhma, which shall be erected "on the highest summits, where they know there are always corpse-eating birds" (Fargard VI, v. 45)—"a building out of the reach of the dog, of the fox and the wolf, and wherein rainwater cannot stay" (Fargard VI, v. 50). The Dakhma, if possible, shall be "of stones, mortar and earth," but if this cannot be afforded "they shall lay down the dead man on the ground, on his carpet and his pillow, clothed with the light of heaven and beholding the sun" (Fargard VI, v. 51). The corpse remains in the possession of the Drug until it "has been rained on, until the Dakhma has been rained on, until the unclean remains have been rained on, until the birds have eaten up the corpse" (Fargard V, v. 14). When, however, "the dog has seen it or eaten it up, or when the flesh-eating birds have taken flight toward it, then the Drug Nasu rushes away to the regions of the North" (Fargard VII, v. 3). The Dakhmas themselves are centres of horrible pollution. The fiends rush to them in companies and revel, taking food and voiding filth. Disease of every sort is rife. "There death has most power on man from the hour when the sun is down" (Fargard VII, v. 58). There is no action more worthy of merit than to pull down these terrible places once their end has been served. Whosoever does this, "his sins in thought, word and deed are atoned for," "the stars, the moon and the sun shall rejoice in him. Ahura Mazda himself shall give him welcome from the decaying world into the undecaying one" (Fargard VII, vv. 51, 52). More difficult than the actual disposal of the dead is the exorcising of the fiend from the persons or the belongings of those who have from some contact with dead bodies or polluted objects become themselves possessed. Various ceremonials are prescribed to meet various degrees of defilement. The case of one who has touched the corpse of a man or a dog in which the Nasu is still present is to be dealt with as follows: Three holes are dug in the ground and filled with gomez. The unclean person washes himself therein. After this a yellow dog with four eyes or a white dog with yellow ears is placed in front of him. The process is repeated and is followed by a washing with water. The exorcist then commences to chase the Drug Nasu from the body. Commencing at the "forepart of the skull" he sprinkles with "the good waters" in such systematic fashion that the Nasu is driven ever lower until at last it is confined to the left toe, from which it is at length triumphantly driven to the accompaniment of the fiend-smiting chant: "Keep us from our hater, O Mazda, and Ârmaiti Spenta! Perish, O fiendish drug! Perish, O brood of the fiend! Perish, O world of the fiend! Perish away, O Drug! Rush away,

O Drug! Perish away, O Drug! Rush away, O Drug! Perish away, O Drug! Perish away to the regions of the north, never more to give unto death the living world of the holy spirit" (Fargard VIII, v. 72).

Fargard XIII, XIV and part of XV deal with the treatment of the dog—an animal of the greatest consideration amongst a Cattle People. The dog is "the good creature among the creatures of the good spirit that from midnight until the sun is up goes and kills thousands of the creatures of the evil spirit" (Fargard XIII, v. 1). His duties are to watch over his master's goods and to guard the cattle and sheep. The dog must be properly fed and cared for. Lack of attention to a bitch with young, of such a nature as to cause her death or that of any of her litter, is to be regarded as wilful murder. The man who kills a dog "kills his own soul for nine generations" (Fargard XIII, v. 3). But the dog also may on due occasion be mutilated, or even in extremity be put to death.

Fargard XIX. Angra Mainyu "the deadly, the Daêva of the Daêvas," rushed forth against Zarathustra, inciting the Drug to destroy him. "The unseen death, the hellborn," was routed as Zarathustra raised loudly the chant: "The will of the Lord is the law of holiness," and followed the chant "swinging stones in his hand, stones as big as a house" (vv. 1–11). The fiend, seeing that he could do nothing with violence, attempted bribery, offered to make him the "ruler of the nations." The offer is contemptuously rejected and the Evil One driven back. Ahura teaches Zarathustra the great invocation to all the good beings and the good things in the Universe, by which the onslaughts of the Daêvas can be triumphantly repelled. A revelation is made concerning the rewards or penalties that lie beyond death. For three days "the hellish evildoing Daêvas" assail the soul. Then "the fiend named Vizaresha carries off in bonds the souls of the wicked Daêva worshippers who live in sin"

MAZDAISM

(v. 29). The souls of the righteous rise above the Kinvat Bridge, and are conducted by a beauteous maiden into the presence of the heavenly gods. Again Zarathustra utters a great invocation to all the powers of goodness. Angra Mainyu and his Daêvas fly—"they run away, they rush away, the wicked evil-doing Daêvas into the depths of the dark horrid world of hell" (v. 47).

FARGARD XX. As Mazdaism is pre-eminently a religion of life, the healing of disease is regarded as a high and holy thing. The first physician was "Thraita . . . who first of the healthful, the wise, the happy, the wealthy, the glorious, the strong man of yore, drove back sickness to sickness, drove back death to death, and first turned away the point of the poniard, and the fire of fever from the bodies of mortals" (v. 2). Mazda himself assisted by bringing down healing plants.

FARGARD XXI. Angra Mainyu is the source of disease—"the ruffian, Angra Mainyu the deadly, wrought by his witchcraft nine diseases and ninety and nine hundred and nine thousand and nine times ten thousand diseases" (v. 2).

There are certain prohibitions contained in the Vendîdâd which have not previously been noted and which are important.

1. Self-abuse—a deadly sin (Fargard VIII, v. 27).
2. Unnatural lust—the sinner becomes a Daêva before and after death (Fargard VIII, v. 31–32).
3. Intercourse with a woman who is quick with child (Fargard XV, v. 8).
4. The procuring of miscarriage (Fargard XV, v. 14).

(h) YASTS

The Yasts are for the most part acts of devotion addressed to various gods or great spiritual beings.

I. ORMAZD YAST. This Yast is of particular importance on account of the lists given of the names of Ahura Mazda.

He is the Herdgiver, the Strong One, Perfect Holiness, Creator of all good things, Understanding, Knowledge, the Producer of Weal, the Beneficent, the Harmless One, the Unconquerable, the Maker of True Account, All-seeing, the Healer, the Creator, the Lord. He is the protector and Well-Wisher of men, the Liberal King. He does not deceive nor can he be deceived. He destroys malice. He is the Energetic One, the Wise One, He who does good for a long time (vv. 7-15). Whenever the believer pronounces the names and attributes of Ahura he is safe from the weapons of his enemies and from the assaults of the fiends.

II. HAPTAN YAST. This is a song of praise to Ahura and to the Amesha-Spentas. The mention of "Mercy and Charity" is interesting.

III. ARDIBEHIST YAST. Of all means of healing the Holy Word is the most potent. Pride, Scorn, Hot Fever, Slander, Discord and the Evil Eye fly before it as do "the most lying words of falsehood" (vv. 8-9). The daêvas are smitten. Angra Mainyu himself admits the victorious power of the Righteous Order.

IV. ABÂN YAST. This describes the worship of the water goddess, Ardvi Sûra Anâhita. She demands sacrifice "with libations cleanly prepared and well strained, together with the Haoma and meat" (v. 7). She is represented as being worshipped by the great heroes of the Aryan race to whom she grants victory in battle. Men of strength pray to her for "swift horses and supremacy of Glory" (v. 86). Maids beseech her for strong husbands and women for "a good delivery" (v. 87). All her foes, the fever-stricken, liars, cowards, the jealous, women, the unfaithful, the leper, the blind and the deaf; the wicked, the destroyer and the niggard; the hump-backed or bulged forward, and the fiend with decayed teeth are forbidden to drink of her libations (vv. 92-93).

V. Khôrshêd Yast. "The undying, shining, swift-horsed sun" is in an especial sense a creature of Ahura. Light is the natural symbol of the good, darkness of evil. During the night "Daêvas born of darkness" have their hour, but when the dawn comes and the earth is flooded with light all good things rejoice and become clean.

VI. Mâh Yast. The worship of the moon.

VII. Tîr Yast. Tistraya is "the bright and glorious star whom Ahura Mazda has established as a lord and overseer above all stars" (v. 44). He it is who brings the rains and thus gives "ease and joy on the fertile countries" (v. 9). His enemy is the drought fiend—the Daêva Apaosha. The combat between them is long and doubtful, but Tistraya is strengthened by the offering to him of "the libations, with the Haoma and the Holy meat" (v. 7). He is victorious, and as a result the "life of the waters will flow down unrestrained to the big-seeded cornfields, to the small-seeded pasture fields and to the whole of the material world" (v. 29). "Behind him travels the mighty wind made by Mazda and the rain and the cloud and the sleet, down to the several places down to the fields . . ." (v. 33) ". . . the wind blows the clouds forward, bearing the waters of fertility, so that the friendly showers spread wide over . . ." (v. 40). There is promise of blessing to those who perform to Tistraya the rightful offering. But if they be forgotten or performed unworthily or by wicked persons "a murderer or a whore" (v. 60), then will come plagues and hostile hordes.

VIII. Gôs Yast. Gôs, "the cow," keeps the flocks in health. To her the heroes of the Iranian race are represented as offering sacrifice and praying for blessings both spiritual and material.

IX. Mihir Yast. This is devoted to the praise of Mithra, "the lord of wide pastures, who is truthspeaking, a chief in assemblies, with a thousand ears well shapen, with ten thousand eyes, high, with full knowledge, strong, sleepless and ever awake" (v. 7). He is "as worthy of sacrifice, as worthy of prayer, as . . . Ahura Mazda" (v. 1). Mithra and Ahura are "the two great imperishable, holy gods" (v. 145). Mithra is a god of war—the especial champion of the Aryan race—"victory making, army governing . . . power wielding, power possessing. Who sets the battle a-going, who stands against armies in battle, breaks asunder the lines arrayed" (vv. 35–38). Before him the Daêvas and the fiends flee away. Beside his chariot are bows, arrows, spears, two-edged steel hammers, swords, maces of iron and "a club cast out of red brass, of strong golden brass; the strongest of all weapons, the most victorious of all weapons" (v. 132). With these weapons he smites through the heavenly spaces. They fall crashing on the skulls of the Daêvas. Of a truth he is "a stout and strong warrior," victorious and armed with a well-fashioned weapon, watchful in darkness and undeceivable. He is the stoutest of the stoutest, he is the strongest of the strongest" (vv. 140–141). Sacrifice is offered to him in the usual form. As an all-powerful god he is besought for all manner of blessings: "riches, strength and victory; good conscience and bliss, good fame and a good soul; wisdom and the knowledge that gives happiness; the victorious strength given by Ahura, the crushing Ascendant of Asha Vahista, and conversation (with God) on the Holy Word" (v. 33). Associated as he is with the sun, he is regarded as "lord of all countries" (v. 145). His face "looks over all the seven Karshvares of the earth" (v. 64). He is the great giver of prosperity: "increase giving, fatness giving, cattle giving, sovereignty giving, sun giving, cheerfulness giving and bliss giving" (v. 65).

X. Srôsh Yast Hâdhôkht. Sraosha is the god "of the incarnate Word." He smashes the skulls of the Daêvas, but is "dear and friendly" in the houses of faithful men.

XI. Rashn Yast. Rashnu is "the smiter, destroyer of thieves and bandits." He is "watching the doings of men and making the account . . ." (v. 8).

XII. Farvadin Yast. Ahura Mazda gives praise to the Fravashis—or souls—of good men and things without whose aid it would be impossible for him to carry on the conflict with the fiendish creatures of Angra Mainyu " . . . they come to help me . . . they bring assistance unto me, the awful Fravashis of the faithful" (v. 19). In times of fearful peril the people, hard-pressed by the foe, call upon the souls of the ancient heroic dead. They come by the thousands and tens of thousands to "fight in the battles that are fought in their own place and land, each according to the place and house where he dwelt of yore" (v. 67). Beginning with Zarathustra, "the first Priest, the first Warrior, the first Plougher of the ground" (v. 88), the Yast gives a long roll of the heroes and saints of the Aryan race. All those who are worthy receive worship: "the souls of the holy men and women, born at any time, whose consciences struggle or will struggle, or have struggled for the good" (v. 154). Among these Zarathustra is exalted "the Lord and Master of all the material world, the man of the primitive law; the wisest of all beings, the best ruling of all beings, the brightest of all beings, the most glorious of all beings, the most worthy of sacrifice amongst all beings, the most worthy of prayer amongst all beings . . . worthy . . . as much as any being can be, in the perfection of his holiness" (v. 152).

XIII. Bahrâm Yast. Verethraghna—the genius of victory —is "the best armed of the heavenly gods." He is "the strongest in strength . . . the most victorious in victory . . . most glorious in glory" (v. 3). His blessings are those which make for the strength of the body.

XIV. Dîn Yast. The goddess Kista gives "swiftness of the feet, the quick hearing of the ears, the strength of the arms, the health of the whole body, the sturdiness of the whole body, and the eyesight of the vulture . . ." (v. 13).

XV. Ashi Yast. This goddess, the daughter of Ahura Mazda, enlivens the intelligence and bestows heavenly wisdom. She is a giver of riches. She will not accept the libation of the "man whose seed is dried out . . . or the courtesan . . . or young boys and girls who have known no man" (v. 54).

XVI. Astâd Yast. Ahura Mazda is represented as being especially the god of the Aryans. He has blessed them with prosperity and power. The non-Aryans are destroyed.

XVII. Zamyad Yast. There is prophecy of the ultimate victory of good "when the dead will rise, when life and immortality will come . . . when the creation will grow deathless—the prosperous creation of the Good Spirit—and the Drug shall perish" (v. 12).

XVIII. Vanant Yast.

XIX. Yast Fragment. This Yast deals with the various indulgences which are granted to those who recite the "praise of Holiness." Special merit is acquired if their recitation takes place after sleeping, after eating, during cohabitation, at the time of dying; when a man professes "good thoughts, good words and good deeds" and rejects "evil thoughts, evil words and evil deeds" (v. 7) and at the sacrifice of the Haoma.

XX. Yast Fragment. On the first night after the death of one of the faithful the soul stays near the head singing the Ustâvâiti Gâtha. The soul is supremely happy. This continues for three nights. At the next dawn his own conscience, in the form of a beautiful maid, is blown toward him on a sweet-scented wind. His good deeds have made her beautiful. At the first step the faithful soul finds himself in the Paradise of Good Thought, at the second in that of the Good Word, at the third in that of the Good Deed and at the fourth in that of the Endless Lights, where he is welcomed by the faithful departed before him, and by Ahura Mazda. Here he eats the sanctified food. As for the wicked, he sits for three nights singing a song of lament and is then borne away by a foul-scented wind and plunged into the hells of Evil Thought, Evil Word and Evil Deed. Finally, he reaches the Endless Darkness and is given the food "of poison and poisonous stench" (v. 36).

XXI. ÂFRÎN PAIGHAMBAR ZARTÛST. This is the blessing of Zarathustra on Vistaspa. He prays that the king may have long life, that sons may be born to him, that he may be beneficent, fiend-smiting, well-armed, strong, glorious and beautiful of body, a wise chief of assemblies, rich in cattle and in horses, holy, "beloved by the gods and reverenced by men" (v. 4); victorious, free from sickness and death.

XXII. VISTASP YAST. Blessings of every sort are invoked upon Vistaspa. If he receives well the teaching of Zarathustra he will be "rich in children, and rich in milk; rich in seed, in fat, in milk" (v. 13). Wealthy men are commanded to be liberal to the poor. Charity ever stands at the door in the persons of the poor brethren. Only the followers of Angra Mainyu "shut (to the poor) the door of the house" (v. 37).

(*i*) SUMMARY OF MAZDAISM

Those Aryan tribes amongst whom arose the Mazdayasnian faith may have entered Media and Persia at much the same period as the Greeks poured into Hellas. They were nomads, whose only wealth was in cattle—migrating from pasture to pasture—ever wandering and ever at war. They possessed little culture and neither cohesion nor national self-consciousness. Their religion was similar to that of the Aryan invaders of India. On every side except the north and the west they were shut in by great mountains, stretches of desert, or wide seas. To the west lay the mighty empire of

Assyria, and from the north the Scythian hordes were a constant menace. Gradually, as numbers increased, the nomad life became more difficult, and at last impossible. Permanent settlements were made. Agriculture was practised to some extent. National self-consciousness commenced to make itself felt. This period of consolidation may have lasted for some hundreds of years. The Gâthas show that the process was by no means finished at the time when Zarathustra became the religious leader of the people. There were still some who desired to revert to the wandering habits of their ancestors. Of Zarathustra himself we know nothing except what can be inferred from the Zend Avesta. He was probably the last and greatest of a long line of prophets who had steadily evolved a high and lofty faith from the primitive polytheism of the migratory clans. Prior to his call there had been a period either of religious conflict or revival. The people are represented as calling in an agony to Ahura Mazda for a leader and teacher. He names Zarathustra. This calling of a mere man is regarded with the bitterest disappointment. But Zarathustra hears the call and before long his teaching has apparently been delivered with such power as to have gained him a position of unquestioned primacy in the priesthood of the Cattle People. His influence is paramount in religion and in national affairs generally. For some time it would appear that his mission was almost entirely that of preaching and teaching. He endeavoured to direct men's attention to the fundamental ideas and attitudes of religion. They must make decisions in the light of reason and of conscience. The response to his message seems to have been widespread and the effect lasting. Religion amongst such a people could hardly become purely speculative. Of necessity it would deal with practical affairs, and the priest would become identified with everyday life—the ploughing, the planting of grain, the welfare of the cattle, civil disputes and the practical application of moral law. So we can see Zarathustra, the teacher, prophet, priest and lawgiver of the tribes, busily employed about the work of revival, renascence and settlement. Some part of his life seems to have passed happily enough after the initial struggle against incredulity. But darker days came. The Daêva worshippers, probably Scythian hordes from the north, threatened to overwhelm the Aryans. The struggle was long and desperate. Zarathustra became the centre and soul of national resistance. There were periods of terrible disaster. The future was dark, but the prophet never lost his conviction of ultimate deliverance, even when treacherous desertion had made the triumph of evil seem almost certain. His faith was in the long run justified, and it would seem that in the end the tribes maintained their freedom and their faith. There are scattered passages which give an impression of selfish self-seeking, but on the whole Zarathustra appears as the shepherd of his people, devoting his life to their interests, spiritual and material, and to the extension of the Kingdom of God.

The essential elements of the Zarathustrian doctrine as revealed in the Gâthas are:

1. The belief in Dualism. Running through the whole of the Universe there is a tremendous conflict between Good and Evil. Nothing is or can be neutral. Ahura Mazda, who is altogether good and the creator of all good things, good beings and men, has been struggling from the beginning of time with Angra Mainyu, the creator of evil and evil beings.

2. The Kingdom of Ahura is made up of all beings, all attitudes, all material things which make for life. Obedience, Righteousness, and Holiness are its foundations. Good harvests and abundant flocks, health and happy homes, progress and prosperity are its visible signs amongst men.

3. The Evil One and his followers are thieves, liars, murderers and bringers of drought. Their pleasure is to destroy life and to spread disease, pollution and death.

4. The struggle, though age-long, is not eternal, for in the end righteousness will prevail. The Kingdom of Ahura, already established and growing, will be everywhere victorious, and the reign of evil overthrown. The methods by which this is to be accomplished are two-fold:

(*a*) The growth in men's souls of a knowledge of God. Through the quiet operation of the Holy Spirit in the lives of good men the kingdom is spread from one to another.

(*b*) At the end of the age of conflict the Evil One and his followers will be violently overthrown, their strength utterly broken and they themselves miserably cast down to the lowest regions of Hell.

5. There is a sure insistence on the immortality of the soul. After death the faithful ones, having left behind them their corruptible bodies, will go safely over the Kinvat Bridge and reach the blessed abode of Heaven, there to live for ever with Mazda in his home of song. The wicked are cast down to the abyss.

6. Zarathustra himself is apparently a monotheist. Ahura Mazda is the only God mentioned in the Gâthas. The great personifications of Piety, Sovereign Power, the Good Mind, the Righteous Order and Obedience are either special manifestations of Himself or comparable to the angels of Christian theology. Ahura stands by Himself, as the Creator of the Heavens and the Earth, the Sustainer of the Universe, the Eternal, the Unchangeable, the Living Lord of all good life.

7. With the narrowness that accompanies nationalism, particularly in its earlier and struggling stages, Ahura was

MAZDAISM

represented only in the vaguest way as the God and Father of all men. While there is nothing to contradict a theory of universalism He is besought as the national god of the Aryans to grant them victory in battle. All other peoples are Daêva worshippers and are, therefore, naturally supposed to be outside the circle of His providence.

8. Zarathustra frequently displays an intolerant and often bloodthirsty spirit. If any sinner has the temerity to give false teaching the bystanders are to make no reply, but are to immediately hew him down with their halberds. He prays for the death of Bendva, an enemy chieftain. Vengeful hate inspires him to rally his people against their oppressors.

9. The Gâthas, rich as they are in some of the sublimest elements of spiritual religion, do not exhibit any clear-cut ethical system. Men are exhorted to righteous living, but little is said of those things which go to constitute good life. Zarathustra was probably satisfied with the existing codes, and considered that the real need of his people was a deepening of spiritual experience, a greater certainty of the holiness and righteousness of God and a sure faith in the ultimate victory of good.

The Yasna, Vendîdâd, Yasts and minor sections are of a later period than that of Zarathustra. They agree in the main with the propositions outlined in the Gâthas, but introduce some fresh material, elaborate points which have not been dealt with in detail, and materially modify the theory of monotheism.

The Mazdayasnian Confession was a credal statement which probably outlined the minimum of belief essential for salvation. It is a re-statement in short form of the actual Zarathustrian position. In the Yasna Concluding, however, worship is directed not only to Ahura but to every good being, man or thing to be found throughout the whole creation. The Yasna and the Yasts mention numerous gods and goddesses all subordinate in some degree to Ahura, but still essentially belonging to a divine order. Sacrifice is offered to these deities, and they are besought for various blessings. The explanation, no doubt, lies in the fact that ancient Aryan tribes were polytheistic. Religious reformation and development led the loftier souls, and perhaps temporarily even the whole nation, to a higher level of belief, but the new atmosphere was too rarified for the multitude, and old deities once more made their appearance. Haoma, the god of wine; Mithra, a god of war; the sea goddess Anahita and others took again their ancient places. The new and high development was still maintained as the essential basis of orthodoxy, but the old stood side by side with the new. Zarathustrian priests of post-Reformation times were probably prepared to sanction interpolations into the liturgy for the sake of unity in the Church. The whole position is surprisingly similar to the development within the Roman Catholic Church of the adoration of saints, many of whom on examination prove to be favourite gods or heroes of paganism in another guise.

A very great deal of space is taken up with the description of the various ceremonials for purification and for the exorcising of fiends. Mazdaism degenerated very largely into a wearying round of empty ceremonies to counter defilements that existed in the imagination only. This was the result of an insistence on certain spiritual attitudes without an equal insistence on moral conduct. There were sacrificial and sacramental expressions, prayer and praise, sonorous liturgies, an extraordinarily high conception of the nature of God, of the Kingdom of God and of the ultimate victory of good, but the ethical bases of man's contacts with his fellow-man are not stressed as being of fundamental importance. This does not mean that there is no recognition of the necessity for moral living. Far from this being the case, a search reveals numerous inhibitions and some constructive rules for right

MAZDAISM

living. The faithful are forbidden either directly or by inference:
1. To rob, assault with violence or commit murder.
2. To lie or break a contract.
3. To be jealous, scornful, proud, malicious or sowers of discord.
4. To be niggardly or cowardly.
5. To practise witchcraft.
6. To live as a courtesan.
7. To indulge in self-abuse or unnatural lust.
8. To have intercourse with women quick with child or to procure miscarriage.

They are commanded:
1. To be bountiful, givers of alms and charitable.
2. To be kind to animals.
3. To be truthful.
4. To be merciful.

While these precepts cover a wide field and touch upon some of the most important principles of human conduct they are incidental and not central in the Mazdean scriptures.

Women are regarded as being equally capable with men of good action and of sharing in the future life. Their sphere is apparently restricted to the home in which they are subordinate to the head of the house.

The religion of Mazda is in a narrow sense the possession of a small people, but in its larger sense it has burst its bounds and flowed into the life of the race. The ideas of God as the Creator, the Lord of Saving Power, our Friend, our Brother, our Father; of the Kingdom of God embracing all good life; of the ideal life of man consisting of good thought, good word and good deed; of man's life strengthened by the indwelling of the Spirit; of the immortality of the soul and the Heaven of Endless Light are too great and true not to have lived.

CHAPTER VIII

INDIA

(a) EARLY HISTORY

Before the dawn of history three primitive stocks, the Tibeto-Burmans, the Kolarians and the Dravidians, peoples dark in colour, flat-nosed and of a low grade of culture, crossed the Himalayas and entered into possession of the vast areas of the Indian Peninsula. They were the earliest settlers of whom we have record, and they still form the base of the great majority of Indian peoples. At a time which it is sheerly impossible to date—perhaps 2000 B.C., perhaps much earlier—occurred some great disturbance that resulted in Aryan hordes moving west, south and south-east from the original Central Asian home of the race. One horde moved into Europe, and keeping to the south of the Danube entered Greece and Italy. Another moved north into Germany and the surrounding countries, while a third, moving to the south and east, ultimately entered India and subdued or drove before it the aboriginal inhabitants. The conquest of the Punjab probably commenced not later than 1500 B.C. and may have been long before that date. The general line of advance was across the great river plain of the north up the Indus and then across to the Jumna and the Ganges. During this great march of a race were composed the hymns of the Rig-Veda. From these we are able to extract a general idea of the movements, of the social and political organization and especially of the religious conceptions of the early Aryan conquerors of India.

The Aryan tribes who broke through the mountain barrier of the Himalayas were fierce fighting men inured to the rigour of continental climates and the hardships incidental to the passage of mountainous regions. Their unit was the tribe at the head of which would be the war chief, whose position was probably hereditary. He would be supported and guided by a council of captains and wise men. Priests also, probably hereditary, would offer sacrifices to the gods, conduct auguries, perform certain magical ceremonies, and also keep some sort of rough historical narrative, in the form of genealogical tables, of the chiefs and the record of heroic deeds of a more or less mythical character. The tribesmen themselves would be self-respecting warriors owing allegiance to the chiefs, but otherwise free men enough except when actually at war. Their only wealth was in cattle. They were devoid of anything in the nature of systematic culture or of developed religion. Great common dangers would sometimes bring about a temporary federation of tribes, but any permanent political organization in a large sense was probably never attempted.

The passage of the Himalayas may well have been the slow work of generations, but once the tribes debouched upon the great plains the conquest of the land would proceed apace. There were few natural barriers that could not, with a little patience, be overcome or passed by. It is extremely doubtful whether the Dravidian and other aboriginal stocks were at that time particularly numerous. Though there was no doubt fighting, and fierce fighting at that, the conquest was probably comparatively rapid. Tribes which for many years had been cramped in their development by huge mountains and hostile neighbours suddenly became lords of wide lands and rulers of great kingdoms. The general change of circumstances and surroundings brought developments and modifications of all sorts. The Rig-Veda describes the period of transition during which the tribes developed from rough and uncultured marauding bands into great kingdoms with a complex social organization, an effective military system, and a highly speculative religion with a detailed ritual. When the first of the hymns was composed about 1400 B.C. the process had commenced; when the canon closed at a period not later than 800 B.C. it was still far from complete. The Rig-Veda is the first document that enables us to get on to anything like sure historical ground, and to abandon conjecture for something approaching certainty.

(b) THE PERIOD OF THE RIG-VEDA

The hymns of the Rig-Veda describe a life that has ceased to be migratory. The wealth of the Aryan tribes no longer consists only in cattle. Harvests are essential to the life of the people. The Storm gods are constantly invoked. They bring the harvests, for it is they "who drench the earth" (M. 1, H. 166).[1] They are besought for "an invigorating autumn with quickening rain" (M. 3). Life, though settled, is far from peaceful. In one great battle "Indra-Agni . . . hurled down by one deed the mighty strongholds of which the Dasas were the lords" (M. 3, H. 12, v. 6). Agni is represented as "the conqueror in battles rich in valiant men" (M. 3, H. 29, v. 9). The gods are besought "to crush all enemies, be they relations or strangers" (M. 3, H. 4, v. 5); to give "valiant offspring" (M. 1, H. 96), "valiant heroes" (M. 1, H. 44); to "deprive . . . enemies of power and to send against them an enemy like an arrow" (M. 1, H. 38); and to give to their worshippers "inviolable and invincible strength" (M. 2, H. 34). The spoils of war are greatly to be desired. The favourites of the Maruts "win rich booty" (M. 1, H. 64). "Help us to booty" is the prayer of the suppliants of Rudra (M. 1, H. 43). "Let us partake of all booty; help us to the wealth that is nearest" is the cry of Agni's worshippers (M. 1, H. 27). The actual position probably was that the Aryans had driven a great wedge into the north of India, embracing the valleys of the Indus and its tributaries, and reaching far toward the Ganges. The aborigines menaced all borders and at the same time were themselves a tempting mark for aggression. Within the wedge itself several kingdoms developed and on occasion fought each other with more fury than they fought the common enemy. The story of one of these ancient wars

[1] M. = Mandala. H. = Hymn.

formed the nucleus of the great Indian epic, the Mahabharata. This huge work of some ninety thousand couplets was not finally completed until some centuries after the commencement of the Christian era. It is therefore quite impossible to regard it as being in any sense an authoritative account of the religious or social life of Aryan peoples prior to 500 B.C. The heroes and their detailed exploits are as mythical as the knights of King Arthur or the peers of Charlemagne. The muster-rolls of the combatants are far less exact than those of the Odyssey. At the same time there remains a substratum of probable fact which gives some sort of a picture of the general state of affairs prevailing amongst the ancient kingdoms of the Punjab. Dhritarâshtra, the blind king of the Kurus, had brought up the children of his dead brother together with his own sons. Bitter rivalry developed in the Court. Yudhisthir, the son of Pandu, was recognized as the heir-apparent, but by the treachery of Duryodhan was driven to the forest with his brothers. The exiled princes hear that the princess of Panchala, a neighbouring kingdom, is to make choice of a husband from all the monarchs of North India. They attend the ceremony in disguise, and by the skill of Arjun with the bow, win the princess, who apparently becomes the wife of Yudhisthir. Strengthened by this alliance the exiles are able to return and to insist upon the partition of Kuruland—although they were compelled to take the inferior position. However, good fortune followed them, and in course of time their new capital of Indra-prastha—supposed to be in the vicinity of Delhi—overshadowed the older Kuru capital of Hastina-pura. The power of Yudhisthir grew so rapidly that he proposed to perform the Rajasuya, or Great Horse Sacrifice. The performance of this ceremonial was in itself a claim to imperial sway. Dhritarâshtra and his sons attended the sacrifice, which was duly performed. The new emperor was now at the very height of his power, but during a visit to his cousin he gambled away wealth, power and freedom, and was doomed to an exile of twelve years, to be spent in the forest and another year in concealment. The time passed, and at the end of the thirteenth year they distinguished themselves by helping their Matsya hosts to repel a cattle-lifting raid organized by Duryodhan. Yudhisthir had honourably kept the terms imposed upon him and now demanded the return of his kingdom. Duryodhan refused, and both sides gathered all their resources for the trial by battle. After furious fighting Yudhisthir was victorious. He regained his former power, and once more having performed the Rajasuya, reigned as Emperor of the North. The story of the Maha-bharata thus bears out the inferences drawn from the Rig-Veda. Cattle-raiding—the pursuit of booty—was a common practice. Newly established Aryan kingdoms were in a state of flux—now dividing up, again coming together, and yet again torn by war. While there is little that gives any definite idea of the conditions of social life or the development of culture, we may presume that there were few large towns and that life was comparatively simple.

The gods of the Vedas are personifications either of natural features or of the powers of nature. The descriptions given show little tendency toward anthropomorphism. The deities are vague and indefinite, and distinctions are not strongly marked. They do not seem to form a hierarchy; first one and then another seem to be all-powerful or the special object of prayer and sacrifice. They pass easily one into the other. Agni is hailed as being Indra, Vishnu, Brahman, Varuna, Mitra, Aryaman, Amsa, Tvashtri, Rudra, Savitri, Ribhu, Bharati and Ida: "In thee, O Agni, with thy mouth all the guileless immortal gods eat the offering which is offered to them" (M. 2, H. 1). This passage must not be pressed too far, but it does give an indication of the tendency to seek the One in the Many—

a wide Universal manifesting itself in many forms, but returning ever to the One. Indra is perhaps the chief deity of the invading Aryans. He is hailed as the creator of light and the giver of wealth (M. 1, H. 6)—the Lord of men to whom are the songs and prayers and sacrifices of men (M. 1, H. 65). He gives victory in battle: "Indra-Agni, you have hurled down by one deed the ninety strongholds of which the Dasas were the Lords" (M. 3, H. 12). The Maruts and Indra work together to give harvest, and upon their co-operation the prosperity of the settlements depends. At one time there is serious danger of a breach. Indra is apparently unwilling to share sacrifices with the Maruts (M. 1, H. 170), whom he accuses of having deserted him in his hour of need (M. 1, H. 165). Reconciliation is indispensable to men (M. 1, H. 170). Finally, this is effected—the Maruts recognizing the supremacy of Indra and admitting that there is none other amongst the gods like to him (M. 1, H. 165). The Maruts—or Storm Gods—are interesting figures. There is a rough, fresh boisterousness about them. They are endowed with terrible vigour. They shake the heavens and the earth, make the rocks tremble and tear asunder "the kings of the forest" (M.1, H. 39). Rain is their great gift to men: "The Maruts, charged with rain, endowed with fierce force, terrible like wild beasts, blazing in their strength, brilliant like fires and impetuous, have uncovered the rain-giving cows" (M. 1, 2, H. 34). They are powerful to grant boons, and men pray to them for "luck, wisdom, inviolable and invincible strength" (M. 2, H. 34), "offspring and wealth" (M. 7, H. 56), "for cows and horses" (M. 5, H. 52). Although they protect mortals, yet men fear rather than love them. The people of Trinaskanda pray "that the straightforward shaft and the stone which they hurl may be far from them" (M. 1, H. 172). Their shining thunderbolts are feared. Not only men but the mountains also trembled as they passed by (M. 1, H. 37). The singers pray, "Have mercy on us, O Maruts, do not strike us" (M. 5, H. 55). They grant immortality (M. 5, H. 55). Varuna is a very great god. The laws of the universe have been founded by him (M. 4, H. 5). Men are in danger of his judgments (M. 4, H. 3). They dread his anger (M. 3, H. 29), and Agni is besought to "Cause Varuna to go away from us" (M. 3, H. 29). Agni—Fire—is the youngest of the gods. He has "a two-fold birth (celestial and terrestrial)" (M. 1, H. 149) and is "well-allied with Heaven and Earth" (M. 3, H. 1). This, apparently, signifies that his presence, pervading the universe and all material things, can be called into immediate and visible action. "This is one of the wonders: when the virgin conceives thee as her child—thou becomest a messenger as soon as thou art born" (M. 4, H. 7). Agni is "enveloped in many mothers, in the wood" (M. 4, H. 7). When the Aryan produced fire by friction on wood the God of Fire manifested himself. While he closely resembles many of the other deities in his power and in the gifts which lie within his bestowal—mighty strength, valiant men, plenty of food, wealth, with good progeny, etc. (M. 2, H. 4)—Agni is represented as standing in a very special relationship with both gods and men. He is the great Mediator. "In thee, O Agni, with thy mouth all the guileless immortal gods eat the offering which is offered to them. Through thee the mortals taste their drink" (M. 2, H. 1). Because Agni is a good sacrificer, "Our human prayer has prospered amongst the immortals who dwell in the great heaven" (M. 2, H. 2). On the one hand he is invoked "to consume with his hottest flames those who violate the .. laws of Varuna" (M. 4, H. 5), while on the other men urge him "to deprecate for us the god's anger" (M. 3, H. 29). While other gods are feared Agni is "the beloved of many" (M. 1, H. 12): "a kind friend to men—sitting in the midst, the lovely one in the house" (M. 1, H. 69); "the dear friend of men, a friend who is to be magnified by his friends" (M. 1, H. 75). He is the father and lord of all people: "men live in his presence before a father's face" (M. 1, H. 127). He is called "the guardian and the father of the weak," "the instructor of the simple" (M. 1, H. 31). Agni is "the most merciful One" (M. 1, H. 94), "the joy-giver ... the Good-Willed One" (M. 1, H. 144), "always listening to him who wishes to be his friend" (M. 1, H. 128). He can be approached in prayer. The "steward of both worlds" (M. 1, H. 59), "the Son of Strength" (M. 1, H. 58), is "easy to invoke" (M. 1, H. 58), and, indeed, he cannot hide himself from prayer. While many of the prayers addressed to him are for material well-being or victory in battle, there are some which reach a loftier level. "May we be of those to whom thou ... art pleased to grant sinlessness ..." (M. 1, H. 94). "Drive away from us sin which leads astray" (M. 1, H. 189). "Release from every guilt on all sides, O Agni, even from great guilt ... from the prison of gods and of mortals ... let us thy friends never be harmed" (M. 4, H. 12). Yet despite the high level of many of the conceptions held with regard to Agni he is considered by the tribes who worship him as being in a particular sense their god. To all others he is terrible. To a group of the Aryan clans Agni is "the king of human tribes—the centre of human settlements ... a supporting column" (M. 1, H. 59), but to the others— the Dasyus and the unfriendly tribes—he is "a slayer of foes" (M. 1, H. 74), the one "who hurlest the Dasyus away" (M. 1, H. 78). "This Agni is the conqueror in battles, rich in valiant men; he by whom the gods have overpowered the Dasyus" (M. 3, H. 29). Rudra is hailed as "the best of all physicians" whose "softly stroking hand cures and relieves" (M. 2, H. 33). He is besought to "put away anguish, put away sicknesses in all directions" (M. 2, H. 33). Though beneficent in his healing actions, Rudra, like all the other gods, is cruel and terrible in battle. In the very hymn in which he is hailed as the possessor of "the best medicines" there rises the anxious prayer: "O Rudra, hurt us not. ... Let thy cowslaying and thy manslaying be far away ..." (M. 1, H. 114). Vata is hailed as the king of the whole of this world (M. 10, H. 168). "May Vata waft medicines healthful, delightful to our heart: may he prolong our lives. Thou, O Vata, art our father and our brother and our friend, do thou grant us to live. O Vata, from that treasure of the immortal which is placed in thy house yonder, grant us to live" (M. 10, H. 186).

The Hymns of the Rig-Veda are not primarily speculative. Material prosperity, victory in battle and strong sons are the boons for which the gods are sought. The ancient Aryan lived largely in the present—anxious to avert the wrath of his gods and to enjoy the stirring life of warrior, pioneer and colonizer. The former could be achieved by sacrifice which, if successfully performed, brought the latter in its train. The detail of sacrifice is not dealt with to any great extent, but it is clear that sacrifices were regarded as being of the utmost importance. They consisted of burnt offerings of beasts, fruits of the field, and libations of Soma juice. The Soma Sacrifice is constantly spoken of, and so great is the importance assigned to it that Soma is in the course of time raised to something like the standing of a deity. "Soma is not a sacred tree inhabited by some spirits of the woods, but the Lord of immortality who can place his worshippers in the land of eternal life and light. Some of the finest and most spiritual of the Vedic hymns are addressed to him, and yet it is hard to say whether they are addressed to a person or a beverage" (*Hinduism and Buddhism*, Vol. 1, p. 58). Thinking with regard to the future life is not prominent. At the same time there are gleams here and there of aspiration for a life beyond. The Maruts are prayed to "Place us all in immortality" (M. 5, H. 55). In a hymn addressed to many of the gods the sage prays: "May I be detached from death, like a gourd from its stem, but not from the immortal" (M. 7, H. 59). Immortality is described as being the gift of the Golden Child (M. 10, H. 121). Although, as has been said, the tone of the hymns is on the whole practical, there is little actual definition of how life should be lived. There is no definite code of moral law and scarcely any indication of basic principles of good life. A good woman—and a very good woman is apparently worth more than a very bad man—is described as one who "finds out the weak, the thirsty, the needy and is mindful of the gods" (M. 5, H. 61). It is extremely doubtful, however, whether these qualities, admirable enough in a woman, would have been regarded as being of a sufficiently masculine nature to adorn the character of her husband. Immorality in women is condemned. "They who roam about like brotherless girls of evil conduct, like women who deceive their husbands, being wicked, sinful and untrue" (M. 4, H. 45). For the men there was no doubt a less exacting standard.

THE RISE OF BRAHMANISM

The Aryan kingdoms were consolidated. The times were apparently peaceful, and prosperous village communities grew up on every side. The enervating climate and material well-being caused the Aryans to abandon their old predatory and marauding habits. A moral equivalent to war was found in the elaboration of sacrificial ceremonials, in philosophical speculations and in a passionate and ofttimes painful quest for spiritual experience and satisfaction. The history of India from the time of the Rig-Veda to 500 B.C. is the history of a development in religion.

(c) THE SACRIFICIAL SYSTEM

A vast and complicated system of sacrifice was gradually developed. This system is described in the treatises known as the Brahmanas, which were certainly of later date than the Vedic hymns. The sacrifices were of various kinds, and the ritual ranged from the very simple to the highly complex, from offerings of melted butter that could be made by the poorest to ceremonials that stretched over a lengthy period and which were so costly that they could be performed only by kings and emperors in whose control was the wealth of nations. While every house had its altar, and while every house father no doubt performed the simpler ceremonials, the greater sacrifices could be rightly performed only by properly initiated priests. If a qualified priest was not available some other person might sacrifice, but was liable to be stopped at once should a priest arrive. Ushasti Kakrayana, an ascetic mendicant priest, is represented as arriving in the midst of just such a ceremonial. He objected, and the celebrants immediately sit down. Finally, he grants them permission to proceed, but demands an offering equal in value to that which they are to receive. In the Satapatha Brahmana the various sacrificial rituals are detailed at great length. There are new and full moon sacrifices (Ks.[1] 1 and 11); the ritual for the establishment of sacred fires (K. 2); the Soma sacrifice (Ks. 3–4); the Rajasuya (K. 5); the regulations for the construction of the Fire Altar (Ks. 6–10); Seasonal Sacrifices (K. 11); the Asvamedha or Horse Sacrifice (K. 13); the Purushanedha or Human Sacrifice (K. 13). To study the whole of this vast literature of sacrifice in detail would be both wearisome and profitless. As it is necessary, however, to have some understanding of why sacrifice was performed, what it was hoped would be achieved thereby, and to what extent the sacrificial system was interwoven with the life of the people, we shall study with some care the Asvamedha, or Horse Sacrifice.

THE ASVAMEDHA

The sacrificer in this case was always a ruling monarch and a member, therefore, of the Kshatra class. The sacrificing priests were, of course, Brahmans, and consequently Spring —the Brahman season—was chosen for the commencement of the sacrifice. The four chief celebrants, the Adhvaryu, the Hotri, the Brahman and the Udgatri are handsomely fed with cows and gold (Ad.[2] 4, B.[3] 1). They partake of a ceremonial meal, and with ghee left over from this feast a grass rope is purified and thus the horse is made pure (Ad. 1, v. 1). The King and four of his wives pass the night in the hall of sacrifice, while offerings are made for the safe progress of the horse (Ad. 4, B. 1). Next morning the horse is haltered, and after the fact has been announced to the gods it is sprinkled with water. A four-eyed dog is killed and plunged under the horse's feet (Ad. 1, B. 2). After the Adhvaryu and the Sacrificer have whispered into

[1] K. = Khanda.   [2] Ad. = Adhyâya.   [3] B. = Brahmana.

the animal's ear, it is then allowed to wander free toward the north-east (Ad. 4, B. 2). For a whole year it is allowed to roam at its pleasure. Armed guards follow to protect it against interference on the part of the king's enemies (Ad. 1, B. 3). As in so long a while the horse will wander far afield, any territory through which it passes unharmed is obviously subject to the will of its master. After the departure of the horse the ceremonial is continued. The priests and the Sacrificer sit down on stools and cushions of gold while the Hotri recounts the Pariplava Legend (Ad. 4, B. 3). Two lute players, a Brahmana and a Ragayana, play before the assemblage. Both the priest and the warrior insist on recognition, and the two players are a compromise to a strained feeling existing between Kshatra and Brahman (Ad. 1, B. 6). For the whole year during which the horse wanders at will oblations, initiatory rites and minor sacrifices are performed. When all the preparations have been completed and the great day of sacrifice has at last arrived the horse and many other victims are bound to stakes (Ad. 2, B. 2). The animals are appeased by the recitation of various verses (Ad. 2, B. 2). The wild beasts, after fire has been carried round them, are dismissed (Ad. 2, B. 4). The horse is then driven by the Adhvaryu and the Sacrificer to a pond, after which, anointed and adorned by the Queen Consort and the other wives of the King, it is once more tied to the central stake (Ad. 2, B. 6). A cloth of gold is spread out, upon which the horse is first quieted and then slain with a golden knife. The other victims are slain with knives of copper or iron. A procession of the King's wives then walk around the victim making amends for the slaughtering and seeking fertility (Ad. 2, B. 8). The Queen is blessed and lies down with the slain horse (Ad. 2, B. 9). The wounds are stitched with copper, silver and gold needles (Ad. 2, B. 10). The omenta are roasted with fire (Ad. 5, B. 2), and then the whole performance is brought to a conclusion by the chanting of the Katushtoma and the offering of oblations. Throughout the sacrifice the horse is offered on behalf of the nobility and the other victims for the peasantry (Ad. 6, B. 2). As the result of the successful performance of the Asvamedha the Sacrificer "becomes complete, and this, indeed, is the atonement for everything, the remedy for everything. Thereby the gods redeem all sin, and even the slaying of a Brahman they thereby redeem" (Ad. 3, B. 1). Other blessings that follow are the birth of sons, cows, oxen, racers, women, warriors, blitheful youth and grain (Ad. 1, B. 9), strength, the attainment of desires, distinction, abundance of food, firm establishment in the possession of lands, and increase of holiness through the birth of a holy Brahman, and an increase in power through the birth of a Raganya skilled in hitting the mark (Ad. 3, B. 7). Such a ceremony, which worked to its climax over a long period of time, gave to a reigning monarch an excellent opportunity to make display of his power and wealth. The processions, the pageantry, and the splendid ceremonial would make an appeal to all classes of the community, who no doubt assembled in vast numbers to watch the final celebration. Apart altogether from the religious meaning, such an act of sacrifice must have taken the same place with the people as a whole as the mystery plays took in medieval Europe. It was a dramatic performance accompanied by singing, playing and the recitation of old epics. In the very earliest times the victim was probably a man, the shedding of whose blood appeased the wrath of the gods. As time went on the horse was substituted. While there is no reason to suppose that human sacrifice was at any time offered by the Aryans in India, the Purushadmedha or Human Sacrifice (K. 13, Ad. 6, v. 2), while describing what has become purely symbolical, probably reaches back to far times, when such a sacrifice was actually offered. The vast sacrificial system which permeated the whole of men's living in those days was probably the central buttress of the power of the Brahman class. It is at least doubtful whether they in the latter times of our period had, as a class, any profound belief in the efficacy of a system which brought them place and wealth.

THE PHILOSOPHY OF THE UPANISHADS

The works commonly known as the Upanishads preceded the rise of Buddhism, and must therefore be regarded as being in the main produced not later than 550 B.C. As these works are of the utmost importance in the development of Hinduism we shall study them separately and then summarize the results.

(d) KHANDOGA UPANISHAD

There is a definite attempt to explain the universe in terms of a unity. "What is the origin of the world? 'Ether,' he replied. 'For all these beings take their rise from the ether and return into the ether. Ether is older than these, ether is their rest. He is indeed the udgitha (Om-Brahman), greater than great, he is without end" (P.[1] 1, K. 9). The ether is identified with Brahman. "The Brahman . . . is the same as the ether which is around us. And the ether which is around us is the same as the ether which is within us. And the ether which is within us, that is ether within the heart. That ether in the heart (as Brahman) is omnipresent and unchanging" (P. 3, K. 12, vv. 7-9). Things may take different forms, but they can finally be interpreted in the terms of the one. "The essence of all beings is the earth, the essence of the earth is water, the essence of water the plants, the essence of plants man, the essence of man speech, the essence of speech the Rig-Veda, the essence of the Rig-Veda the Sama Veda, the essence of the Sama Veda the Udgitha, which is Om" (P. 1, K. 1, v. 2). In the beginning of all things "was that . . . which is one only without a second" (P. 6, K. 2, v. 1). The evolution of differentiation in form is described in two ways. In the first Pragapati

---

[1] P. = Prapâthaka.

"brooded over the worlds, and from them thus brooded on he squeezed out the essences. Agni (fire) from the earth, Vayu (air) from the sky, Aditya (the sun) from heaven" (P. 4, K. 17, v. 1). In the second "It (Brahman) thought, may I be many, may I grow forth. It sent forth fire. The fire thought, may I be many, may I grow forth. It sent forth water. . . . Water thought, may I be many, may I grow forth. It sent forth earth" (P. 6, K. 2, vv. 3-4). "That being thought, let me now enter those three beings (fire, water, earth) with this living Self, and let me then reveal names and forms" (P. 6, K. 3, v. 2). Man emerges as one form of the Universal. His body is a prison—always bound by death. Passion and desire, even the inclination to think "this body is I and I am this body" (P. 8, K. 12, v. 1), lead him away from reality. Only as he breaks from all illusion and realizes that Brahman is within him and that he is Brahman can man ever find final satisfaction. "The intelligent, whose body is spirit, whose form is light, whose thoughts are true, whose nature is like ether (Omnipresent and invisible), from whom all works, all desires, all sweet odours and tastes proceed: he who embraces all this, who never speaks and is never surprised, he is myself within the heart, smaller than a corn of rice, smaller than a corn of barley, smaller than a mustard seed, smaller than canary seed or the kernel of a canary seed. He also is myself within the heart, greater than the earth, greater than the sky, greater than heaven, greater than all these worlds. He from whom all works, all desires, all sweet odours and tastes proceed, who embraces all this, who never speaks and is never surprised, he myself within the heart is that Brahman. When I shall have departed from hence I shall obtain him (that self)" (P. 3, K. 14, vv. 1-4). The true life of man is not in works but in self-discovery. The true end of self-discovery is complete merging of the self with Brahman. Yet works and a high standard of morality are not to be despised. "Penance, liberality, righteousness, kindness, truthfulness, these form his Dakshinas (gifts bestowed on priests)" (P. 3, K. 17, v. 4). Ganusruti Pautrayana, who is described as a righteous man, "was a pious giver—bestowing much wealth upon the people and always keeping open house. He built places of refuge everywhere, wishing that people should everywhere eat of his food" (P. 4, K. 1, v. 1). King Vaisvanara speaks of his kingdom in which "there is no thief, no miser, no drunkard, no man without an altar in his house, no ignorant person, no adulterer, much less an adulteress" (P. 5, K. 11, v. 5). Moral actions are held in high esteem. To a certain degree they are effective. Those whose conduct has been good will quickly obtain some good birth, "the birth of a Kshatrya or a Vaisva" (P. 5, K. 10, v. 7). Good men after death go in the strength of their good deeds to the Devas, but their accumulated good works are quickly used up and they then return by various phases to the weariness of existence. Virtue, then, admirable though it may be, is not enough. Sin brings punishment in its train. "But those whose conduct has been evil will quickly attain an evil birth, the birth of a dog, or a hog, or a Kandala . . . man who steals gold, who drinks spirits, who dishonours his Guru's bed, who kills a Brahman, these four fall and as a fifth he who associates with them" (P. 5, K. 10, vv. 7, 9–10). And yet so greatly do other considerations outweigh conduct that he "who knows the doctrine of the five fires is not defiled by sin even though he associates with them" (P. 5, K. 10, v. 10). Sacrifice, important though it is, likewise fails to remove the boundary of the self and the illusion of desire. "And as here on earth whatever has been acquired by exertion perishes, so perishes whatever is acquired for the next world by sacrifices . . . (P. 8, K. 1, v. 3–6). Brahman is in every man. To win to freedom and immortality, man must discover himself in Brahman, and having overcome desire, be prepared to sink himself in the infinite world of spirit, losing personal identity, but living ever in the eternal sea of passionless consciousness. The primacy of spirit is the base of all aspiration. "Speech is better than a name. Mind is better than speech. Will is better than mind. Consideration is better than will. Reflection is better than consideration. Understanding is better than reflection. Power is better than understanding. Food is better than power. Fire is better than water. Ether is better than fire. Memory is better than ether. Hope is better than memory. Spirit is better than hope. Spirit, then, is all this. He who sees this, perceives this and understands this becomes an ativadin" (P. 7, Ks. 2-15). This may be perceived through the purification of the intellect. "When the intellectual aliment has been purified the whole nature becomes purified. When the whole nature has been purified the memory becomes firm. And when the memory of the highest self remains firm then all the ties which bind us to a belief (in anything but the self) are loosened" (P. 7, K. 26, v. 2). We must not confound "intellectual" in the sense in which it is here used with "knowledge." The way of escape, indeed, is not by knowledge. A man may be learned in all the learning of the age—the Vedas, grammar, the rules of sacrifice to ancestors, the science of numbers, portents and time; in logic and ethics, etymology, pronunciation, ceremonial, prosody, the sciences of demons, weapons, astronomy, serpents, poisons, genii, singing, playing and the fine arts, and yet the end of it all be grief. Not knowledge, but meditation is the path to freedom. Abstinence, self-mortification and meditation lead to the realization and the achievement of the truth. "Those who in the forest follow faith and austerities"—go to Brahman (P. 5, K. 10, v. 1). Vows of silence, fasting, and the hermit life are all forms of abstinence which obtain Brahman. By meditation on the sacred syllables victory can be obtained over death. When a man "has learnt the Veda from a family of teachers according to the sacred rules in the leisure time left from the duties to be performed for the Guru; who, after receiving his discharge, has settled in his own house keeping up the memory of what he has learnt by repeating it regularly in some sacred spot; who has begotten virtuous sons, and concentrated all his senses on the Self, never giving pain to any creature" (P. 8, K. 15, v. 1), then at the hour of death the soul leaves the body and travels by the sunbeam track to the sun, which is the door of Brahman. Entering in to the universal soul the Self becomes "free from sin, free from old age, from death and grief, from hunger and thirst" (P. 8, K. 1, vv. 3–6). Whoever has crossed the boundary of Self, "if blind ceases to be blind, if wounded ceases to be wounded, if afflicted ceases to be afflicted. Therefore, when that bank has been crossed night becomes day indeed, for the world of Brahman is lighted up once for all" (P. 8, K. 4, vv. 1–3). And so the circle is completed. A spark of the divine universal essence leaps for a period into an intolerable isolation from which at last it escapes by entering again into the omnipresent and unchangeable. There is "a light which shines above this heaven, higher than all, higher than everything in the highest world beyond which there are no other worlds" (P. 3, K. 13, v. 7). When a man by abstinence, concentration and meditation has realized that this is the same light which is within him, then all the barriers of the material are rolled away, and he, being thus freed from desire and striving, enters in to perfect freedom.

(e) TALAVAKÂRA OR KENA UPANISHAD

Real knowledge is the recognition of Brahman in all things. All else leads to the "great destruction" of new births (K. 2). The way to wisdom and so to immortality is by "penance, restraint and sacrifice" (K. 4, v. 8). There is an interesting note on the relative position of the gods. "Agni, Vayu and Indra are, as it were, above the other gods, for they touched it (Brahman) nearest. And therefore Indra is, as it were, above the other gods, for he touched it nearest, for he first knew it" (K. 4, vv. 2–3).

(f) AITAREYA-ĀRANYAKA UPANISHAD

There is again definite insistence on the essential unity of all things. In the beginning "all this was self one only: there was nothing else blinking whatsoever" (Ar.[1] 2, Ad. 4, K. 1, v. 1). This self or Brahman, consisting of and resting in knowledge, thought, "shall I send forth worlds?" He sent forth accordingly water, light and material things. Last of all he formed "the Purusha, the Person, taking him forth from the water" (Ar. 2, Ad. 4, K. 1, vv. 2–5). Gods are mentioned by name, but they, like all else, are forms of the universal spirit. "And that Self, consisting of (knowledge), is Brahman, it is Indra, it is Pragapati" (Ar. 2, Ad. 6, K. 1, v. 5). However wide may be the apparent gap between things and living forms, there is a chain of connection throughout. Pragapati, who is represented as the actual creator of the visible universe, is apparently a manifestation of Brahman: "The seed of Pragapati are the Devas. The seed of the Devas is rain.... The seed of rain are herbs. The seed of herbs is food. The seed of food is seed. The seed of seed are creatures. The seed of creatures is the heart. The seed of the heart is the mind. The seed of the mind is speech. The seed of speech is action. The action done (in a former state) is this man, the abode of Brahman" (Ar. 2, Ad. 1, K. 3, v. 1). Speech is one great link: "Friends unite through speech. All beings unite through speech. Therefore speech is everything here" (Ar. 3, Ad. 1, K. 6, v. 13). More important than speech is prana or breath. "Let him know that breath is the beam

[1] Ar. = Āranyaka.

(on which the whole house of the body rests)" (Ar. 3, Ad. 1, K. 4, v. 2). "The eye, the ear, the mind, the speech, the senses, the body, the whole self rests on this breath" (Ar. 3, Ad. 2, K. 1, v. 1). Indra, speaking to a Rishi, says: "I am prana (breath) . . . thou art prana, all things are prana" (Ar. 2, Ad. 2, K. 3, v. 4). In breath the "gods exist all joined together" (Ar. 2, Ad. 3, K. 8, v. 5). Brahman lies hidden beneath the breath. Speech and breath join man with the ultimate. "Speech is united with breath, breath with the blowing air, the blowing air with the Visvedevas, the Visvedevas with the heavenly world, the heavenly world with Brahman" (Ar. 3, Ad. 1, K. 6, v. 8). For the life of man the supremely important thing is to realize the connection between the immortal which pervades the entire universe and that spark of the immortal that is within himself. The physical body is mortal, liable to decay and death, but "its essence is the incorporal conscious self" (Ar. 3, Ad. 2, K. 3, v. 3). He must know himself "reaching as far as the gods . . . and the gods reaching as far as me" (Ar. 2, Ad. 1, K. 8, v. 2). Wherever men express themselves in speech there is Brahman. "As far as Brahman reaches so far reaches speech, wherever there is Brahman there is a word; and wherever there is a word there is Brahman" (Ar. 1, Ad. 3, K. 8, v. 9). Through Brahman there is victory over evil and over rebirth. "Having driven away evil by means of that Brahman (which is hidden in prana) the enlightened man goes to the Svarga world (becomes one with the Hiranyagarbha, the universal spirit)" (Ar. 2, Ad. 5, K. 8, v. 5). The son is a continuation of the life of his father. The connection is very intimate. "Whatever there is belonging to the son belongs to the father; whatever there is belonging to the father belongs to the son" (Ar. 2, Ad. 1, K. 8, v. 1). The father, having performed "all he has to do and having reached the full measure of his life, departs . . . and departing from hence is born again" (Ar. 2, Ad. 5, K. 1, vv. 11–12). The son is then placed in his father's stead "for the performance of all good works" (Ar. 2, Ad. 5, K. 1, v. 10).

(g) KAUSHÎTAKI UPANISHAD

In this Upanishad it is the moon, not the sun, which is the door of the heavenly world. Those who are to be born again descend upon the earth as rain, and, according to their deeds and their knowledge, are born again as "a worm, or as an insect, or as a fish, or as a bird, or as a lion or as a boar, or as a serpent, or as a tiger, or as a man, or as something else in different places" (Ad. 1, v. 2). He who is born as a man passes through the processes of life, and then, if he has by right meditation achieved knowledge, he, "(at the time of death) having reached the path of the gods, comes to the world of Agni, to the world of Vayu (air), to the world of Varuna, to the world of Indra, to the world of Pragapati (Virag), to the world of Brahman" (Ad. 1, v. 3). Here he is welcomed with garlands, fruits and adornments. Coming to the lake Ara "he crosses it by the mind, while those who come to it without knowing the truth are drowned. . . ." At the River Vigara, which again is crossed by the mind alone, he "shakes off his good and evil deeds. His beloved relatives obtain the good, his unbeloved relatives obtain the evil he has done. Being freed from good and freed from evil he, the knower of Brahman, moves toward Brahman" (Ad. 1, v. 5). He approaches Brahman, who catechises him at some length, and then if the answers are satisfactorily given passes into the world of the universal. In the concluding portion of the Upanishad Indra takes the place of Brahman, announcing that he is "prana" and that "he who meditates on me as life and immortality gains his full life in this world and obtains in the Svarga world immortality and indestructibility" (Ad. 3, v. 2). All the stress is laid upon right knowledge and meditation and none at all upon moral living. "And he who knows me thus by no deed of his can his life be harmed, not by the murder of his mother, not by the murder of his father, not by theft, not by the killing of a Brahman. If he is going to commit a sin the bloom does not depart from his face" (Ad. 3, v. 1).

(h) VÂGASENYI-SAMHITA UPANISHAD

The right end of all living things is "to be hidden in the Lord (the Self)." When a complete surrender of life has been made its aspirations, strivings and passions, then "thou mayest enjoy" (v. 1). The material is worthless and transient. Men are told not to covet wealth, probably because it is mere illusion and no abiding reality. The body itself ends in ashes—it is the breath or soul which passes to the air and so to the immortal. Faith is exalted as the way of union with the universal Self encircling all "bright, incorporeal, scatheless, without muscles, pure untouched by evil, a seer, wise, omnipresent, self-existent," he who has disposed "all things rightly for eternal years" (v. 8). Works cannot give that right knowledge which is essential for the attainment of immortality. Those who trust in them "enter into blind darkness" (v. 9). "There are the worlds of the Asuras covered with blind darkness. Those who have destroyed their self (who perform works without having arrived at a knowledge of the true self) go after death to those worlds" (v. 3).

(i) MUNDAKA UPANISHAD

Brahma was the first of the Devas. He was the maker of the universe and the preserver of the world. The knowledge of Brahman, which is the foundation of all knowledge, was revealed by him to his eldest son Atharva. The highest any man can know is that "by which the indestructible Brahman is apprehended" (Mu.[1] 1, K. 1, v. 15). Brahman is described as "That which cannot be seen nor seized, which has no family, and no caste, no eyes nor ears, no hands, no feet, the eternal, the omnipresent (all-pervading), infinitesimal, that which is imperishable, that it is which the wise regard as the source of all beings" (Mu. 1, K. 1, v. 6). From this divine essence proceed all things. As the spider sends forth and draws in its threads, as plants grow on the earth, as from every man hairs spring forth on the head and the body, thus does everything arise here from the indestructible" (Mu. 1, K. 1, v. 7). "As from a blazing fire sparks, being like unto fire, fly forth a thousandfold, thus are various beings brought forth from the imperishable . . . and returned thither also" (Mu. 2, K. 1, v. 1). The right end of man is to obtain a complete union with the imperishable and eternal. "The great Being is Manifest, Near, moving in the cave of the heart" (Mu. 2, K. 2, v. 1). A full realization of his immanence can be attained only "By truthfulness . . . by penance, right knowledge and abstinence" (Mu. 3, K. 1, v. 5) . . . "those who practise penance and faith in the forest, tranquil, wise, and living on alms, depart free from passion through the sun to where that immortal person dwells whose nature is imperishable" (Mu. 1, K. 2, v. 11). While sacrifice and good works are enjoined it is the height of folly for men to trust in them. "Fools dwelling in darkness, wise in their own conceit and puffed up with vain knowledge, go round and round staggering to and fro like blind men led by the blind. . . . Considering sacrifice and good works as the best, these fools know no higher good, and having enjoyed their reward on the height of heaven gained by good works they enter again this world or a lower one" (Mu. 1, K. 2, vv. 8-10). Nothing attained by works, how-

[1] Mu. = Mundaka.

ever pleasant for a season, is permanent. Those foolish men who trust in deeds are subject again and again to old age and death (Mu. 1, K. 2, v. 7). On the other hand, those who have acquired "freedom from all desires . . . having reached Him who is omnipresent everywhere, devoted to the self, enter Him wholly" (Mu. 3, K. 2, v. 5). "As the flowing rivers disappear in the sea, losing their name and their form, thus a wise man freed from name and form goes to the divine Person who is greater than the great" (Mu. 3, K. 2, v. 8).

(j) SVETÂSVATARA UPANISHAD

The reality behind all things is "the high Brahman, the vast, hidden in the bodies of all creatures and alone enveloping everything" (Ad. 3, v. 7). He is the one God "hidden in all beings, all-pervading, the self within all beings, watching over all works, dwelling in all beings, the witness, the perceiver, the only one free from qualities" (Ad. 6, v. 11). By him the Brahma wheel turns. There are evils fronting the life of man—pain, suffering, death—and only "when men shall roll up the sky like a hide will there be an end of misery" (Ad. 6, v. 20). There is but one way of escape. By Sankhya (Philosophy) and Yoga (religious discipline) men can apprehend the cause of things and so be freed from the fetters of life. When the Brahma students "have known what is within this (world) they are devoted and merged in the Brahman free from birth" (Ad. 1, v. 7)—"sufferings are destroyed and birth and death cease" (Ad. 1). The wise who perceive the eternal within themselves pass beyond the darkness to a world in which "The sun does not shine there, nor the moon and the stars, nor these lightnings and much less this fire. When he shines everything shines after him, by his light all this is lighted" (Ad. 6, v. 14). In this world of passionless light "there is no day, no night, neither existence nor non-existence: Siva the blessed alone is there" (Ad. 4, v. 18).

(k) TAITIRÎYAKA UPANISHAD

Various gods are invoked: "May Mitra be propitious to us and Varuna, Aryman also, Indra, Brîhaspati and the wide-striding Vishnu" (V.[1] 1, An.[2] 1). Attention is paid to the technique of speech and the qualities supposed to lie beneath the combinations of letters (V. 1, An. 2). Several triads are mentioned: Heaven, ether, earth; Sun, lightning, fire; Teacher, knowledge, pupil; Mother, child, father; Lower jaw, speech, upper jaw (V. 1, An. 3). Men are exhorted to reverence the gods and their parents and to perform good works. "Do not neglect the (sacrificial) works due to the gods and fathers. Let thy mother be to thee like unto a god. Let thy father be unto thee like unto a god. Whatever actions are blameless, those should be regarded not others. Whatever good works have been performed by us, those should be observed by thee" (V. 1, An. 11, v. 2). Almsgiving should be "with faith ... with joy, with modesty, with fear, with kindness" (V. 1, An. 11, v. 3). The main theme of the Upanishad is, however, concerned with the nature of Brahman and man's relation with the universal. In the beginning was Brahman, and "from that Self (Brahman) sprang ether, that through which we hear: from ether air, that through which we feel and hear: from air fire, that through which we hear, feel and see: from fire water, that through which we hear, feel, see and taste: from water earth, that through which we hear, feel, see, taste and smell: from earth herbs, from herbs food, from food seed, from seed man. Man thus consists of the essence of food" (V. 2, An. 1). "Breath is the common life of all things, but within breath is mind, within mind understanding, within under-

[1] V. = Vallî. [2] An. = Anuvâka.

standing is the inner Self . . . joy, satisfaction, bliss, Brahman" (V. 2, An. 3). "Brahman wished, may I be many—may I grow forth. He brooded over himself like a man performing a penance. After he had thus brooded he sent forth (created) all whatever there is. Having sent forth he entered into it, he became *sat* (what is manifest) and that (what is not manifest) defined and undefined, supported and not supported, endowed with knowledge and without knowledge, as stones real and unreal. The Sattya true became all this whatsoever, and therefore the wise call it the Brahman—Sattya the true" (V. 2, An. 6). Pervading the whole of creation, Brahman is present also within men's hearts. "There is the ether within the heart and in it is the Person consisting of mind golden immortal" (V. 1, An. 6). The future life depends upon a man's knowledge of Brahman. Whoever knows him as the visible and the material, that man is still bound to the wheel of life, but if he knows the Brahman as non-existing he becomes non-existing himself (V. 2, An. 6). The right end of human life is absorption in the Universal. "That from whence these beings are born, that by which when born they live, that into which they enter at their death, try to know that. That is Brahman" (V. 3, An. 1). He who has the right knowledge attains the goal. "He who knows this when he has departed this world reaches and comprehends the Self . . ." (V. 2, An. 8).

(*l*) BRİHAD-ÂRANYAKA UPANISHAD

Yagnavalkya, a philosopher and religious, of very great reputation, evidently spent a considerable deal of his time going from place to place discussing and answering questions concerning the gods, the universe and human life. Eminent professors were held in great reputation and were rewarded with substantial fees. Yagnavalkya for his skill in argument received "a thousand cows with a bull as big as an elephant"

(Ad. 4, B. 1). He is asked to give the number of gods, and replies that there are three thousand and six. In reply to further questions he reduces the number to thirty-three, then to six, to three, to two, to one and a half and finally to one. There are the eight Vasus: Agni (fire), Prithivi (the earth), Vayu (air), Antariksha (the sky), Aditya (the sun), Dyu (the heaven), Kandramas (the moon), Nakshatras (the stars); the eleven Rudras—ten of whom are the vital breaths and the eleventh the Atman or soul; the twelve Adityas, connected with the sun god—one for each month of the year: Indra the god of thunder and Pragapati the god of sacrifice. And yet after all the numbers and all the names there is one god only and he is Brahman, for when they say: "Sacrifice to this or sacrifice to that god, each god is but his manifestation and he is all gods" (Ad. 1, B. 4, v. 6). The primeval Brahman—"that great unborn Self who consists of knowledge" (Ad. 4, B. 4, v. 22)—emerged in the beginning of things from the waters. "Water produced the true and the true is Brahman" (Ad. 5, B. 5, v. 1). The Self was alone in the shape of a Person. He recognized himself. At first he was afraid, but overcoming this found no delight in loneliness and so, dividing himself into two, called into being all manner of beings, things and creatures: the Kshatra powers among the Devas—Indra, Varuna, Soma, Rudra, Parganyas, Yama, Mrityu, Isana; the Vis people—those Devas who are called Vasus, Rudras, Adityas, Visve-Devas and Maruts; "he created the Sudra colour (caste) as Pushan (as nourisher for the earth nourishes all this whatsoever)" (Ad. 1, B. 4, v. 13). So Brahman created all things, "As the spider comes out with its thread or a small spark comes forth from fire, thus do all senses, all worlds, all Devas, all beings come forth from that Self" (Ad. 2, B. 1, v. 20). Brahman is present throughout the universe in various forms, "the material and the immaterial, the mortal and the immortal, the solid and the fluid"

(Ad. 2, B. 3, v. 1). "Everything except air and sky is material, is mortal, is solid, is definite. But air and sky are immaterial, are immortal, are fluid, are indefinite. Everything except the breath and the ether within the body is material, is mortal, is solid, is definite. But breath and the ether within the body are immaterial, are immortal, are fluid, are indefinite" (Ad. 2, B. 3, vv. 2–5). In the forms, then, of breath and of ether he is present within the life of men. Everything is of him and in him. "This earth . . . this water . . . this fire . . . this air . . . this sun . . . this space . . . this moon . . . this lightning . . . this thunder . . . this ether . . . this law . . . this true . . . this mankind . . ." (Ad. 2, B. 5, vv. 1–13). "This Brahman class, this Kshatra class, these worlds, these Devas, these creatures, this everything is that Self" (Ad. 2, B. 4, v. 6). "As clouds of smoke proceed by themselves out of a lighted fire kindled with damp fuel. . . . As all waters find their centre in the sea. . . . As a lump of salt thrown into water becomes dissolved into water . . . thus verily . . . . does this Great Being, endless, unlimited, consisting of nothing but knowledge, rise from out these elements and vanish again in them" (Ad. 2, B. 4, vv. 6–12). He is "the lord of all beings, the king of all beings. And as all spokes are contained in the axle and in the felly of a wheel, all beings and all those selfs (of the earth, water, etc.) are contained in that Self" (Ad. 2, B. 5, v. 15). The all-pervading Brahman is "unseen but seeing, unheard but hearing; unperceived but perceiving; unknown but knowing; there is nothing that perceives but it, nothing that knows but it" (Ad. 3, B. 7). He consists of "knowledge, mind, life, sight, hearing, earth, water, wind, ether, light and no light, desire and no desire, anger and no anger, right or wrong and all things" (Ad. 4, B. 4, v. 5). Birth is for men the great evil. "On being born that person assuming his body becomes united with all evils" (Ad. 4, B. 3, v. 8). He comes immediately under the control of Dharma—the law of the Deed.

"Now as a man is like this or like that, according as he acts and according as he behaves so will he be; a man of good acts will become good, a man of bad acts bad. He becomes pure by pure deeds, bad by bad deeds. And here they say that a person consists of desire. And as is his desire so is his will; and as is his will so is his deed: and whatever deed he does that he will reap" (Ad. 4, B. 4, v. 5). Those whose lives have been a record of good deeds do not lack their reward. They pass to worlds wherein they enjoy the results of their right living. But this enjoyment is of limited duration, and when the stock of good works has, as it were, been used up they are born again. "And as a caterpillar after having reached the end of a blade of grass and after having made another approach (to another blade) draws itself together towards it; thus doth the self after having thrown off this body and dispelled all ignorance and after making another approach to another body draws himself together toward it" (Ad. 4, B. 4, v. 3). For those who have lived wickedly or ignorantly "there are indeed those unblessed worlds covered with blind darkness" (Ad. 4, B. 4, v. 11), from which they may return as "worms, birds and creeping things" (Ad. 6, B. 2, v. 3). Birth, governed by Dharma, being so evil a thing the whole end of man is to break free from the wearisome succession of births. No life of virtue or of sacrifice will give him this freedom. "Nay, even if one . . . should perform here on earth some great holy work it will perish for him in the end" (Ad. 1, B. 4, v. 15). From the heavens the divine voice of thunder may repeat again and again "be subdued, give, be merciful" (Ad. 5, B. 2, v. 3), and yet, well pleasing though a life of charity and mercy may be, it will bring no release. The way of escape lies in the right knowledge of Brahman. "Those who know Brahman go to him and return no more" (Ad. 6, B. 1). This knowledge cannot be bought. Maitreyi asks: "My Lord, if this whole earth full of wealth belonged to me, tell me, should I be immortal by it or no?" (Ad. 4, B. 5, v. 3). "No," replied Yagnavalkya, "like the life of rich people will be thy life. But there is no hope of immortality by wealth" (Ad. 4, B. 5, v. 4). The whole of desire must be centred on Brahman. Husband, wife, sons, wealth, cattle, the Brahman class, the Kshatra class, the worlds, the Devas, the Vedas the creatures—not any of these must be dear for their own sakes, "but that you may love the Self" (Ad. 4, B. 5, v. 6). Brahmanas seek to know the Universal "by the study of the Vedas, by sacrifice, by gifts, by penance, by fasting, and he who knows him becomes a Muni" (Ad. 4, B. 4, v. 22). Finally, the lust of this world being altogether cast out, and "wishing for that world (for Brahman) only, mendicants leave their homes" (Ad. 4, B. 4, v. 22), and, whatever state and power may have been theirs, live as hermits in the forest practising austerities. "When all desires which once entered his heart are undone, then does the mortal become immortal, then he obtains Brahman. And as the slough of a snake lies on an ant hill dead and cast away, thus lies this body, but that disembodied immortal spirit is Brahman only, is only light" (Ad. 4, B. 4, v. 7). In his life the victorious one may have done good or evil—neither the one nor the other is supremely important, for "whether he says that for some reason he has done evil: or for some reason he has done good—he overcomes both, and neither what he has done nor what he has omitted to do burns (affects) him" (Ad. 4, B. 4, v. 22). There is a strong hint in this Upanishad as to the difficulty of reconciling the claims of the Kshatra (warrior) and Brahman (class) to real supremacy. The solution is a triumph of diplomacy. "There is nothing beyond the Kshatra, and therefore at the Ragasaya sacrifice the Brahmana sits down below the Kshatriya. He confers that glory in the Kshatra. But Brahman is (nevertheless) the birthplace of the Kshatra; therefore, though a king is exalted, he sits down at the end (of the sacrifice) below the Brahman as his birthplace. He who injures him injures his own birthplace. He becomes worse because he has injured one better than himself" (Ad. 1, B. 4, v. 11).

(m) MAITRÂYANA-BRÂHMANA UPANISHAD

Life is full of all manner of evil: "Bewilderment, fear, grief, sleep, sloth, carelessness, decay, sorrow, hunger, thirst, niggardliness, wrath, infidelity, ignorance, envy, cruelty, folly, shamelessness, meanness, pride, changeability . . . inward thirst, fondness, passion, covetousness, unkindness, love, hatred, deceit, jealousy, vain restlessness, fickleness, unstableness, emulation, greed, patronizing of friends, family pride, aversion to disagreeable object, devotion to agreeable objects, whispering, prodigality" (P. 3, v. 5). Even the enjoyment of so-called pleasure is useless in a world of this sort, for "he who is fed on them is seen to return (to this world) again and again" (P. 1, v. 4). Men who think themselves wise are deceived by the vain show and "wander about floundering" and "deceived like the blind led by the blind" (P. 7, v. 9). The greatest of all snares, the very origin of "the net of bewilderment," is egotism— the exaltation of the human self—"for if a man looks at the world egotistically, then taking the diadem of passion, the earrings of greed and envy, the staff of sloth, sleep and sin, and having seized the bow whose string is anger and whose stock is lust, he destroys with the arrow, which consists of wishes, all beings" (P. 6, v. 28). If men can but see it, the real goal of life is not the satisfaction of desire, but complete freedom from desire. Foolish men are blinded by what is near and immediate. "Though they have been told there is a grove before them they cling to a small shrub" (P. 7, v. 8). They believe that in "children, wife and house" they can find fulfilment of being, and do not know that true blessedness can only be found in "identity with Brahman" (P. 6, v. 28). The truly wise are like the King Brihadratha, who "went into the forest because he considered this body as transient and had obtained freedom from all desires" (P. 1, v. 2). "The slavery of desire can be broken and union with Brahman attained by the practising of Yoga, which consists in the oneness of breath, mind and senses and then the surrendering of all conceptions" (P. 6, v. 25). When Yoga has been perfectly achieved by "concentration of the mind on the object of meditation, restraint of the breath, restraint of the senses, meditation, fixed attention, investigation, absorption" (P. 6, v. 18), then all desire being overcome the ascetic "pure, clean, undeveloped, tranquil, breathless, bodiless, endless, imperishable, firm, everlasting, unborn and independent, he stands on his own greatness, and having seen (the Self) standing in his own greatness he looks on the wheel of the world as one who has alighted from a chariot (looks on its revolving wheel)" (P. 6, v. 28).

(n) KATHA UPANISHAD

The Katha Upanishad consists in the main of a dialogue between Nakoketas, who has been sacrificed by his father, and Yama, the god of death. The material is represented as being entirely inadequate. "These things last till tomorrow. . . . No man can be made happy by wealth" (Ad. 1, V. 1, vv. 26–27). A distinction is made between what is good and what is merely pleasant. "The good is one thing, the pleasant another. . . . It is well with him who clings to the good; he who chooses the pleasant misses his end" (Ad. 1, V. 2, v. 1). Those who choose the seen and the temporal and allow themselves to be filled with desire are "Fools dwelling in darkness, wise in their own conceit, and puffed up with vain knowledge," who "go round and round staggering to and fro like blind men led by the blind" (Ad. 1, V. 2, v. 3). For that man who has allowed himself to be deluded by the things of time and sense there is the doom of rebirth—"he has to take body again in the worlds of creation" (Ad. 2, V. 6, v. 4). The real goal of life is identification with Brahman, the true and the great, who dwells as the sun in the bright heaven, as the air in the sky, as the sacrificer in the fire, as the guest in the Soma libation, who "dwells in men, in gods" (Ad. 2, V. 5, v. 2). While in one place "study, sacrifice, almsgiving" (Ad. 1, V. 1, v. 17) are enjoined and in another it is laid down as an essential that men should turn away from their sin, liberation from the chains of life cannot be attained by moral rectitude. The great freedom can be won only by meditation and the practice of Yoga—"the firm holding back of the senses" (Ad. 2, V. 6, v. 11). The man who is "free from desires and free from grief, who is tranquil and subdued, whose mind is at rest, is able to perceive Brahman within himself. At the dissolution of the body he passes beyond to the heavenly world where "there is no fear. Thou art not there, O Death, and no one is afraid on account of old age. Leaving behind both hunger and thirst and out of the reach of sorrow all rejoice in the world of heaven" (Ad. 1, V. 1, v. 12). This passage by itself might give some idea of the possibility of continued personality in that world of light in which "the sun does not shine . . . nor the moon and the stars, nor these lightnings" (Ad. 2, V. 6, v. 15). It is not so, however. The right knowledge of Brahman leads to complete absorption. "As pure water poured into pure water remains the same, thus, O Gautama, is the self of a thinker who knows" (Ad. 2, V. 4, v. 15). And so in the end, when desire has been completely overcome, when personality is no longer valued, when Brahman has been perceived by right meditation, a man "reaches the end of his journey . . . reaches indeed that place from whence he is not born again" (Ad. 1, V. 3, vv. 8 and 9).

(o) SUMMARY OF EARLY BRAHMANISM

In the period of the Satapatha Brahmana and the Upanishads the caste system had been established at least in its main outlines. The Kshatra or warrior caste were the soldiers, rulers and administrators. The Brahmans were the priests and the philosophers. While regarded by the Kshatras as being the second order in the State, they were through their control of the sacrificial system probably in actual fact the more powerful of the two. The Vaisyus were the free husbandmen and traders of the Aryan race. Below these were the toiling Sudras, the descendants of the conquered aborigines who, in process of time, had become hewers of wood and drawers of water for their "twice born conquerors." It is scarcely necessary to comment further on the political ordering of the Aryan kingdoms or on the sacrificial system which formed the popular conception of religion. The one we shall be dealing with at a later period, while the other was to a very large extent transitory, and without far-reaching permanent effects. The great development of this period was the philosophy and religion of the Upanishads. It is impossible to stress too strongly the importance of these documents. They are fundamental in the whole after-history of India, and have conditioned to an extraordinary degree the whole outlook, the social life, and the joys, sorrows, hopes and fears of millions of the human race for a period of two thousand five hundred years.

The fundamental conception is that of Brahman. In the numerous descriptions given of him there is barely a trace of anthropomorphism. Although in one passage he is described as a person, he definitely lacks many of the main elements of personality. He can scarcely be called God, although he is the creator of the universe and the sustainer of its life. Brahman is a vast misty consciousness without form, from which everything arises and to which everything returns. He is the life-stuff which forms the essence of all living beings. The sum of all life is Brahman—and Brahman is its goal. He is the soul of all things and all things are merely emanations of himself. He was from before all time, and will be for evermore, changing in form but ever the same in substance. Brahman is an ocean of passionless consciousness full of light, in which everything is seen and known, but whose vast surface is unstirred by any tempest of passion. The formlessness of Brahman enables the Hindu philosopher to interpret all things in terms of a unity. There is no need for the exclusion of anything in the conception of a life force that can be masculine, feminine and neuter, and which can contain good and evil indifferently. For most primitive peoples the conception of the Divine Being turns on his good or evil will towards themselves and the measure of power with which he asserts his will. The god or gods must be interested in them. While Brahman is perhaps conscious of men as one might imagine an ocean to be conscious of the fishes swimming in it, he is certainly not interested in them or concerned about them.

Such a being is not sufficient for ordinary men, and in consequence the philosophic conceptions of Brahman were supplemented by the worship of other beings of a somewhat more definite nature, most of whom were, as we should expect, the deities of the old Vedic pantheon, such as Agni and Indra. These deities were still little more than personifications of natural phenomena, but being connected with season or locality possessed that definiteness which men need when they direct their prayers towards the supernatural. Thus we have a system which is apparently as polytheistic as that of the Rig-Veda. And yet to the philosopher it was not so in the least, because whether there were three gods worshipped or three million, there was still but one, because all these, many or few, were alike manifestations of the universal and eternal which, although multiple in form, was still one in essence.

The individual personality of the members of the human race is not regarded as being in any sense a breach of the unity of all life. Men are sparks flying up from the central fire, and though for a space they are separated from the glowing immensity of the eternal, yet they are still fire of its fire, and in the end they sink back into it unchanged as it is unchangeable. The awareness of self, the sense of separateness induced by temporary isolation, and the inability to see past the barriers of the physical and the material, imposed by the very condition of birth, is evil—wholly evil. Life, considered egotistically, is a delusion and a snare. All those things so greatly coveted by man, all those satisfactions of instinctive desire, are but bandages to the eyes of his soul. As long as he looks upon these things and seeing them seeks them, he is doomed to the continuing evil of rebirth. Like Bunyan's "Man with the Muckrake" he spends his life gathering straws, unaware of the angel and of the crown—and he is doomed to rake the straws of life after life. So fundamentally evil is the life of man that there is no mending of it. Freedom from birth is the quest of the thinkers of the Upanishads. Man, on entering the world, becomes subject to Dharma—the Law of the Deed. Right living, the performance of good deeds and of holy works will, after death, lead him to a heaven of good works, where for a period he will enjoy every pleasure, but from whence he is surely born again. Evil deeds lead to darkness, but from this also there is rebirth, although in lowly form. Dharma, then, although it may alleviate the hard condition of men bound to a wheel of successive and perhaps endless births, has a negative effect only. An infinite number of lives crowded with good works will never bring the freedom so ardently sought. This can only be obtained by the man who realizes that he is of one essence with Brahman, and that he is indeed separated from the infinite only by those barriers of egotism which we know as desires. If he can by the practice of asceticism and by meditation on the Infinite break altogether the power of desire, then he, at the time of death, will leave behind the material, and knowing that he is Brahman and Brahman is himself he sinks back into that vastness and becomes one with it. So freedom is attained, and for that man there is no longer birth. The chains are broken, the isolation and loneliness are passed. The intolerable burden of individuality has rolled away and a serene unbroken tranquillity replaces the fitful and feverish restlessness of human life. While the whole idea of the evil of birth and the weariness of life is based on a premise of pessimism, it is not fair to say that the quest of the Hindu religious is for annihilation. His search is for a higher form of life, and he sees this not in the growth, purification or exaltation of his own personality, but in the complete mergence of his self with the great universal Self. When he has shaken off all the bonds of desire he does not lapse into nothingness, but sees with the eyes of Brahman, is conscious with the consciousness of Brahman, and is for ever at rest in that wide sea of restfulness which is bliss eternal.

In all religions in which the thoughts and aspirations of man reach out to the spiritual these questions sooner or later present themselves:

1. Is God personal?
2. Is He moral?
3. Can men obtain unification with Him by moral living, by a purely spiritual experience, or by experience and a moral life combined?

The seers of the Upanishads reply that God is not personal, that He is unmoral, and that unification with Him is a matter solely of spiritual experience.

(*p*) THE REVOLT AGAINST BRAHMANISM

As Brahmanism consolidated its position by the control of the sacrificial system and the unique spiritual and even temporal position claimed by the members of the priestly class, its tyranny commenced to cut deep into the very life of peoples who had not entirely forgotten the meaning of freedom. The young Brahman, Ambattha, is represented as saying: "There are these four grades, Gotama, the nobles, the Brahmans, the tradesfolk and the work people. And of these four, three—the nobles, the tradesfolk and the work people—are verily but attendants on the Brahmans. So, Gotama, that is neither fitting, nor is it seemly that the Sakyas, menials as they are—mere menials—should neither venerate, nor value, nor esteem, nor give gifts to, nor pay honour to the Brahmans" (*Ambattha Sutta*, c. 1, v. 15). Such language, such an attitude toward free men, rich and secure, of a proud and ancient fighting-stock would inevitably arouse antagonism. To demand of a Kshatriya that he become the mere slave of a class that in the days of the conquest was subordinate to his own, was to precipitate a conflict. In the sixth century B.C. there arose a widespread revolt against Brahmanism. The issue at stake was the life of India during what we know as the historical period.

Many schools of thought put forward their philosophies. An old Buddhist text mentions sixty-three of them, and there were probably more. (*Cambridge Modern History*, Vol, I, c. 6, p. 150). Some of these differed in everything save their common antipathy to Brahmanism. Others were so closely akin that they quickly amalgamated. Some simply faded away, others were absorbed ultimately into the very faith with which they contended, while two in particular—the religion of the Jains and the religion of Buddhism—have lasted until our own time. Wandering teachers debated with each other every conceivable philosophical principle—the nature and end of man, the gods and their relation to men, the soul and its destiny, the place of prayer and sacrifice, the importance of works. One remarkable feature of the tremendous conflict was the absence, as far as we can trace, of any widespread persecution of heretics. There was an altogether remarkable tolerance and a very gracious courtesy extended to all manner of strange professors. Anyone who, on a venture of faith, became a wandering mendicant and commenced to expound some body of teaching lacked neither an audience nor a meal.

EARLY BUDDHISM

(q) THE LIFE OF GOTAMA, CALLED THE BUDDHA

The Republic of the Sakyas lay at the foot of the Himalayas. According to ancient tradition the population comprised some half-million souls. The clan was prosperous and probably more warlike than its southern neighbours. While Brahmanism had no doubt a considerable hold the predominant warrior type had maintained in a great degree the old Aryan freedom. To Suddhohana, of the house of Gotama, the Raga or president of this clan, and to his wife, Maya, was born about 563 B.C. a son Siddhartha—the Buddha of history. How many of the stories concerning him are true, how many are pure myth, it is impossible for us to say with any certainty. We can safely reject much as being obviously silly invention; but much is so humanly true as to be well worthy of credence.

The highborn lad was brought up from infancy as the darling of his father's Court. A white canopy was held over him continually, for it was commanded: "Let not cold or heat or straws or dust or dew annoy him" (V.[1] 3, p. 16, par. 34). As quite a small boy he sat in the hall of judgment with the Raga his father and received the training in law that befitted a future ruler. Three palaces were built for him, and he was surrounded with every luxury and with every pleasure that was likely to appeal to the senses of youth. All that was ugly, evil or unpleasant was kept far from him. No hint of death or sorrow, no sight of sickness or of sin was to be seen in this artificial paradise. But one day, as the young lord drove through his pleasure park, an afflicted, decrepit old man crossed the path. Siddhartha learned, to his amazement, that old age was the common

[1] V. = Volume in Sacred Books of Buddhists.

lot and went back to his splendid rooms "brooding, sorrowful and depressed, thinking: Shame then, verily, be upon this thing called birth, since to one born old age shows itself like that" (V. 3, p. 19, par. 2). His father, much disquieted and dreading lest the boy should go out into "the homeless state," surrounded him still more with sensuous pleasures. Again the youth gave himself entirely to the enjoyments of sense until, once more driving abroad, he came upon "a sick man, suffering and very ill, fallen and weltering" (V. 3, p. 20, par. 6). From his charioteer he learned that all were liable to disease. Once more he brooded upon the evil of birth which made men the prey of such misfortunes, but being more abundantly surrounded with all delights he relapsed again into a life of selfish pleasure. A third time they drove into the park, and on this occasion Siddhartha beheld a great concourse of mourners surrounding a funeral pyre, and was shocked at beholding the corpse and realizing that all life ended in sorrow and separation, and that death spared neither king nor queen, nor, indeed, any creature. Again, after a lapse of time, he went forth, and this time met a yellow-robed, shaven-haired ascetic, and learned that this wanderer was "thorough in the religious life, thorough in the peaceful life, thorough in good actions, thorough in meritorious conduct, thorough in harmlessness, thorough in kindness to all creatures" (V. 1, p. 22, par. 14). The meeting with the ascetic was the turning-point of his career. He returned home to find the palace ablaze with lights and all the people rejoicing that a son was born to him. Power, wealth, pleasure of every kind, youth, health, wife and child, everything a man could desire was his. But the tragedy of life, the enigma of sorrow, were pressing upon him, demanding an answer that he could in no wise give, while he was surfeited with every luxury. At midnight he rose from his bed. In the antechamber were dancing-girls lying around asleep. The sight of them filled him with loathing. In an instant his mind was definitely made up. He is said to have taken one last look at his sleeping wife and child, and then, turning away, went out into the wilderness a homeless ascetic, to wrestle with himself and the universe until he could find some way of salvation. Almost at once he was tempted by Mara, the Evil One, who offered him world empire if he would give up his quest after truth. But the Buddha-to-be pressed steadfastly on, "a pilgrim now in search of the right and in quest of the excellent road to peace" (V. 5, p. 115). He came first to Kalama, an ascetic and professor of repute, but on finding that his doctrine was insufficient, as it merely led to the attaining of "the Nought and not to renunciation, passionless cessation, peace, discernment, enlightenment and Nirvana" (V. 5, p. 116), Siddhartha turned away from this teacher and continued his search. He then came to Uddaka Ramaputta, but found that his doctrine "merely led to attaining the plane of neither perception nor non-perception" (V. 5, p. 117). So, quite unsatisfied, he went to Ureveka—a place entirely suitable for "a young man whose heart is set on striving." Here for a space of six years he, with five companions, sought by the practice of frightful austerities to find peace and enlightenment. He starved himself with rigour, subsisting on a grain of rice or a single jujube fruit a day, until "his belly clave to his backbone." His raiment consisted of filthy rags taken from the dust heaps. For great lengths of time he never quitted the standing for a sitting posture—and then again squatted or couched himself on thorns. His body was a loathly accumulation of dirt. The most awesome depths of a forest were his lairs—and in such solitariness did he dwell that the sight of a wandering herdsman caused him to dart from "thicket to thicket, from hill to hill." In the winter he was frozen and in the summer scorched. The cowherds' boys mocked, teased and pelted him (V. 5, pp. 53-56), but the fame of his austerities rang through North India "like the sound of a great bell hung in the canopy of the sky."

> "Now scorched, now froze in forest dread alone,
> Naked, and fearless set upon his quest,
> the hermit battles purity to win" (V. 5, p. 55).

And the end of it all was that when, in a state of extreme exhaustion, he fell down apparently dead, the realization was forced upon him that all his sufferings and torments had brought him no nearer to the end of his quest. To the disgust of his five devoted disciples he from that time abandoned the way of austerities, took regular food and returned to a normal although abstemious and temperate life. Some time later, having now become an outcast indeed, he wandered along the banks of the Nairanjara and sat down beneath the shade of a great tree—known to posterity as the Bo tree—the tree of wisdom. He fell into a deep meditation, considering all the wasted strivings of so many years. The lure of power and wealth, the desire for love and home life again surged up within him. The temptation was strong, but he struggled on toward victory, and as evening fell he attained to perfect enlightenment, and entered into the peace for which he had sought so long and with such pain. "Subject in myself to rebirth—decay—disease—death—sorrow—and impurity, and seeing peril in what is subject thereto, I sought after the consummate peace of Nirvana, which knows neither rebirth nor decay, neither disease nor death, neither sorrow nor impurity; this I pursued and this I won: and there arose within me the conviction, the insight, that now my Deliverance was assured; that this was my last birth, nor should I ever be born again" (V. 5, p. 117 f.). He had won enlightenment for himself. He was now a Buddha. The question immediately arose in his mind as to whether he should withdraw into obscurity and silence, or whether he should go out to proclaim a gospel. The difficulties in the way of such a proclamation were great. Human nature was not then more impressionable than now.

> "Must I then preach what I so hardly won?
> Men sunk in sin and lusts would find it hard
> to plumb this Doctrine—upstream all the way;
> abstruse, profound, most subtle, hard to grasp—
> Dear, lusts will blind them that they shall not see
> —in densest mists of ignorance befogged" (V. 5, p. 118).

For himself he desired only the quietness, but while he doubted a vision of Brahma Sahanpati appeared urging him, for the sake of "the world undone . . . quite undone," to take up the task:

> "Lead on thy pilgrim train—
> through all the world thy doctrine preach
> —among the hearers some will understand" (V. 5, p. 119).

Moved with compassion for mankind, he thought first of his old teachers, Kalama and Uddaha Ramaputta, but both were dead. And so he went on his way to the Ispatria Deer Park at Benares, where dwelt the Five Almsmen who had served him so well in the days when he strove by austerities to purge himself. The five saw him coming afar off. To them the Buddha was but "the recluse Gotama, the man of surfeits," who had abandoned his struggle and reverted to surfeiting. They agreed to treat him with coolness and to offer none of the courtesies usually paid by Eastern disciples to their master. But as he drew nearer those Five Almsmen "proved less and less able to abide by their compact: some came forward to relieve me of my bowl and robes: others indicated my seat: while others brought water for me to wash my feet: but they addressed me by name and by the style of reverend" (V. 5, p. 122). They questioned him, and after long discussion became his first followers. During the rainy season the number of the believers slowly grew. Much time was spent in instruction, and when the dry weather came again the Buddha called all together and said: "Beloved Rahans, I am free from the five passions which like an immense net hold men and angels in their power; you, too, owing to my teaching, enjoy the same glorious privilege. There is now laid on us a great duty, that of working effectually for men and angels, and gaining for them also the priceless blessing of salvation. Let us therefore separate, so that no two of us shall go the same way. Go ye now and preach the most excellent law, explaining every point thereof, unfolding it with diligence and care . . ." (*Encyclopædia Britannica*, vol. 4, p. 429). So Buddhism set out to save the world. For more than forty years the Buddha, "the Lord the Arahat all enlightened," lived the life of a mendicant teacher, proclaiming his new gospel to all sorts and conditions of men. To the poor and the simple in mind the message was given in story and parable, to the philosopher in the terms of the philosophy of the day. Behind it all was a real passion for humanity showing itself in kindly words and deeds, and an enthusiasm which could maintain itself only on a profound spiritual experience. The new doctrine won immediate recognition. King Bimbisara gave to the Buddha the garden known as the Bamboo grove, famous ever after as the place in which he spent many rainy seasons and preached many of his great sermons. Gotama was received with the greatest honour at Kapolavastu, his old home, and won many of his relations, including Nanda his half-brother, and even his own son Rahula. The order of mendicant monks grew with every passing year—and devout and believing laymen were multiplied exceedingly. Women pressed in, and against the Buddha's wish he was reluctantly constrained to establish an order of nuns, of which his widowed wife, Yasodhara, was one of the first members. The priestly Brahmans strongly opposed the new doctrine, and are even alleged to have instigated attempts on the life of Buddha. Their wealth and prestige were threatened, and the final success of the new faith meant the entire overthrow of the sacrificial system, the abandonment of caste, and the substitution of a moral code based on the principle of kindly life for the vague and often unmoral spirituality of Brahmanism. Yet despite the opposition, Buddha remained the central figure of his time, attracting to himself men of every condition. At the great assembly held some time before his death there were assembled one thousand and two hundred and fifty Arahants—fully enlightened members of the order. The story of his death is fully told. When he had turned eighty years of age and his body "was like a worn-out cart," he was at the beginning of the rainy season seized with "a sore sickness, and sharp pains came upon him even unto death." The Exalted One, "ever mindful and self-possessed, bore them without complaint." By a great effort of will he overcame the sickness and kept his hold on life until the appointed time should come. Accompanied by Ananda, his own personal attendant, he journeyed slowly, teaching as he went, until he reached Kusinara, "a wattle and daub town" of the Mallas. The inhabitants came out in great numbers to take their farewell. Then came a certain wanderer by the name of Subhadda, who had a feeling of uncertainty which he hoped the Exalted One would resolve for him. Ananda would have spared his dying master the fatigue of the interview, but he himself hearing the voices called in Subhadda and spoke with him until the wanderer, reaching certainty, entered the Order as an Arahant—"he was the last disciple whom the Exalted One himself converted" (V. 3, p. 169). Ananda was given certain instructions concerning the future of the Order, and then the Buddha, turning to the brethren who had come to that place, uttered his last words: "Behold now, brethren, I exhort you, saying: Decay is inherent in all component things. Work out your salvation with diligence" (V. 3, p. 173). He then passed through all the stages of rapture—"and passing out of the last stage of rapture he immediately expired" (V. 3, p. 175).

> "When he who from all craving want was free,
> Who to Nirvana's tranquil state had reached,
> When the great sage finished his span of life,
> No gasping struggle vexed that steadfast heart.
> All resolute and with unshaken mind
> He calmly triumphed o'er the pain of death;
> E'en as a bright flame dies away so was
> The last emancipation of his heart" (V. 3, p. 176).

When the brethren perceived that the Buddha was indeed dead some gave themselves up to an utter abandonment of grief, crying and bewailing: "Too soon has the Exalted One died. Too soon has the Happy One passed away. Too soon has the Light gone out of the world" (V. 3, p. 177). But the Arahants "bore their grief, collected and composed." Of those who could not restrain themselves was Ananda, the beloved disciple. To the scandal of the gravely controlled elders of the order he wept aloud. When reproved for this breach of decorum his only excuse was: "But he was so kind."

(r) BUDDHIST THEORY

In the Agganna Suttanta there is given an account of the beginning of things. At the end of an age this world passed utterly away. The living beings on it had been reborn in the world of Radiance, where for a period they enjoyed every delight. After ages of time the world commenced to evolve as "one world of water, dark and of a darkness that maketh blind. No moon, no sun appeared, no stars were seen, nor constellations, neither was night manifest, nor day. . . ." The beings from the World of Radiance came to life again in this chaos as human beings. Dry land formed itself from the waters: "Even as a scum forms on the surface of boiled milky rice that is cooling." The earth had a savoury taste "even as the flawless honey of the bee, so sweet was it." Some of the beings of a greedy disposition first tasted, and then breaking off great lumps of the earth feasted upon it. Craving had entered into them, and as a result life became increasingly material and degraded. The living beings lost their self-luminance, which departed to the heavenly bodies, became increasingly solid, and at length became divided into male and female with every degree of divergence in personal characteristic. "In them passion arose and burning entered their body. They in consequence thereof followed their own lusts." As desire arose and more and more dominated the life of man they built huts to hide their doings from others, they commenced to hoard grain, and then found it necessary to make boundaries where aforetime there had been none. Then came theft and after punishment, and so "did stealing appear and censure and lying and punishment became known." Evil deeds became so prevalent that at length they chose out the most capable and said to him, "Come now, good being, be indignant at that whereat one should rightly be indignant, censure that which should be rightly censured, banish him who deserves to be banished. And we will contribute to thee a portion of our rice. And he consented and did so. . . ." Thus the social order of the nobles came into being. The Brahman class was formed from those who, putting aside evil, lived lives of austerity and meditation. The Vaisyu caste was composed of trades-folk and the Sudras of those who lived on hunting and other trifling pursuits.

The background of this account was no doubt common belief of the time. Whether the Buddha believed it literally is of no consequence. By means of it he was able to demonstrate what was the foundation of his system—namely, that life was evil and that evil depended upon and grew forth from desire. This conception, in which, of course, he was entirely orthodox, is reinforced time and again throughout the teaching. "Thus then is it, Ananda, that cognition with name and form as its cause: name and form with cognition as its cause: contact with name and form as its cause: sensation with contact as its cause: craving with sensation as its cause: grasping with craving as its cause: becoming with grasping as its cause: birth with becoming as its cause: old age and death with birth as its cause: grief, lamentation, ill, sorrow and despair all come into being. Such is the coming to pass of this whole body of ill" (V. 3, p. 52). "And what Bikkhus is the Aryan truth regarding ill? Birth is painful, old age is painful, death is painful, grief, lamentation, suffering, misery and despair are painful, painful, is it not, to get what is wished for, in a word, the Five Groups that arise from Grasping are connected with pain" (V 3, p 337) The wish arises in man: "Ah! If only we were not subject to birth, if only we could avoid being born" (V. 3, p. 339). Life is hindered, obstructed and entangled by the Five Hindrances:

"The hindrance of worldly lusts.
The hindrance of ill-will.
The hindrance of torpor, and sloth of heart and mind.
The hindrance of flurry and worry.
The hindrance of suspense" (V. 2, p. 312).

and like to be overwhelmed by the Deadly Floods, the Deadly Taint of Lusts, the deadly taint of Becomings, and the Deadly Taint of Ignorance.

From this life, so painful and subject to so many ills, therefore so little to be desired, there is no plain or easy way of escape. Man is doomed to a continual round of rebirth. Buddha, speaking of himself, says: "I call to mind my diverse existences in the past, a single birth, then two . . . a hundred thousand births, many an aeon of disintegration of the world, many an aeon of its reintegration, and again many an aeon both disintegration and of its reintegration. In this or that former existence I remembered such and such was my name, my sept, my class, my diet, my joys and sorrows and system of life. When I passed thence I came by such and such subsequent existence wherein such and such was my name and so forth. Thence I passed to my life here" (V. 5, p. 15). This vast procession of lives is passed between purgatory and "the consummate peace of Nirvana." A man whose life has been evil passes to the state of "woe and misery." He is pegged down with red-hot pegs, trimmed with axes and razors, and driven harnessed "over a fiery expense all aflame and ablaze." After all this he is cast into Great Purgatory, which is

"Four square, four doored, quadrangular
    roofed with steel
 with incandescent floor of molten steel
 a hundred leagues this way and that its range extends"
                                (V. 6, p. 250).

From thence he is plunged into Great Filth Purgatory, wherein needle-mouthed creatures successively rip away his skin and his hide, his flesh, his tendons and his bones till they can "devour his marrow" (V. 6, p. 259). The next hell is that of Ember Purgatory, where he is driven to climb up and down in a forest of silk cotton-trees a league high "with prickles half a yard long, all afire and aflame and ablaze" (V. 6, p. 259). Passing through the Sword-leaved Forest the sufferer is plunged into the great Caustic River. Dragged from this torment by a fish-hook, he is questioned as to what he wants, and if he replies that he is hungry, then the wardens of purgatory, "prizing his mouth open with a red-hot crowbar, thrust into his mouth a red-hot ball of copper." If he says that he is athirst "they pour into his mouth molten copper and bronze, all afire and aflame and ablaze" (V. 6, p. 260). And after all this he is cast once more into Great Purgatory.

Foolish thinking and wrong living may cause "the fool, who in this world was fond of tastes and has committed evil deeds, after the body's dissolution to be reborn," as a grass-eating animal, a dung-eating animal, a denizen of darkness, an aquatic creature or an organism that lives in decaying matter. Any reborn into such a life experience the greatest difficulty in escaping from it. A blind turtle coming to the surface of the sea once in a century would more quickly find the single aperture in a floating yoke, driven at the mercy of the winds, than would one born into the animal world become a human being again. Even so he is born into "one of the low stocks—outcastes, trappers, rush-plaiters, cartwrights and rat-catchers—that he is reborn into a life of vagrancy and want and penury, scarce getting food and drink for his belly or clothes to his back. He grows up ill-favoured and unsightly, misshapen, a weakling, blind, or deformed or lame or a cripple. . . . He misconducts himself in act, word, and thought, and so again becomes liable for a state of misery and woe or to purgatory" (V. 6, p. 252).

On the other hand, those who live rightly, or at the time of their death have a right outlook, "pass to a future state of bliss in heaven. Now heaven is all that is called pleasing, pleasant and agreeable—it is far from easy to picture the happiness of heaven" (V. 6, p. 253). If after a great space of time the wise and good man should be reborn again as a human being it will be "into one of the higher stocks—rich nobles or Brahman or masters of houses—that he is reborn to a life of affluence, riches and wealth, with abundance of gold and coins of silver and with abounding substance and abounding possessions. He grows up well-favoured and well-liking, with the loveliest complexion, with plenty of food and drink and clothes and carriages and garlands and scents and perfumes: he conducts himself aright in act, word and thought, and his right conduct brings him at the body's dissolution after death to well-being and satisfaction in heaven" (V. 6, p. 255). In the succession of births men "fare according to their past" (V. 6, p. 255), although not always according to the immediate past. Cases are mentioned in which the apparently evil attain to bliss or the apparently good are tormented in purgatory. There is, as it were, a process of ripening, and in the brief span of one life the effects of this process are not always discernible. "If with non-murderous habits here, and so forth, and with the right outlook the man is reborn into a state of misery and woe or purgatory, this is because either aforetime or thereafter he had done evil deeds which result in painful experiences, or else at the time of his death he had secured and chosen the wrong outlook. His non-murderous habits here, and so forth, and his previously right outlook are experienced in their ripening either here and now or in his rebirth or in some other way" (V. 6, p. 277). The whole position is admirably summed up in the Aggañña Suttanta. "Now a Khattiya, Vasettha, who has led a bad life, in deed, word and thought, whose views of life are wrong, will, in consequence of his views and deeds, when the body breaks up, be reborn after death in the Waste, the Woeful Way, the Downfall, Purgatory. And a Brahman too . . . a Vessa too . . . a Sudda too, who has led a bad life, in deed, word and thought, whose views of life are wrong, will in consequence of his views and deeds, when the body breaks up, be reborn after death in the Waste, the Woeful Way, the Downfall, Purgatory. Again Vasettha, a Khattiya . . . or Brahman . . . or Vessa . . . or Sudda, who has led a good life in deed, word and thought, whose views of life are as they should be, will in consequence of his views and deeds when the body breaks up be reborn after death in a happy bright world. Again Vasettha, a Khattiya . . . a Brahman too . . . a Vessa too . . . a Sudda too . . . who has lived a life both good and bad, in deed, word and thought, whose views of life are mixed, will in consequence of his mixed views and deeds, when the body breaks up, be reborn after death suffering both happiness and unhappiness" (V. 4, p. 92 f.). The Chain of Causation—the insistence on the intimate connection between deeds and rebirth, is the first outstanding doctrine of Buddhism. There are passages in the earlier Upanishad, from which, no doubt, the idea evolved, but it was the Buddhist who first laid it down as a fundamental principle that future existence was determined by conduct. In the passages that have been quoted dealing with rebirth into states of happiness we must be very careful to remember that the happiness therein described is after all only relative and is bounded and terminated by birth and death, which are in themselves such great evils as to entirely overshadow any transient pleasure that the higher grades of human life or even the heavenly world can give. The result of rebirth is always "decay, disease, death, sorrow and impurity" (V. 5, p. 114).

The Buddha did not, however, regard his mission as

being merely to give an adequate description of life as he believed it to be. At a very great cost he had won enlightenment and salvation for himself, and he was under a strong impulse to deliver this message of hope to men. For himself he was sure that he had reached the end of birth and that he would not after his present life be born again in any state. Passing out from the misery of life he would cease to be. Never again would he bear the burden of existence. This consummation had been attained by a definite victory over wrong thoughts, wrong attitudes of mind, wrong ways of life. While he himself was in that age the supremely enlightened one, others might learn and practise his system and so attain the same goal. In his last great speech to his disciples the dying teacher is reported to have said: "Which . . . O brethren, are the truths which when perceived I made known to you, which when you have mastered, it behoves you to practise, meditate upon and spread abroad, in order that pure religion may last long and be perpetuated, in order that it may continue to be for the good and happiness of the great multitudes; out of pity for the world, to the good and the gain, and the weal of gods and men?

They are these:

> "The four earnest meditations.
> The fourfold great struggle against evil.
> The four roads to saintship.
> The five moral powers.
> The five organs of spiritual sense.
> The seven kinds of wisdom.
> The Aryan eightfold path."

On one occasion the Exalted One addressed the brethren, saying: "The one and only path Bhikkus leading to the purification of beings, to passing far beyond grief and lamentation, to the dying out of ill and misery, to the attainment of right method, to the realization of Nirvana,

INDIA

is that of the Fourfold Setting Up of Mindfulness" (V. 3, p. 327). The term "mindfulness" has been variously translated as Conscience, Attention, Meditation, Memory, Contemplation, Insight and Thought (V. 3, p. 323 f.). It is of the greatest importance in the system of Buddhist theory and consists of four aspects.

1. MINDFULNESS CONCERNING THE BODY

The disciple must pay heed to certain attitudes. He must sit cross-legged and holding the body erect, inhale and exhale with conscious deliberation. Then "ardent, self-possessed and mindful" he must so concentrate his mind as to reach a perfect awareness of his whole body and all its functions. He must consider that it is something that comes to be and something that passes away again. He must reflect upon every part of it, remembering that it is but a skinful of impurities and made of earth, water, heat and air. When his body performs any of the functions natural to it—eating, drinking, chewing, reposing, sitting, sleeping, watching—he must be perfectly aware of them. Not only must he contemplate his body as an actuality of the present, but also as a decomposed and broken thing reduced from all form to a rotten powder. The body must be known for exactly what it is and what it will be (V. 3, pp. 327–333).

2. MINDFULNESS AS TO FEELINGS

In a similar way the disciple must be completely aware of all feelings. Every state of consciousness must be considered in its coming on and in its passing away. . . ."A brother, when affected by a feeling of pleasure, aware of it, reflecting. I feel a pleasurable feeling: So, too, is he aware when affected by a painful feeling, or by a neutral feeling, or by a pleasant or painful or neutral feeling concerning spiritual things" (V. 3, p. 333).

3. Mindfulness as to Thought

Every thought must be intelligently recognized for what it really is. . . . "A brother, if his thought be lustful, is aware that it is so: or, if his thought be full of hate, or free from hate, or dull, or intelligent or attentive, or distrait, or exalted or not exalted, or mediocre, or ideal, or composed or discomposed, or liberated or bound, he is aware in each case that his thought is so" (V. 3, p. 334).

4. Mindfulness as to the Ideas which Affect Character

Meditation upon the Five Hindrances, sensuous desire, ill-will, sloth and torpor, flurry and worry and doubt, provides a method of severe self-examination. The Bhikku then considers the five groups that arise from grasping—material from its beginning and its passing away, feeling, perception, dispositions and cognition, all of which are connected with pain. Cravings are then traced down to their origin in the sense of sight, hearing, smell, taste, touch and imagination, the six internal and external spheres of sense. From this point onward the meditation proceeds on constructive lines. The innermost thought has been laid bare, every feeling has been classified for exactly what it is, and the searcher for the truth, having, as it were, made a general confession and received absolution, is now ready to fix his cleansed and purified mind on the seven factors of enlightenment—mindfulness now fully developed, truth-seeking, energy, joy, serenity, rapture and equanimity. As he meditates upon these he is aware if any be absent, he is aware if any not hitherto present rise into consciousness. The last stage is now reached. The brother meditates on the Four Aryan Truths concerning the nature of Ill which consists of the pains and miseries of life. As the coming of Ill arises from the Graspings and the Cravings, he being clearly aware of its nature, reaches the point where he can envisage its complete cessation. Finally, at the thought, "This is the way leading to the cessation of Ill," he is able to contemplate the "Aryan Eightfold Path—to wit, right view, right aspiration, right speech, right doing, right livelihood, right effort, right mindfulness, right rapture" (V. 3, pp. 335–343).

Meditation is preparatory to the actual Fourfold Great Struggle against Evil:

1. To check the rise of evil and to prevent wrong states of consciousness from arising (V. 6, p. 6).

2. To shed evil and wrong states that have already arisen (V. 6, p. 6).

3. To encourage the rise of right states which have not yet arisen (V. 6, p. 7).

4. To ensure that right states which are there already shall be stablished and ordered aright, multiplied and developed, shall wax apace and grow to perfection (V. 6, p. 7). These struggles must be maintained with resolution, earnest striving, perseverance and the exertion of the whole of a man's mind and heart.

The truth-seeker has now become wholly mindful. All bad states of consciousness have been rooted out—all good ones are growing stronger, and he is now able to proceed by the Four Roads which lead to Saintship. Which are the four ways? In the first place a brother practises that way which is compounded of concentration and effort with desire. In the second place a brother practises that way which is compounded of concentration and effort with energy. In the third place a brother practises that way which is compounded of concentration with effort with a (dominant) idea. In the fourth place a brother practises that way which is compounded of concentration and effort with investigation (V. 3, pp. 246–247).

The Five Moral Powers and the Five Organs of Spiritual Sense are now brought to bear on the dominant idea. They are Faith, Energy, Mindfulness, Concentration and Insight (V. 4, p. 257).

These again are supplemented by the Seven Kinds of Wisdom, or factors of enlightenment: "the factor of mindfulness, of study, of doctrines, of energy, of zest, of serenity, of concentration, of equanimity" (V. 4, p. 235).

In the formula of the Aryan Eightfold Path we have summed up the whole of Buddhist theory in relation to practical life.

1. RIGHT VIEWS

To every strenuous seeker after truth who endeavours in all honesty to translate his thought into action the necessity of this becomes apparent. To such a seeker as the Buddha, right views were of paramount importance. For thirty years he had lived a life of selfish, careless pleasure, for other years he had tormented himself in fearful ways because of wrong views, and only after wasted time and sore travail had he attained enlightenment, and such rightness of view as enabled his life to be well lived, and so "Right Views come first." If a man has really Right Views, Right Thoughts are operative; if he has really Right Thoughts, Right Speech is operative; if he has really Right Speech, Right Action is operative; if he has really Right Occupation, Right Mindfulness is operative; if he has really Right Mindfulness, Right Concentration is operative; if he has really Right Concentration, Right Knowledge is operative, and if he has really Right Knowledge, then Right Deliverance is effectual (V. 6, pp. 197–198). The whole of life is based on Right Thinking—to get a clear conception of what is right, it is necessary first of all to comprehend what views are wrong. Beliefs such as that "there is no such thing as alms or sacrifice or oblations; that there is no such thing as the fruit and harvest of deeds, good and bad; that there are no such things as this world or the next;

that there are no such things as parents or a spontaneous generation elsewhere; that there are no such things as recluses and Brahmins who tread the right path and walk aright, who have of and by themselves comprehended and realized this and other worlds and make it all known to others" (V. 6, pp. 194–195) are wrong. Lustful, spiteful and cruel thoughts, lying, spiteful and savage speech, chattering; the refusal to give alms, sensuality, all forms of cheating and insatiate greed are the result of Wrong Views. Right Views, even when accompanied by Cankers, are the opposite of all these. They lead, moreover, to right comprehension, and after a critical study of the Doctrine to Enlightenment, to the embracing of reason, to the avoidance of misconduct in speech and to Right Occupation. "If a man has really right views, for him wrong views are ended: ended too for him are the hosts of bad and wrong dispositions which grow up in the train of wrong views while as the train of right views, hosts of right dispositions march up to perfected development" (V. 6, p. 198).

2. RIGHT ASPIRATIONS

The aspirations of the heart must be completely and wholly right. It is immutable Deliverance which is the prize and the heart and the goal of the Higher Life (V. 5, p. 143). Nothing else must satisfy. A young man "for faith's sake" may go forth from home to homelessness on pilgrimage (V. 5, p. 139). His views concerning birth, decay, death, sorrow, and all ills may be right. He may be a seeker after that which will make an end of ill, and yet if he allow his aspirations to be satisfied by presents, esteem and repute, by consciousness of his own virtue, steadfastness or powers of rapt concentration, or if he be intoxicated by his own success in winning mystic insight, he may grow remiss and so fall a prey to ill. Nothing but the focussing of aspiration steadily upon the highest of all goals will lead to Eternal

Deliverance. To obtain the highest, the mind must be fixed upon it without variation or shadow of turning. The Buddhist path demands the whole of a man's spiritual energy. The prize of their high calling is not to be won save by the whole-hearted.

3. RIGHT SPEECH

Speech should be slow and unhurried, so that it may be coherent and intelligible and without any strain. No ill effects can follow slow and measured utterance (V. 6, p. 288). Men should avoid all affectation and use whatever is the recognized parlance (V. 6, p. 288) of a province or district. If a man is a liar, deliberately lying in the interests either of himself or of other people or for some trifling gain (V. 6, p. 182); if he is a slanderer to whom "discord is the pleasure and delight, and joy and motive of his speech" (V. 6, p. 182); if he is a "reviler, rough and harsh, hurtful and wounding to others, fraught with anger and discord" (V. 6, p. 182); if he is a tattler whose talk is "trivial and ill-timed, frivolous, leading nowhere and void of profit" (V. 6, p. 182), then "wrong dispositions wax apace, while right dispositions wane" (V. 6, p. 182). The man of right speech "abstains from lies." "He is a promoter of harmony and a restorer of amity. Concord is the pleasure and joy and delight and motive of his speech. . . . What he says is without gall, pleasant, friendly, hearty, urbane, agreeable, and welcome to all. . . . He speaks in season and according to the facts, he is profitable in his speech, even of the doctrine and of the rule." In such a one "wrong dispositions wane while right dispositions wax apace" (V. 6, p. 183). Questioned as to whether a truthfinder would ever say anything displeasing to others, Buddha replied that such would depend absolutely upon the facts of the case. Pointing to a small child he asked the father whether if the boy were to get a stick fixed firmly in its mouth he would pull out the stick even if this caused the child pain and loss of blood. The father replied that he would "out of pity for the child." In precisely the same fashion a truth-seeker will, at the right season, mention some disagreeable truth "out of pity for creatures" (V. 5, p. 284). Speech, then, must be used always for edification and fellowship, never for hurt and division.

4. Right Conduct

Right behaviour is that "which conduces to the harm neither of one's self nor of others, nor of both together, wherein wrong states of consciousness wane, while right states wax apace" (V. 6, p. 61). A very clear and definite code is outlined for the seeker:

(*a*) "Putting away the killing of living things, Gotama the recluse holds aloof from the destruction of life. He has laid the cudgel and the sword aside, and ashamed of roughness and full of mercy he dwells compassionate and kind to all creatures that have life."
(*b*) The recluse must live temperately and without grasping. He may accept such gifts as are necessary—his daily bread and clothes—but he will refuse all luxuries, such as garlands, scents, unguents, lofty beds, silver, gold, uncooked grain, raw meat, women slaves or live stock.
(*c*) He must observe chastity.
(*d*) He must never swerve from the truth faithful and trustworthy, he breaks not his word to the world.
(*e*) He must be an encourager of those who are friends, a peacemaker, a lover of peace, impassioned for peace, a speaker of words that make for peace.
(*f*) His speech must be blameless, in no way frivolous, but words worthy to be laid up in the heart.

(g) He must abstain from causing injury even to seeds or plants.

(h) He must eat but one meal a day and absolutely abstain from the use of intoxicating liquor. . . . He indulges not in arrack or spirits or strong drink.

(i) He abstains from every form of theft, whether by the use of false weights or by the practice of highway robbery with murder and violence.

(j) He must practise the utmost sobriety of life, avoiding all ordinary pleasures and excitements, such as singing, dancing, plays, acrobatic feats, combats of men or animals and pageants; all games of skill and chance.

(k) Fortune-telling, soothsaying, prophesying, black and white magic, the invoking of oracles, the practice of medicine are strictly forbidden.

"These, brethren, are the trifling matters, the minor details of mere morality" (V. 2, pp. 1–26).

5. A Harmless Livelihood

This follows as a natural corollary to the injunctions concerning Right Conduct. All Buddist laymen would need to consider their occupations in case they should lead to a breach of the moral law: The life of a soldier, a medical man, a rich merchant, a soothsayer, or a public entertainer would, of course, be inadmissible. The highest life is, naturally, that of a recluse who, realizing that home life is but a "hole and corner" one, gives away all his substance, and parting from his friends goes out into homelessness. Keeping the whole of the moral code, he gains mastery over all his faculties, and having purged his heart of all worldly appetites and filled it with lovingkindness and compassion for all that lives (V. 5, p. 130), he gains the victory over all hindrances and dwells serene.

6. Perseverance in Well-Doing

The mere setting out upon a right path is NOT sufficient. It MUST be persevered in until the end. Temptations pursue the seeker, and as we have seen his very success in preliminary stages may lead on to his undoing. There must be established "a mindfulness which knows no distraction."

7. Intelligent Activity

As described under Mindfulness.

8. Right Rapture

"There are four modes of being addicted and devoted to pleasure, Cunda, which conduce absolutely to unworldliness, to passionless cessation, to peace, to higher knowledge, to enlightenment, to Nibbana. What are the four? Firstly, Cunda, when a brother aloof from sensuous appetites, aloof from evil ideas, enters into and abides in the first Jhana, wherein there is initiative and sustained thought, which is born of solitude and is full of zest and ease. Secondly, when suppressing initiative and sustained thought he enters into and abides in the second Jhana, which is self-evoked, born of concentration, full of zest and ease, in that, set free from initial and sustained thought, the mind grows calm and sure dwelling on high. Thirdly, when a brother no longer fired with zest abides calmly contemplative while mindful and self-possessed, he feels in his body that ease whereof Aryans declare: He that is calmly contemplative and aware he dwelleth at ease, so does he enter into and abide in the third Jhana. Fourthly, by putting aside ease and by putting aside malaise, by the passing away of the joy and the sorrow he used to feel, he enters into and abides in the fourth Jhana, rapture of utter purity of mindfulness and equanimity wherein neither ease is felt nor any ill" (V. 4, p. 124).

Every step of the Eightfold Path has now been trodden. All ties are loosed, and that which has endured the storms of so many aeons is now ready for its final dissolution. The seeker who has reached this stage is Arahat—all-enlightened —he has indeed reached the Delectable Land and awaits but the final step to the goal. When a brother by the destruction of the Deadly Floods . . . "has by himself known and realized and continues to abide here in this visible world, in that emancipation of mind, that emancipation of heart which is Arahatship—that is . . . a condition higher still and sweeter still for the sake of which the brethren lead the religious life under me" (V. 2, p. 201). The Arahats are those "in whom cankers are dead, who have greatly lived, whose task is done, who have cast off their burthen, who have won their weal, whose bonds are broken, who by utter knowledge have won Deliverance" (V. 6, p. 22). They have attained the passionless peace of Nirvana, and when the body wears out they pass from existence "E'en as a bright flame dies away" (V. 3, p. 176). Having entirely overcome the bond of Desire which has been the focussing-point of their aeons of rebirth it is not possible that they will be born again.

The gods of the Vedas were definite enough and were certainly worshipped with fervour. Those of the Upanishads were vague and formless, but sufficiently definite for worship and to be regarded as influences to be reckoned with. Great Brahman was passionately sought after by those who desired to lose all personality in him. What is the position of the gods in the theory of early Buddhism? A hierarchy of Divine beings was accepted as fact . . . "the gods in the heaven of the Four Great Kings . . . the Four Great Kings . . . the Thirty-three and their king Sakka . . . the Yama Gods . . . and their king Suyama . . . the Tunta Gods . . . and their king Santusita . . . the Nimmana-rati Gods . . . and their king Sunimmita . . . the Paranimmitu Vasavitti gods... and their king Vasavatti... the gods of the Brahma world, and over all Brahma the Great Brahma, the Supreme One, the Mighty One, the All-seeing One, the Ruler, the Lord of All, the Controller, the Creator, the Chief of all appointing to each his place, the Ancient of days, the Father of all that are and are to be" (V. 2, p. 280). And yet to the Buddhist the gods are irrelevant. There is no salvation in them, no final knowledge. A brother experiencing doubt worked himself into an ecstasy, and in his ecstatic state attained to the worlds of the gods and finally came into the presence of Brahma himself. He put his questions, but the All-seeing One admitted his inability and admitted that his greatness depended upon the ignorance of the other gods. For an answer he referred the questioner to the Buddha. When Gotama had won enlightenment, the Supreme Brahma appeared to him and besought him to preach for the weal of gods and men. The gods themselves stand in need of enlightenment. They are subject to birth and death, and they likewise suffer from Desire and would be rid of it. Sakka, the King of the Thirty-three, seeks leave to question the Exalted One, who thought: "For a long time now this Sakka has lived a pure life. Whatever questions he may ask of me will be to good purpose and not frivolous" (V. 3, p. 309). After the questions had been answered, Sakka, touching the earth with his hand... called aloud thrice: "Honour to the Exalted One, to the Arahant, to the Buddha Supreme."

Now, while he was speaking... "the stainless, spotless eye for the Truth arose in Sakka, the ruler of the gods, to wit: 'Whatsoever thing can come to be that must also cease to be'" (V. 3, p. 320). The references to Brahma and Sakka are probably in the nature of a parable, but they make the Buddhist position abundantly clear. The gods may be real and, within certain limits, powerful. They may perhaps enjoy heavenly pleasures, but they differ only in degree from men. Their state of exaltation is merely the result of good Karma, and they are still liable to ill. In consequence, it is useless to offer them prayers and sacrifices or to expect from them any aid.

Men are forced back upon themselves. They may put their faith in the teaching of the Buddha, but scarcely in his person. The teacher himself vanishes, but the teaching is left. The way has been made clear, but the individual must fight the good fight himself, relying on none but himself. High thinking and moral living alone will bring him to Nirvana. Starting from its own premises, Buddhism is an optimism, an overcoming and triumphant faith. All life is evil, dominated as it is by Desire, and the completest victory is the casting out of all desire for life. When this has been achieved the nightmare of existence is broken. The fevered dream dissolves and the man plunges into a sleep peaceful and passionless, from which there is no waking, because "he is not." But to describe Buddhism as an optimism is only true if we admit that life is an insupportable ill, otherwise it is a pessimism, very sober and steadfast and courageous, but a pessimism nevertheless. There is a certain grandeur about it. It is such a faith as would commend itself to the brave souls of a dying aristocracy, who saw their end in clear prospect, but would be *grand seigneur* to the end—not faltering nor bowing the head nor deviating from an established knightly code, but still tired and hopeless, welcoming the end because it brought rest and utter forgetfulness.

The Gospel of Deliverance from life was free to all, if they could attain to self-mastery. Gods, women, men of all castes and conditions could, if they were able, attain to saintship, and within the boundaries of the faith there were no divisions except those of attainment in the faith. Such a conception cut right across the caste edifice, which the Brahmans had built up with such care, and which was becoming with the passing of time an ever more efficient means of dominating the life of society. Buddhism was a tremendous challenge to Brahmanism. Even within the lifetime of the Buddha the new faith met with an astonishing success.

CHAPTER IX

CHINA

(a) THE BOOKS OF THE SHÛ KING, 2357–627 B.C.

The books of the Shû King give a history of China from about 2357 B.C. There are considerable gaps in the narrative as we now have it, due to the fact that some periods probably never found an historian and to the further fact that we possess only a mutilated copy of what was once the whole work, due to the attempted destruction of the classical literature by the Emperor Khin in 213 B.C.

In the Book of Thang and the Book of Yu we have references to the very earliest times. No great weight can be placed upon the facts referred to as the documents are not contemporaneous and it is impossible to tell what documents went to their making. A great Ruler of this period is credited with laying the foundations of Chinese civilization. This man, Ti Yao, was reverential, intelligent, accomplished and thoughtful.... He was sincerely courteous and capable of (all) complaisance (V.[1] 3, p. 32). He placed able and virtuous men in official positions. He (also) regulated and polished the people (of his domain), who all became brightly intelligent. (Finally) he united and harmonized the myriad states, and so the black-haired people were transformed. The result was universal concord (V. 3, p. 32). Yao's achievement was probably not as great as the chronicler would suggest, but he was probably the first chieftain to make a realm and reign. At one period the prosperity of the community was threatened by an inundation. The Minister of Public Works was unable to cope with it, and Yao sought everywhere for some capable person. A certain

[1] V. = Volume in S. B. E.

man named Shun was recommended as being one who had by his filial piety reduced an obstinately unprincipled father, an insincere step-mother and an arrogant step-brother to harmony and self-government. Although domestic qualifications of this sort would from our point of view scarcely be sufficient credentials for an engineer they impressed Yao very strongly. As a further test of fitness he married his two daughters to Shun, and as the latter apparently survived this stern trial he was appointed General Regulator. For three years he carried out every duty of State at its appointed season, and at the end of this time was raised to the kingship. He is reputed to have carried on the work of organization. Weights and measures were standardized, ceremonies and sacrifices regulated, the country divided into twelve departments with properly appointed responsible officials in control. A penal code was laid down and enforced, but the severity of punishment was tempered with mercy. "Let me be reverent! let me be reverent!" He said to himself: "Let compassion rule in punishment!" (V. 3, p. 41). The welfare of his people was the constant care of this shepherd of men. He was indeed the father of his people, wearying himself to procure their food, to secure their safety, to guard them from the unruly, to lead them with gentleness into the paths of duty so that they should be straightforward but mild; strong but not tyrannical; impetuous and yet not arrogant. In order that every care of the State should be efficiently discharged he instituted triennial examinations, as a result of which the undeserving were degraded and the deserving advanced (V. 3, p. 45). His charge to his successor Yu and the responses of Yu show a remarkable conception of sovereignty: "To obtain the views of all; to give up one's opinion and follow that of others; to keep from oppressing the helpless and not to neglect the straitened and poor" (V. 3, pp. 46-47). Yu said, "The virtue of the Ruler is seen in (his) good government and that government in the nourishing of the people" (V. 3, p. 47). Shun, in demonstrating the worthiness of Yu to succeed him in his high office, describes him as "full of toilsome earnestness in the service of the country and sparing in your expenditure on your family, and this without being full of yourself and elated—you (again) show your superiority to other men. You are without any prideful assumption, but no one under heaven can contest with you the palm of ability" (V. 3, p. 49). The virtue of the Ruler is to be seen in his choice of Ministers, thus making it possible for the people to be rightly governed. The finest type of official is the one who displays nine virtues: viz. "AFFABILITY combined with DIGNITY; MILDNESS combined with FIRMNESS; BLUNTNESS combined with RESPECTFULNESS; APTNESS for government combined with REVERENT CAUTION; DOCILITY combined with BOLDNESS; STRAIGHTFORWARDNESS combined with GENTLENESS; an easy negligence combined with DISCRIMINATION; BOLDNESS combined with SINCERITY; and VALOUR combined with RIGHTEOUSNESS" (V. 3, p. 54). The ideal State is one in which Ruler and Ruled are one in their pursuit of the common good.

> "When the members (work) joyfully
> The head rises (grandly),
> And the duties of all the offices are fully discharged.
>
> "When the head is intelligent
> The members are good,
> And all affairs will be happily performed" (V. 3, p. 62).

As we have seen, for the recalcitrants punishments were provided. These might be used with moderation, but the idea was clearly held that by means of punishment the future infliction of punishment might be done away with. In other words, it was definitely held that crime could be abolished by the use of force. A contrary view is, however, put forward in the story of the Lord of Miao, who was in open rebellion and continued so throughout a period of thirty years. At length the army was withdrawn—the leader remembered how Shun in his early days had brought a wicked family to practise virtue by his own respectful service and virtuous example. "It is virtue that moves heaven," said Ki; "there is no distance to which it does not reach. Pride brings loss and humility receives increase; this is the way of heaven" (V. 3, p. 52). So new plans were made, and "The Ti set about diffusing on a grand scale the virtuous influences of peace" (V. 3, p. 52), and within seventy days the rebel lord came in and made his peace. The dynasty of Hsia—Yu and his descendants ruled from 2205-1766 B.C., a period of 439 years. In the "Tribute of Yu" we have a general description of the economic system of old China. The land had been surveyed and graded for the purpose of equitably assessing taxation. As tribute was actually paid in goods, and as the rivers offered facilities for transport, there may have been considerable interchange of commodities between the various provinces. There is little to suggest luxury or anything approaching the imperial magnificence of Babylon or Egypt, but there is a strong presumption that prosperity was widespread and the people content. Silk was produced over a wide area and woven into fabrics, sometimes of an ornamental nature dyed azure and purple. A fine cloth was made from the dolichos fibre, and the wild people bartered grass dresses and fans. Oyster pearls and coloured stones were gathered and used for personal adornment. Hemp, bamboo, bow-staves and timber were exchanged. Ivory was apparently known. There is no direct reference to pastoral industries except the mention of skins and hides. This, coupled with the fact that the growing of grain is only casually referred to, indicates that the common necessities were produced in every settlement to the amount required and that exchange was carried on only in the special products of each. Gold, silver, copper, coal and iron were all worked to some extent. Flints were in demand for the making of arrow-heads and for use as grindstones and whetstones. Yu carried on the work of development—felling forest, clearing rivers, and banking marshes

With the "Speech at Kan" made by Khi, the successor of Yu, we reach documents that are probably contemporaneous with the events they describe. "The documents which follow the 'Tribute of Yu,' commencing with the speech at Kan delivered in 2197 B.C. by Yu's son and successor, may all be received as veritable documents of antiquity" (V. 3, p. 19). The speech itself is an exhortation addressed by the Ruler to his archers, spearmen, and charioteers before battle. The next of the line, Thai King, was an utterly worthless ruler. Giving himself over to reckless dissipation, he completely neglected the cares of State. The palace was given over to lust, serious business was abandoned for the pleasures of the chase, drunkenness replaced the old sobriety, and "lofty roofs and carved walls" the simplicity of the ancient kings. The rottenness spread, and in the reign of King Khang, who succeeded his unworthy brother, we find the Marquis of Yin receiving orders to destroy without mercy the worst offenders.

The dynasty of Thang "superseded Hsia" (1766 B.C.) and held the kingdom for fully three hundred years. Kieh, the last monarch of the house of Hsia, was a man of many crimes. A cruel and arrogant king, he exhausted and oppressed his people until at last they became utterly indifferent to his service; and Khang Thang, rising up against him, took his seat and banished him. The new Ruler was somewhat conscience-stricken by his own proceedings and feared that in future times rebellious men might use them as an excuse for their own wrong-doing. His doubts were allayed by the speech of Khang-hui, "Oh! heaven gives birth to the people with (such) desires that without a Ruler they must fall into all disorders, and Heaven gives birth to the man of intelligence to regulate them" (V. 3, p. 87).

Kieh, by his evil conduct, had utterly forfeited the good will of heaven. "God viewed him with disapprobation" and "caused our Thang to receive his appointment" (V. 3, p. 87).

In Thang's inaugural speech there is a very noble conception of the King as the representative man—a servant, and, if need be, the suffering servant of his people. "The good in you I will not dare to keep concealed, and for the evil in me I will not dare to forgive myself. I will examine these things in harmony with the mind of God. When guilt is found anywhere in you who occupy the myriad regions let it rest on me—the One man" (V. 3, p. 91). One legend says that after a drought of seven years' duration it was suggested that human sacrifice be offered. Thang said: "If a man must be the victim, I will be he" (V. 3, p. 91). He was succeeded in 1754 B.C. by his grandson Thai Kia, to whom I Yen the chief Minister delivered a discourse on the right behaviour of kings. The young Ruler had before him the great example of his grandfather—a man who had paid "careful attention to the bonds that held men together. He listened to expostulation and did not seek to resist it; he confirmed to (the wisdom of) the ancients; occupying the highest position, he displayed intelligence, occupying an inferior position he displayed his loyalty; he allowed (the good qualities of) the men (whom he employed) and did not seek that they should have every talent; the government of himself he seemed to think that he could never (sufficiently) attain" (V. 3, pp. 93-94). He sought out wise men and vigorously punished those who engaged in illicit pleasures or extravagance. I Yen urged Thai Kia to heed their warnings, for "(the ways) of God are not invariable: on the good-doer he sends down all blessings and on the evil-doer he sends down all miseries" (V. 3, p. 95). The young king, however, paid small heed to the excellent advice of the sage and fell into evil courses. Expostulation after expostulation was without effect, and at last the Minister resorted to the drastic expedient of removing the youth from the scene of his temptations and confining him for a period of three years in the vicinity of his grandfather's tomb. This provided a lasting reformation, and the young man returned to the Court sincerely virtuous. In his valedictory speech, when laying down his high offices, I Yen emphasizes the fact that Heaven extends its protection to virtue alone. "It was not that Heaven had any private partiality for the lord of Shang, it simply gave its favour to pure virtue" (V. 3, p. 101). And not only Heaven but the common people also turn naturally to virtue. "It was not that Shang sought (the allegiance) of the lower people—the people simply turned to pure virtue" (V. 3, p. 101). Good and evil do not wrongly befall men, but Heaven sends down misery or happiness according to their conduct" (V. 3, p. 101). From the time of Thai Kia to Pan-kang, the next king to be mentioned in the Shû King, there is a gap of three centuries.

The reign of Pan-kang extended from 1401–1374 B.C., and is remarkable as that in which the dynasty began "to be called Yin" (V. 3, p. 103). This ruler, perhaps owing to a change in the course of the Ho, found it advisable to remove the capital to another site. The mass of people being comfortably settled objected strongly to a move which appeared to them unnecessary. By a judicious mixture of exhortation, cajolery and sound argument, with a strong hint regarding the possible cutting off of certain rebellious noses, the move was safely made. The community was reorganized with the same paternal regard for the common good. "Oh! ye chiefs of regions, ye heads of departments, all ye, the hundreds of officers, would that ye had a sympathy (with my people). I will exert myself in the choice and guidance of you: do ye think reverently of my multitudes— I will not employ those who are fond of enriching themselves; but will use and revere those who are vigorously, yet reverently, labouring for the lives and increase of the people, nourishing them and planning for their enduring settlement. . . . Do not seek to accumulate wealth and precious things, but in fostering the life of the people seek to find your merit" (V. 3, p. 112).

After Pan-kang there is another gap until we come to the reign of Wai Ting (1324-1264 B.C.). On his accession he was doubtful whether his merit was equal to the great responsibility to which he had been called. While he meditated on the matter he dreamt that God had appointed for him an assistant whose face appeared most clearly to him in the vision. Search was made throughout the land, and at last there was found a builder by the name of Yueh whose face corresponded exactly with that seen by the king in his dream. This personage was at once raised to the position of Chief Minister. He stressed on the king the value of learning and especially the wisdom of copying the perfect patterns of antiquity. "That the affairs of one not making ancients his masters can be perpetuated for generations is what I have not heard" (V. 3, p. 117). After an interval of seven more reigns we come to the last ruler of the dynasty of Yin, Kan-hsia—a dissolute and pleasure-loving man under whom the prosperity of the country suffered greatly. The chief of the West broke out in open rebellion. The state of the kingdom went from bad to worse. "The great deeds of our founder were displayed in former ages, but by our maddened indulgence in spirits we have destroyed (the effects of) his virtue in these after-times. (The people of) Yin, small and great, are given to highway robberies, villainies and treacheries. The nobles and officers imitate one another in violating the laws, and there is no certainty that criminals will be apprehended. The smaller people (consequently) rise up and commit violent outrages on one another" (V. 3, p. 122). These calamities were the result of the angers of Heaven against a king who "has no reverence for things which he ought to reverence" (V. 3, p. 123). Wu, a great noble, was raised to the chieftainship of the insurgents. In the three speeches known as the Great Declaration he describes the fearful crimes of the degenerate king who "does not reverence Heaven above and inflicts calamities on the people below." Abandoned to drunkenness and reckless in lust he has dared to exercise cruel oppression. He extended the punishment of offenders to all their relatives. He has put men into office on the hereditary principle. He has made it his pursuit to have palaces, towers, pavilions, embankments, ponds and all other extravagances to the most painful injury of you the myriads of the people. He has burned and roasted the loyal and good. He has ripped up pregnant women" (V. 3, p. 125). Conduct of this sort is abhorrent in the eyes of Heaven. The cup of his iniquity is full, and although he has a great following and Wu but a handful, there can be no doubt of the overthrow of a tyrant against whom "the innocent cry to Heaven" (V. 3, p. 127).

In the great battle that ensued "the blood flowed till it floated the pestles of the mortars" (V. 3, p. 136). Wu was completely victorious. After offering sacrifice he disbanded the greater part of his army, overturned the remnants of the tyranny, distributed treasure and food, and then proceeded to settle the distracted Government in accordance with the Great Plan. This document is no doubt of greater antiquity than King Yui, whose reign commenced in 1122 B.C., but was probably repromulgated by him as an avowal of his intention to walk in the good ways of the ancient kings. The welfare of the community can best be served when there is a combination of virtue in the multitude and perfection in the King. The basic qualities required are respectfulness manifesting itself in gravity, orderliness, deliberation and sagacity. As the sovereign is "the pattern" of excellence, and should therefore concentrate in himself the five sources of happiness, i.e. long life, riches, soundness of body, and serenity of mind; love of virtue, and the constant fulfilling of the will of Heaven, it is of the utmost importance that he shall conform to the highest possible standard. He must advance the able and good; receive those who abstain from evil; refrain from oppressing the friendless and childless; he must be unselfish and impartial. In times of tranquillity his rule must be correct and straightforward; in a time of violence it must be strong; in a period of order, mild. The ruler must keep power firmly in his own hands. He must be the fountain of honour, the rewarder of the just and the terror of the unjust. When the affairs of the kingdom were in doubt recourse was to be made to divination by means of the tortoiseshell stalks and various states of the weather. If all their matters are rightly observed, then the kingdom will be rightly governed and enjoy happiness while avoiding the six extreme evils: shortening of life; sickness; distress of mind; poverty; weakness (V. 3, pp. 139–149). Two years after the conquest Wu was attacked by so severe an illness that all hope of his recovery was abandoned. The Duke of Kau, his brother, offered sacrifice and prayed to the great kings, their ancestors, that his brother should be spared and he taken in his stead. "I am possessed of many abilities and arts which fit me to serve spiritual beings, and moreover he (Wu) was appointed in the Hall of God to extend his aid all over the kingdom so that he might establish your descendants in this lower earth" (V. 3, p. 153). The King lived and naturally it was firmly believed that the ancient kings had used their ghostly power on his behalf. Later, when all the facts were known, the incident redounded greatly to the credit of Kau, who owing to malicious rumours had fallen somewhat into bad repute. Wu died in 1116 B.C., and his successor Khang found the business of ruling an extremely difficult one. "I who am but a little child am in the position of one who has to go through a deep water" (V. 3, p. 157). There was rebellion and war on the frontier. The auguries were good, but the princes and rulers were

A STUDY IN CREATIVE HISTORY

not willing to face the hardships of an expedition. Yet though others hold back, "I, the little child, dare not disregard the charge of God—I dare not but do my utmost to complete the plans of the Tranquillizing King" (V. 3, p. 159). The expedition was apparently successful, and during the greater part of Khang's reign he proceeded to reorganize and settle the dominions that had become so disturbed during the reign of the tyrant Kau-hsia. In the change to various governors we see once again the old Chinese conception of government and obtain also a glimpse of the special difficulties of the period. Thang is exhorted to study "the old established ways." The utmost care must be used in the infliction of punishments. "(Deal firmly yet orderly with evil) as if it were a disease in your own person" (V. 3, p. 167). Crimes of open violence, murder and robbery are bad and must be punished, but far "more detestable are the unfilial and unbrotherly" (V. 3, p. 169). These must be punished without thought of pardon. Wicked officials or teachers are more blameworthy than any others. Drunkenness is very severely dealt with. States great and small have been ruined by indulgence in spirits, and the King is most anxious that young nobles shall not use liquor except at sacrifices, and then in strict moderation. So deeply had the vice eaten into the life of the community that the severest measures were contemplated for stamping it out. "If you are informed that there are companies that drink together, do not fail to apprehend them all and send them here to Kau, where I may put them to death" (V. 3, p. 178). The great constructive work of the reign was the building of the City of Lo. This task was entrusted to the great Duke of Kau. The site was chosen by divination, and on the completion of the work the city was consecrated by great and suitable sacrifices—the slaying of victims and the pouring out of libations. The Government of the new centre was vested in the Duke, who seems indeed to have ruled the kingdom in all except name and to have treated the young sovereign as a beloved son whom he instructs in all the care of kingship and warns against all the temptations of power, especially that he should indulge in no luxurious ease, "But follow the example of the great ones of old who, meanly dressed, mild and humble, hardly allowed themselves leisure even to eat." The new dynasty was faced with great difficulties. The King was young and inexperienced, if not weak. The old officials of Kau were restless, if not openly rebellious, and we find the Duke, now pleading with a well-tried colleague not to leave him in such an extremity, now reminding mutinous chiefs that if they did not take advantage of the leniency with which "I have spared your lives, I will proceed to severe punishments and put you to death" (V. 3, p. 218). In the Officer of Khu we have a sketch of the departmental system into which government had even then crystallized. "I appoint," says the King, "the Prime Minister, who presides over the ruling of the (various) regions, has the general management of all the other officers and secures uniformity within the four seas; the Minister of Instruction, who presides over the education in the states, diffuses a knowledge of the duties belonging to the five relations of society and trains the millions of the people to obedience; the Minister of Religion, who presides over the sacred ceremonies of the country, regulates the services rendered to the spirits and manes and makes a harmony between high and low; the Minister of War, who presides over the (military) administration of the country, commands the six hosts and secures the tranquillity of all the regions; the Minister of Crime, who presides over the prohibitions of the country, searches out the villainous and secretly wicked and punishes oppressors and disturbers of the peace; and the Minister of Works, who presides over the land of the country, settles the four classes of the people and secures at the proper season the produce of the ground" (V. 3, pp. 228–229). The study of History was especially recommended to those who held any office in the public service. Khang died in 1778 B.C. and was succeeded by his son Kao. The time of stress was over, and as a result of the efforts of Wau-Wu, Khang and especially of the great Duke of Kau, the land was now tranquillized. In the reign of a succeeding monarch, Mu, we have the High Chamberlain very earnestly exhorted to see that all the officers "in your department and my personal attendants are upright and correct, that they strive to promote the virtue of their sovereign and together supply my deficiencies" (V. 3, p. 253). The charge to the Marquis of Lu concerning punishments was probably given about the year 952 B.C. In an historical preamble the king points out that punishments may be terribly abused. Among the people of Miao they did not use the power of goodness, but the restraint of punishments. They made the five punishments engines of oppression, calling them the laws. They slaughtered the innocent and were the first also to go to excess in cutting off the nose, cutting off the ears, castration and branding. "All who became liable to those punishments were dealt with without distinction. . . . The people were gradually affected by this state of things and became dark and disorderly . . . there was no fragrance of virtue arising from them but the rank odour of their (cruel) punishments" (V. 3, p. 256). One of the worst results of this state of affairs was the fact that men "declared their innocence to Heaven," and owing to their misery entered into illicit spiritual relations with the unseen world—thus going past the properly appointed Minister of Religion.

The great Ti inaugurated a better age by properly codifying the law, applying it fearlessly and without favour, and yet with moderation and humanity, the result being that "all were rendered diligent in cultivating their virtue" (V. 3, 259). This great example should always be held in mind by those concerned with the administration of the law. Judges must be diligent, taking every care to see that they examine carefully. They must not be swayed by the influence of any man, even that of the King himself. Female solicitations must not be listened to; no private grudge must be allowed to interfere with justice, while bribes must not on any account be accepted. Should, indeed, anyone endeavour to prevent justice by the use of such methods, his crime is to be held equal to that for which the accused person is standing trial. The law must have been very minutely codified. We read that "set against the five punishments there are 3,000 crimes" (V. 3, p. 262). Great care must be taken to make the punishment fit the crime. Generally speaking, the criminal is to receive the benefit of the doubt. If the crime is undisputed but the intention doubtful a fine may often take the place of physical suffering or mutilation. Fines were to be assessed in varying weights of copper. In cases where an act resulting in apparent crime was proved to be due to pure misadventure no penalty whatever was to be imposed. "I think," said Mu, "with reverence of the subject of punishment, for the end of it is to promote virtue" (V. 3, p. 264). Two centuries after Mu we have some records of Phing, another Tranquillizer, who succeeded in driving out a tyrant and once more stabilizing the Government. In his time the country was threatened by the inroads of barbarous tribes from the west.

THE PHILOSOPHY OF ANCIENT CHINA

(b) THE SHIH KINGS

THE PHILOSOPHICAL AND RELIGIOUS CONCEPTIONS OF ANCIENT CHINA ARE TO BE FOUND MAINLY IN THE SHIH KINGS, THE ANALECTS AND THE GREAT LEARNING

The main teachings of the Shih Kings are:

1. God is "great and sovereign" (V. 3, p. 343), and "beholdeth the world in majesty" (V. 3, p. 389). The appointment of kings is in His hands. "Long ago God appointed the martial Thang to regulate the boundaries throughout the four quarters" (V. 3, p. 307). While His favour and protection remained with the sovereign there could be "no anxieties, no doubts," for "God is with you" (V. 3, p. 342). It was He who appointed the wheat and the barley for the sustenance of men, and the king was most like to God when he gave his people food. "Thou didst prove thyself the correlate of Heaven, thou didst give grain food to our multitudes" (V. 3. p. 320). The Heavenly power is greatly concerned with the affairs of men. "Let it (Heaven) not say that it is high aloft above men. It ascends and descends about our doings; it daily inspects us wherever we are" (V. 3, p. 330). According to men's deeds, which are regulated so much by the example of the King, God rewards or punishes. If their conduct is good then follow peace, prosperity and good government, but if there has been contemptuous indifference, mockery, boastfulness and flattering, a departure from the established rules of propriety, then God reverses His usual course of procedure and the lower people are full of distress" (V. 3, p. 408).

2. Blessing of ancestors is keenly sought after by means of prayer and sacrifice. Their presence is invoked also by

music. "The drums resound harmonious and loud to delight our meritorious ancestor. The descendant of Thang invites him with this music that he may soothe us with the realization of our thoughts" (V. 3, p. 304). In the great feasts that formed an integral part of ancestor worship the spirits were supposed "to happily enjoy the offerings" (V. 3, p. 366). As a result, "Their filial descendant receives blessing. . . . They will reward him with great happiness" (V. 3, p. 366).

3. The ritual of sacrifice seems to have been highly developed from the earliest times. Sacrifices were of two sorts: libations of "clear spirits" and "well-tempered soups" and meat offerings—"fish, rams and bulls." The first part of a great sacrifice has to be carried out with "correct and reverent deportment" (V. 3, p. 366). The victims are slain and cooked. The representatives of the dead take their places. Trays of meat and the cup are passed round. The eating and drinking are apparently ceremonial only. Wives are "still and reverent." Scrupulous attention is paid to form and rule. "Every smile and word are as they should be." Everyone is much exhausted at the strain of having performed every ceremony without error. At the end the officer of prayer announces to the filial descendants the blessing of his spirit ancestors, "Fragrant has been your filial sacrifice, and the spirits have enjoyed your spirit and viands. They confer on you a hundred blessings. Each as it is desired. Each as sure as law. You have been exact and expeditious. You have been correct and careful. They will ever confer on you the choicest favour in myriads and tens of myriads" (V. 3, p. 367). To the sound of music the filial descendants and the guests withdraw. Another feast is then held of not quite such a solemn character, in which freer rein is given to mirth and enjoyment.

4. Morality in any definite fashion is hardly touched upon. A reference to the whole duty of women is interesting. "It will be theirs neither to do wrong nor to do good. Only

about the spirits and the food will they have to think. And cause no sorrow to their parents" (V. 3, p. 351). In other words, the whole moral law for women can be summed up in the words "be obedient."

5. Incidental references give some idea of the general economic development of old China. Wheat, barley, millet, rice, beans and maize were all cultivated in the public and private fields. Sheep, oxen, horses and pigs were all known. A reference to silken robes shows that the silk industry was established. Fish were raised in ponds. The Government revenue was met by a levy: "Bright are those extensive fields, a tenth of whose produce is annually levied" (V. 3, p. 370). In general there is a picture which differs little from agricultural China of our own day. The harvest is brought home with rejoicing and stored in the granaries. The great ones of the land apparently took the major share: "Yet some provision must be made for the desolate. . . . Yonder shall be young grain unreaped, and here some bundles ungathered; yonder shall be handfuls left on the ground and here ears untouched for the benefit of the widow" (V. 3, p. 373).

(c) THE YÎ KING

The Yî King consists of sixty-four hexagrams, which are alleged to date back to the farthest antiquity; an explanatory text ascribed to King Wan and his son, the famous Duke of Kau (1143–1105 B.C.); and various appendices which were added at later periods. In the main the whole is a book on divination—a practice exceedingly prevalent in those times. The linear figures themselves might well have been produced before the days of writing. They were regarded as being pregnant with meaning, and an immense deal of intellectual ability was devoted to the unravelling of these supposed mystic meanings. One example will make the method of the explanatory text clear.

XXXII. The Hang Hexagram

Hang indicates successful progress and "no error in what it denotes. But the advantage will come from being firm and correct, and movement in any direction whatever will be advantageous.

1. The first line (from the foot) divided shows its subject deeply desirous of long continuance. Even with firm correctness there will be evil. There will be no advantage in any way.

2. The second line undivided shows all occasion for repentance disappearing.

3. The third line undivided shows one who does not continuously maintain his virtue. There are those who will impute this to him as a disgrace. However firm he may be, there will be ground for regret.

4. The fourth line undivided shows a field where there is no game.

5. The fifth line divided shows its subject continuously maintaining the virtue indicated by it. In a wife this will be fortunate. In a husband, evil.

6. The topmost line divided shows its subject exciting himself to long continuance. There will be evil" (V. 16, pp. 125 ff.).

From the above one can easily imagine the possibilities for fortune-telling and magic-mongering latent in the sixty-four figures worked out in such detail and capable of numerous combinations. To us such preoccupation is childish, but it appeared natural and desirable to such a sage as Confucius, who is reported to have said: "If some years were added to my life I would give fifty to the study of the Yî and might then escape falling into great errors" (V. 16, p. 1). Our business in studying the Yî King will be to gather the main ideas it contains concerning the general life and thought of the times. These are:

1. God is seen in His work of production bringing His plans into action. He rejoices, He struggles, He is comforted, He enters into rest, and finally brings His works to completion (V. 16, p. 425). He is a Spirit pervading His creation. "When we speak of Spirit we mean the subtle (presence and operation of God) with all things" (V. 16, p. 426). This presence is the unfathomable factor "in the movement of the inactive and active operations" (V. 16, p. 357). Help comes from Heaven to men. Upon the proper union of Heaven and earth all human prosperity depends—all this springs from the fact that in it Heaven and earth are not in communication with each other, and all things in consequence do not have free course; and that the high and the low (superiors and inferiors) are not in communication with one another, and there are no well-regulated states under the sky" (V. 16, p. 224). Heaven aims to make an end of confusion and to bring order. In one passage the over-world is represented as being overwhelmingly on the side of the poor. It is the way of Heaven to diminish the full and augment the humble. It is the way of earth to overthrow the full and replenish the humble. Spiritual Beings inflict calamity on the full and bless the humble (V. 16, p. 226). So great is the influence of Heaven that men may well doubt if anything at all can be done advantageously without the help of the Great Giver and Maintainer of life.

2. The superior man is the salt of the earth. He is benevolent, able to preside over other men; being "the assemblage of excellencies, he is fit to show in himself the union of all

propriety; benefiting all creatures, he is fit to exhibit the harmony of all that is right; correct and firm, he is fit to manage all affairs" (V. 16, p. 408). Withdrawal from the world does not cause him regret, nor does disapproval trouble his mind. Sincere and earnest he guards against depravity. Others may recognize his goodness, yet he makes no boast of it. Active and vigilant, yet careful and apprehensive, he fulfills the whole of his duty with loyalty and good faith. Careful in his speech and of a complete sincerity, knowing what he wants and having within himself a principle of righteousness, he can occupy "a high position without pride and a low position without anxiety" (V. 16, p. 411). Everything is done by him at the right time. His right conduct flows from his inner virtue. He is a discriminating student who puts the result of his learning into practice. All his actions are in harmony with Heaven. Reverencing true virtue in himself, the right actions of his life are not solitary and disjointed, but part of a harmonious whole.

3. In the third appendix an account is given of the economic development of the country. Apparently the earliest inhabitants were nomads living by hunting, and their first invention was the net used both for the snaring of birds and animals and also for catching fish. Settlement followed and with it the growth of agriculture. Wooden ploughs were made, and "The advantages of ploughing and weeding were then taught to all under heaven" (V. 3, p. 383). Markets for exchange were then opened. At this period proper houses were built. Canoes were made for river transport, oxen broken to carts and horses to chariots. Villages were roughly fortified and provided with the wooden-tongued tocsin bells. The mortar and pestle and the bow and arrow came into common use. The knotted record ropes of very ancient times were replaced by written records.

(d) LAO-TZE

The philosopher Lao-Tze was an old man when Confucius was in his prime. He taught that the universe and living beings all resulted from the action and interaction of two primordial forces: "Tao," which consisted of matter and active force, and "Ki," the breath or subtle essence which pervaded everything and caused the actions and reactions from which came shape, form and the somewhat illusory life of gods and men. Beings appeared for a little while, played their part for a brief space on the stage of life and were then quickly lost to view in the mysterious abysses. Life itself is worthless, and man's best hope is to await quietly the everlasting rest beyond the grave. It is sheer folly to strive for the ordinary satisfactions of life. As nothing is profitable and as nothing endures the whole range of desire is vexation and illusion. Abstention is wisdom and action is folly. Every man has within himself an essential spark of life to which indeed he owes his birth. By means of a special system of regulated breathing he is able to build up this spark, so that when the hour of death comes the physical body can be cast away like an outworn garment and the living spirit goes out alive into immortality. Governments should apply this thinking. Any real development or culture should not be attempted. The people should be isolated, kept in ignorance, and any sign of ambition should be repressed. Their heads should be emptied and their stomachs filled, their spirits weakened and their bones strengthened. He detested war probably because of its outrageous violence, its passion, and its complete denial of his principle of quietism. Governments should interfere as little as possible with the life of the people.

(e) THE LIFE OF CONFUCIUS

Confucius was born in the year 551 B.C. Times were troubled. The feudal aristocracy had become too strong for the central authorities, and as a result the land was full of oppression, robbery and war. The boy belonged to an ancient and honourable, although apparently impoverished, family. A natural student, he devoted himself at a very early age to the acquisition of learning. As he said about himself later: "Even in a hamlet of ten houses there must be men as conscientious and sincere as myself, but none as fond of learning as myself" (An.[1] 5, c. 27). The poverty of his own youthful student days gave him life-long sympathy for poor students. "From he who has brought his simple present of dried fish, seeking to enter my school, I have never withheld instruction" (An. 7, c. 27). He was married at the age of nineteen, and at about the same time he entered the official service of the State of Lu. A few years later his scholarship had become so widely recognized that a school of disciples commenced to grow up around him. None except earnest seekers were welcome: "I expound nothing to him who is not earnest. . . . When I have demonstrated one angle and he cannot bring me back the other three, then I do not repeat the lesson" (An. 7, c. 8). His main subjects of instruction were "culture, conduct, conscientiousness and good faith" (An. 7, c. 23). He allowed no discussion of "prodigies, prowess, lawlessness and the supernatural" (An. 7, c. 20). For a number of years he continued this scholar life. His disciples were multiplied and his reputation grew. A visit to the philosopher Lao-Tze and to the Imperial City of Lo, with an exile of eight years' duration, were the main incidents of nearly thirty years of "research into the history, literature and institutions of the Empire." In his fifty-first year Duke

---

[1] An. = Analects (Soothill).

Ting gave him charge of a department. His administration was so successful that he was promoted successively to the Office of Works and to that of Chief Justice. As an officer of the Ducal House "He ... weakened the private families. He exalted the Sovereign and depressed the Ministers. Transforming government went abroad. Dishonesty and dissoluteness were ashamed and hid their heads. Loyalty and good faith became the characteristics of the men and chastity and docility that of the women. Strangers came in crowds from other states. . . . Confucius became the idol of the people and flew in song through their mouths" (Legge, cited from *Intro. Analects*, Soothill, p. 44). This was his highest point. The rival prince of Ch-i by a gift of dancing-girls and horses, so debauched the mind of Ting that Confucius, realizing the utter hopelessness of working longer with him, went again into exile wandering from place to place. In 484 B.C. he was invited to return home. The remaining years of his life were spent in literary work. He died in 479 B.C. In his own village the Sage "bore himself with simplicity, as if he had no gifts of speech" (An. 10, c. 1). Although when occasion demanded he was both ready and clear, bold to those of his own rank, respectful to high dignitaries, "nervous though self-possessed" in the presence of the Prince. Every ceremony demanded by the etiquette of the day was performed with scrupulous attention to detail. Great care was paid to the cut and quality of his clothes. He was no ascetic as far as food and drink were concerned. His viands were of the best, and he would not eat "anything discoloured nor that smelt, nor that was under- or over-cooked or not in season. He would not eat anything improperly cut nor anything served without its proper seasoning. However much meat there might be, he did not allow what he took to exceed the flavour of the rice, only in wine he had no set limit short of mental confusion" (An. 10, c. 8). Neither at table nor in bed did he converse, and after every meal he solemnly set aside a little for sacrifice. He was thoughtful for others, and "When a friend died with no one to fall back upon he would say, 'I will see to his funeral'" (An. 10, c. 15). Innovation was hateful to him. Correctness of conduct and of ceremonial were the very essence of his being. He was the kind of man who "would not sit on his mat unless it was straight" (An. 10, c. 9), nor would he shoot a bird sitting. Confucius was a high though kindly gentleman, an accurate scholar, although in no sense an original thinker, an able administrator of a conservative type, a man guided by a high sense of duty rather than by what we might call a social passion. He was the finest flowering of two thousand years of developing civilization. His idea of a life well spent was "to comfort the aged, be faithful to my friends, and cherish the young" (An. 5, c. 25).

THE TEACHING OF CONFUCIUS

THE ANALECTS

Confucius' whole aim was a practical one. Theory interested him little, and fields of speculation which have in all ages had an irresistible attraction for great thinkers were deliberately ignored by him. He was concerned directly with conduct and character in the affairs of everyday life, and especially with these as they displayed themselves in good government and right social relationships. He was a conservative reformer—a man who, living in troubled and unhappy times, looked backward to a golden age and taught that a return to the old standards was the way of salvation. Individual men were not ends in themselves but units of a prospectively good society. All progress toward the normal would, however, appear to be brought about by the right living and right influence of noble men. At one period of his life Confucius apparently considered the possibility of taking up his abode among the uncivilized and barbarous eastern tribes, whereupon someone remarked: "But they are so uncivilized, how can you do that?" The Master responded: "Were a man of noble character to dwell among them, what lack of civilization would there be?" (An. 9, c. 13). Government by moral excellence should be the pole star of all in positions of authority. Example is worth more than penalty. "If you govern the people by laws and keep them in order by penalties they will avoid the penalties yet lose their sense of shame. But if you govern them by your moral excellence and keep them in order by your decorous conduct they will retain their sense of shame and also live up to standard" (An. 2, c. 3).

The good influences must come from above. Confucius was on one occasion asked if the lawless should not be executed for the good of the law-abiding: "What need, sir, is there of capital punishment in your administration? If your aspirations are for good, sir, the people will be good. The moral character of those in high position is the breeze, the character of those below is the grass. When the grass has the breeze upon it, it assuredly bends" (An. 12, c. 19). If this be true, then the character and the outlook of princes, feudal lords and Government officials will be of the utmost importance. What they are the people will be. In his aphorisms with regard to right living it is of course men of this class that the Sage has particularly in mind.

Let us consider first the qualities that go to the making of the thoroughly upright man. There are five essentials which constitute virtue. "They are respect, magnanimity, sincerity, earnestness and kindness. With respect you will avoid insult, with magnanimity you will win all, with sincerity men will trust you, with earnestness you will have success, and with kindness you will be well fitted to command others" (An. 17, c. 6). These are, as it were, the isolated essentials of character. A man might possess them all and yet be led astray by foolishness, loose speculation, harmful candour, warped judgment, insubordination and intractability, and unless he has the fusing and perfecting quality of a love to learn" (An. 17, c. 8). It is in the calm light of knowledge that Confucian morality grows not in the fervour of inspiration. Moral life is the normal life. "Man is born for uprightness" (An. 4, c. 16). The good man is a lover of his kind. He must be careful of his actions towards his fellows: "Do not do to others what you would not like yourself; then your public life will arouse no ill-will nor your private life any resentment" (An. 12, c. 2). "A right direction of life must be followed up by kindness to others" (An. 7, c. 5). Sympathy is the one word which could be adopted as a life-long rule of conduct. Love your fellowmen is the very meaning of virtue.

We must be careful, however, not to push this too far and read into the word love connotations which might be familiar to us but were certainly not intended by the Sage. The really virtuous man is competent not only to love but also "to hate men" (An. 4, c. 3). The principle of loving one's enemies being advanced on one occasion Confucius repudiated it. "What do you think about the principle of rewarding enmity with kindness?" "With what, then, would you reward kindness?" asked the Master, and then went on, "Reward enmity with just treatment and kindness with kindness" (An. 14, c. 36). The sense of which would seem to be that one's enemies are to be recognized as such and that the general principle of kindness and love does not apply to them. Justice is sufficient.

In every relationship of life duty must come first. Success is of no consideration beside it. "The wise man is anxious about his duty not about poverty" (An. 15, c. 31). Public position, advancement, the acquisition of wealth should never be balanced against right conduct. A man may be happy in poverty if his honour is untouched: "The Master said, Wealth and rank are what men desire, but unless they be obtained in the right way they are not to be possessed. Poverty and obscurity are what men detest; unless it can be brought about in the right way they are not to be abandoned" (An. 4, c. 5). "To see the right and not to do it is cowardice" (An. 2, c. 24).

The three main duties of life are: (1) Filial—those which men owe to their ancestors, parents and families. "When there is anything to be done. . . . the young should take the burden of it" (An. 2, c. 8). Everything must be done with reverence. (2) Service to friends. (3) Service to the Prince. "He who transfers his mind from feminine allurements to excelling in moral excellencies; who in serving his parents is ready to do so to the utmost of his ability; who in the service of his Prince is prepared to lay down his life; and who in intercourse with his friends is sincere in what he says. . . . I should certainly call him educated" (An. 1, c. 7). The good man will take delight in good pleasures only. "To seek pleasure in the refinements of manners and . . . in discussing the excellencies of others . . . in making many worthy friends these are beneficial" (An. 16, c. 5). He will abhor unbridled enjoyment, looseness and gadding, conviviality, forwardness, reticence and blindness to the desires of his superiors. The youth must guard against lust, the mature man against combativeness and the old man against acquisitiveness. Reverence is an essential of character. "The man of noble mind holds three things in awe: he holds the Divine will in awe, he holds the great in awe and he holds the precepts of the Sages in awe" (An. 16, c. 8). Confucius said: "The wise man has nine points of thoughtful care. In looking his care is to observe distinctly; in listening his care is to apprehend clearly; in his appearance his care is to be kindly; in his manner his care is to be respectful; in speaking his care is to be conscientious; in his duties his care is to be earnest; in doubt his care is to seek information; in anger he has care for the consequences; and when he has opportunity for gain his care is whether it be right" (An. 16, c. 10).

How can men become so set toward virtue that "They look upon the good as if fearing not to reach it, and upon evil as if tasting scalding water"? (An. 16, c. 11). The answer is to be found in right education. "Let the character be formed by the poets; established by the laws of Decorum, and perfected by Music" (An. c. 8, v. 8). Great attention is paid to Poetry. "Poetry is liable to stimulate the mind; it can train to observation, it can encourage social intercourse, it can modify the vexations of life; from it the student learns to fulfil his more immediate duty to his parents and his remoter duty to his Prince, and in it he may become widely acquainted with the names of birds and beasts, plants and trees" (An. 17, c. 9). The government of the State will depend upon the Prince and the educated official class. If they are all that has been described above, then all will be well with the people.

The things which the ruling and administrative class should particularly aim at are: (1) To arrange for "sufficient food, (2) sufficient forces, (3) and the confidence of the people" (An. 12, c. 7). When people have become numerous it is the business of the Government to enrich them, educate and guard them. The whole State can only be secure and prosperous when it is rooted and grounded in faith. Again and again Confucius emphasizes the importance of a right influence on the part of the officials. "If good men ruled the country for a hundred years they could even tame the brutal and abolish capital punishment" (An. 13, c. 12). Under a good Government those who live near are happy and the distant are attracted. Right behaviour on the part of a good ruler makes "all within the four seas his brothers" (An. 12, c. 5).

The Sage has no love for war, or indeed for violence of any kind. When asked his views regarding military training, he abruptly declared, "as to military matters I have never studied them" (An. 15, c. 1). On one occasion when war was contemplated between two States Confucius strongly urged the responsible officials to persuade their Chief to abandon his offensive preparations. Yet the Sage was not a pacifist. He no doubt detested war upon general principles, but nevertheless we find that he accepted the principle of military training (An. 13, c. 29). After a certain royal murder he appeared before Duke Ai, saying: "Ch'en Heng has slain His Presence. I beg you to take vengeance on him" (An. 14, c. 22).

While he thinks in terms of an official class we must remember that this class was one not so much of privilege as of duty. "It is not right to refuse to serve one's own country" (An. 18,

c. 7). It is therefore not surprising to find that the sympathies of Confucius are very largely with the poor: "The wise man succours the needy; he does not add to the rich" (An. 6, c. 3). The five rules of proper administrations are: "That the ruler be beneficent without expending the public revenue; that he exact service without arousing satisfaction; that his desires never degenerate to greed; that he be dignified without disdain; and that he be commanding but not domineering" (An. 20, c. 2). Success must not be measured by apparent results. "Duke Ching of Chi had a thousand teams of horses, but on the day of his death his people knew of no virtue for which to praise him. Po-I and Shu-Chi starved to death at the foot of Mount Shou Yang, and down to the present the people still praise them" (An. 16, c. 12).

THE GREAT LEARNING

There is strong reason to believe that the Great Learning, unlike the Analects, which are the reports of disciples, was actually written by Confucius himself. The book is a treatise on government. There is a unity running through all things. Where effects are visible there is a cause. "Things have their roots and their branches. Affairs have their end and their beginning" (G. L.,[1] c. 1, v. 3). To obtain a well-ordered kingdom the ancients "first ordered well their own States. Wishing to order well their States, they first regulated their families. Wishing to regulate their families, they first cultivated their persons. Wishing to cultivate their persons, they first rectified their hearts. Wishing to rectify their hearts, they first sought to be sincere in their thoughts. Wishing to be sincere in their thoughts, they first extended to the utmost their knowledge. Such extension of knowledge lay in the investigation of things. Things being investigated,

[1] G.L. = Great Learning (Legge).

knowledge became complete. Their knowledge being complete, their thoughts were sincere. Their thoughts being sincere, their hearts were then rectified. Their hearts being rectified, their persons were cultivated. Their persons being cultivated, their families were regulated. Their families being regulated, their states were rightly governed. Their stations being rightly governed, the whole kingdom was made tranquil and happy. From the Son of Heaven down to the mass of the people all must consider the cultivation of the person the root of everything besides" (G. L., c. 1, vv. 4–6). Here again we have the stress laid upon the personal influence of the governing class. While self-culture is urged for all, it must not be forgotten that the sovereign and his officials set the standard and that they are the root which, if it be neglected, nothing can be well-ordered. Sincere, upright, earnest men, if they have knowledge, are the ones to guide things aright.

(f) SUMMARY OF ANCIENT CHINESE THINKING

Two main schools of thought arose in ancient China, the Confucian and the Taoist. The first was the larger and the more important of the two. It can be said generally to embrace the teaching of the Shû King, the Shi King, the Lî King, the Great Learning and the Analects. In giving to this the name "Confucian" we must remember that the Sage himself was not its prophet, but rather its editor, commentator and interpreter, as well as being one of its most perfect exponents. The Taoist, though not of such great importance, contained principles that were destined to have a profound influence on Chinese life.

CONFUCIAN THEORY

God is the Creator and the Sustainer of the Universe. He is kindly and well-disposed toward men and a definite influence in affairs, rewarding or punishing according to their deserts, raising up and overthrowing kings and ever working out definite plans. The conception of the Deity is vague and imperfect. He was very remote from the ordinary life of men and could be approached only through the king and certain high officials. Nearer, more intimate, and more potent in ordinary matters were the spirits of the dead. Every household did sacrifice to their ancestors and prayed to them for happiness. It was in the worship of the spirits that every man found access to the spiritual world. The mighty kings of old maintained their position and became to some extent the colleagues of God. The term Heaven apparently conveys the idea of the action of the whole spirit world rather than that of the Deity alone.

Under Heaven human society depended upon kings.

A STUDY IN CREATIVE HISTORY

Never perhaps in all literature has the conception of kingship as a benevolent and paternal authority reached such a lofty level as in these old Chinese writings. The monarch rules by Divine Right. The Great God is concerned for the toiling masses of the people and appoints the One man to be their shepherd and guardian. He must rule with no thought of pomp, luxury or power, but with the single idea of the welfare of the people whose servant he is. His personal character is the greatest single influence in the State. On his example all lesser men tend to mould their lives. The monarchy is hereditary, but if a king should abuse his power and thus lose the favour of Heaven his subjects are acting rightly in deposing him and raising up another in his stead. Below the king and responsible to him are the members of the official class, to each of whom is assigned a definite task—the control of a province or the administration of a department.

In the actual working of government there seems to have been a definite struggle between those who believed in the use of moral suasion alone and those who believed in it to a certain extent yet wished to add to it the restraining influence of punishments. The penal code was elaborate and many of the penalties cruel in the extreme. Punishments were regarded by some with reverence as being a sure means of doing away with crime and so perfecting society. Others, including Confucius himself, put practically the whole weight upon the constructive influence of upright living and were outspoken in their condemnation of retributive justice. To what extent this was actually demonstrated by the Sage during his own period of active administration we do not know. An ideal of life and character was laid down, and the realization of this by the king, the officials and the mass of the people was the essential factor in the well-being of the community. This standard was a high one. The superior man must display respect, magnanimity, sincerity, earnestness and kindness—qualities which if widely practised rapidly make for a good society. Duty must be the watchword of every well-lived life—first to the family and then to the Prince. The man who can live well in his own family circle, displaying reverence for his elders, forbearance in face of provocation and benevolence to his dependants is one who can presumably be trusted with the affairs of the larger family. The fatal defect in the whole system is its lack of passionate faith and its insistence on knowledge as the spring of action. While the moral standard was a high one the narrowing of the scope of learning to a study of the ideal past and the refusal to investigate the mystical life was a barrier to progress. Upon this system the main effect of Taoism would be to accentuate the tendencies toward inertia.

CHAPTER X

GREECE

(a) THE TROJAN WAR

"And these were the circumstances which, set forth in the full blaze of epic and tragic poetry, bestowed upon the legend its powerful and imperishable influence over the Hellenic mind. The enterprise was one comprehending all the members of the Hellenic body, of which each individually might be proud, and in which, nevertheless, those feelings of jealous and narrow patriotism, so lamentably prevalent in many of the towns, were as much as possible excluded. It supplied them with a grand and inexhaustible object of common sympathy, common faith and common admiration" (Grote, Vol. 1, p. 277, l. 4).

Herodotus mentions that certain Phoenicians, landing at Argos, sailed away with Io, the daughter of Gracchus. Cretans—Greeks probably—carried away Europa, the child of the Phoenician king of Tyre. The Argonauts, sailing to Aea in Colchis, bore away Medea and refused to make reparation. A generation later, Alexander, son of Priam, made prize by violence of Helen—a Lacedaemonian girl. The result was the invasion of Asia and the Trojan War. While Herodotus is guarded, even sceptical with regard to these alleged facts, there is little reason to doubt that the stories are in essence true. The Greeks, wandering from their Caucasian homelands, had entered and subdued the peninsula probably between 1500 B.C.-1000 B.C. By the latter date the older Mediterranean civilizations had been absorbed or destroyed. Cnossus was in ruins. Any temporary Cretan ascendancy, hinted at in the legend of Theseus, had long been shaken off. Greek ships were sweeping the Aegean, trading and ravaging. The Phoenicians were established in Tyre on the Palestinian coast and other Asiatics throughout Asia Minor. Before we have any sure historical record, Greek migration commenced toward the Asiatic coast and the islands adjacent. Clashes were inevitable. No doubt there many rapes of women, some of them notable enough. The islands of the Aegean would see many a bloody quarrel between sailors of differing race, and many a piratical act. We have only to think of the English Channel in the days of Edward III to imagine what small bickerings must have inflamed the passions of the opposing peoples. According to Herodotus both Persian and Greek agree that the actual cause of the first great conflict of East and West was the abduction of Helen. A great struggle occurred probably on or about the site of the historical Ilium.

The Homeric and other early poems, although believed as literal fact for many centuries, contain great exaggerations, and much that is imaginary. But the mere fact of this unquestioned belief had a tremendous effect upon the thought and action of subsequent times. Herodotus (Bk. II, p. 53) supposes Homer to have lived about 400 years before his own time—say 880 B.C.-831 B.C. Grote considers the poems to have been not later than 776 B.C., the date of the first Olympiad. The writer of the *Iliad* would thus be describing manners, customs and outlook that would be, at the latest, typical of Greece at the dawn of real history. It is quite possible that the ideas may go much farther back and may even be representative of a period perhaps two centuries earlier. A brief examination of the *Iliad* and of the *Odyssey* gives an idea of the beginnings of the great interaction of East and West which it is our business to study. The facts mentioned in the poems may not even be true, but the Greek of, say, 500 B.C., believing them to be true, would think and act as if they were. In History they have, then, the actual influence of authenticated fact.

1. The *Iliad* shows us a definite league of the West against the East. For the first time we have muster-rolls, probably very inexact, but definitely setting one contingent against the other. Twenty-nine detachments of Greeks composed the army which Agamemnon reviewed on the banks of Seamander (*Iliad*, Bk. II, ll. 508–881). They were drawn from the Peloponnesus, Crete, the Aegean Islands, Rhodes and Northern Greece as far almost as the Haliacmon. The fifteen detachments of the Trojan host (*Iliad*, Bk. II, ll, 938–1020) represent the eastern and northern seaboards of Asia Minor and an indefinite portion of the hinterland. To Homer the territories mentioned would comprise the greater and certainly the most important part of the then known world. Consequently the events he described would be to him and to the men of his time international affairs of the first magnitude. Men's knowledge of the world grew from a centre roughly represented on the map by the Aegean Sea. This conflict in the dim dawn of history marked definitely a division which all subsequent events tended to mark with increasing clearness.

2. The struggle gave solidarity to the numerous tribes of Greeks. The heroic legend of the *Iliad* was the common property of the whole of Greece. The rape of Helen was an insult to all the "long-haired Greeks." The stern struggle on the plain—

> "Then well might he his favouring fortune bless
> Who in that bloody field took part and passed
> By sword or spear unwounded. . . .
> For many a Trojan, many a Greek that day
> Prone in the dust, and side by side, were laid"
> (*Iliad*, Bk. IV, ll. 617–622)

the storming of the wall; the desperate fight about the dark-prowed ships when—

> "the dark earth ran with blood,
> Yet loosed not Hector of the stern his hold,
> But grasped the poop and on the Trojans called:
> 'Bring fire!'"
>
> (*Iliad*, Bk. XV, ll. 825-828)

while Ajax Telamon, expecting death, summons the Greeks to a last rally—

> "Friends, Grecian Heroes, ministers of Mars (Arês),
> Quit ye like men!"
>
> (*Iliad*, Bk. XV, ll. 847-848)

the rally of the Greeks and the exploits of Patrocles, when—

> "with shouts confused
> The Trojans fled"

his death; the rescue of his body by Ajax and Menelaus; the rage of Achilles; his fierce rush across the plain when—

> "his flying steeds
> His chariot bore, o'er bodies of the slain,
> And broken bodies trampling"
>
> (*Iliad*, Bk. XX, ll. 569-571)

the headlong flight of the Trojans, and the death of Hector were episodes which fired the imaginations of generations of Greek youth. The *Iliad*, more than any other Greek poem, fixed not only a standard of endurance and valour, but also the fact of a common unity in arms of all the "brass-clad Greeks." There were times when this fundamental conception of Greek oneness was broken by disloyalty, but generally it held firm through the great age of Greece.

3. The Homeric Poems put into definite form the religious beliefs of Paganism at a time when the influence of Semitic religion was practically unfelt. Early Greek religion was purely anthropomorphic. The gods were larger and more powerful men, who took an active part in human affairs. They initiated action:

> "The eyes of Jove (Zeus),
> Sweet slumber held not. . . .
> . . . . with winged words
> Thus to a phantom form gave command:
> 'Hie thee . . . to Agamemnon's tent,
> There all as I command thee truly speak.
> Bid that he arm in haste the long-haired Greeks
> To combat.'"
>
> (*Iliad*, Bk. II, ll. 2 . . . 14)

And again when it was the purpose of the gods to break the truce:

> "Pallas (Athênê) meanwhile, amid the Trojan host,
> Clad in the likeness of Antenor's son,
> Searched here and there, if haply she might find
> The godlike Pandarus . . .
> She stood beside him and addressed him thus:
> 'Bend then thy bow at Atreus' glorious son.'"
>
> (*Iliad*, Bk. IV, ll. 97–114)

The gods were intimately connected with the affairs of men. They always regarded with special favour definite cities, tribes and even individual men:

> "To whom the stag-eyed Juno (Hêrê) thus replied:
> 'Three cities are there dearest to my heart:
> Argos and Sparta, and the ample streets
> Of rich Mycenae.'"
>
> (*Iliad*, Bk. IV, ll. 59–61)

And again:

> "Two goddesses for Menelaus fight—
> Thou, Juno (Hêrê), Queen of Argos, and with thee
> Minerva, shield of warriors. . . .
>
> .   .   .   .   .
>
> While laughter-loving Venus (Aphroditê) at the side
> Of Paris standing still averts his fate."
>
> (*Iliad*, Bk. IV, ll. 7–12)

Some of the heroes are actually the children of gods or goddesses by a human parent:

> "Anchises' valiant son Aeneas ...
> him mid Ida's jutting peaks
> Immortal Venus (Aphroditê) to Anchises bore."
> (*Iliad*, Bk. II, ll. 947–949)

Sarpedon is the son of Zeus—Achilles of Thetis. For their favourites the gods schemed and even fought. Their intervention was of the most direct sort.

When Paris was in peril at the hands of Menelaus:

> "Venus (Aphroditê)
> ... her fav'rite's peril quickly saw
> And broke the throttling strap."
> (*Iliad*, Bk. III, ll. 436–438)

Later Aphroditê is actually wounded by Diomed. (Bk. V, ll. 427–430). Arês fought in the Trojan ranks, but Diomed, strengthened by Athênê:

> "thrust forward in his turn
> His pond'rous spear ...
> It pierced the flesh."
> (*Iliad*, Bk. V, ll. 973–977)

In and behind every considerable action we have god or goddess guiding, restraining or strengthening, moved by prejudices and passions which are always entirely human. They could be propitiated by gifts and sacrifices.

> "Thou with the elder women seek the shrine
> Of Pallas (Athênê); bring your gifts and on the knees
> Of fair haired Pallas (Athênê) place the fairest robe.
>
> .   .   .   .   .
>
> And at her altar vow to sacrifice
> Twelve yearling kine....
> So she have pity on the Trojan State."
> (*Iliad*, Bk. VI, ll. 317–323)

A STUDY IN CREATIVE HISTORY

They heard and answered prayer. Chrysès, the priest of Hermês, seeks his daughter—a captive in the Grecian camp. Agamemnon repulses him with an almost incredibly brutal speech. The old man prays to his god:

> "if e'er my offer'd gifts
> Found favour in thy sight: if e'er to thee
> I burned the fat of bulls and choicest goats,
> Grant me this boon."
> *(Iliad, Bk. I, ll. 48–51)*

The reply of the god was immediate and terrible:

> "Nine days the heavenly archer on the troops
> Hurled his dread shafts."
> *(Iliad, Bk. I, ll. 64–65)*

The gods were immortal, but subject to hurt and injury even from human weapons. Arês complains to Zeus:

> "Diomed
> ... but now encountered me;
> Barely I 'scap'd by swiftness of my feet,
> Else mid a ghastly heap of corpses slain
> In anguish had I lain; and if alive
> Yet liv'd disabled by his weapon's stroke."
> *(Iliad, Bk. V, ll. 1002–1008)*

Sometimes the anthropomorphism is distinctly humorous as when:

> "Mars (Arês) cried out aloud with such a shout
> As if nine thousand or ten thousand men
> Should simultaneous raise their battle-cry."
> *(Iliad, Bk. V, ll. 978–980)*

His somewhat bedraggled entry into the presence of his father, who orders him to "cease his whining prayers," is delightful. Hêrê, "whom I can scarce control" (Bk. V, l. 1017), seems to have harassed her august spouse considerably. He on occasion responds with "cutting words and taunting tone, the wrath of Juno (Hêrê) to provoke" *(Iliad*

GREECE

Bk. IV, ll. 115-116). Zeus might threaten her with "lightning," but like a true woman she gains her end by stratagem, and borrowing the girdle of Aphroditê lulls her lord to sleep while Poseidôn rages among the Trojan ranks. Life after death was believed in but held to be a cheerless prospect. Soul and body were separate. The blow which stretched some hero lifeless on the battlefield opened a vent through which the soul "fled wailing to the viewless shades."

"My soul shall from my body be divorced," says Priam, in gloomy prophecy. Hector falls by the hand of Achilles:

"And to the viewless shades his spirit fled
Mourning his fate, his youth and vigour lost."
(*Iliad*, Bk. XXII, ll. 430-431)

The spirit of the slain Patroclus appears to Achilles:

"Hasten my funeral rites that I may pass
Through Hades gloomy gates; ere those be done
The spirits and spectres of departed men
Drive me far from them, nor allow to cross the abhorred river."
(*Iliad*, Bk. XXII, ll. 84-88)

When he had spoken:

"with a wailing cry
Vanished, like smoke, the spirit beneath the earth."
(*Iliad*, Bk. XXIII, ll. 118-119)

When Ulysses visited the infernal regions and sacrificed, the nations of the dead swarmed round him shrieking. When the shade of Tiresias, the Theban, seer, had drunk the blood of the sacrifice, he was able to speak:

"Why hapless Chief! leaving the cheerful day,
Arriv'st thou to behold the dead and this unpleasant land?"
(*Odyssey*, Bk. XI, ll. 110-114)

The hero's mother holds "plaintive" converse with him, wondering:

> "how hast thou entered still alive
> This darksome region?"
> (*Odyssey*, Bk. XI ll. 185-186)

Agamemnon appeared and drank the blood:

> "shrill he wailed
> And querelous: tears trickling bathed his cheeks,
> And with spread palms through ardour of desire
> He sought to enfold me fast, but vigour none
> Or force, as erst, his agile limbs informed."
> (*Odyssey*, Bk. XI, ll. 474-478)

Death, then, to the Greek of Homer's time meant not annihilation but a continuation of existence in the gloomiest surroundings—under conditions so miserable that the proud Achilles would prefer to live as a serf in the hire of a poor man than hold rule over all the shades.

The gods might be active in human affairs, but they were in no sense an inspiration to good living, to high and lofty morality, or to what we might call holiness. They were to be placated from fear or wheedled for gifts. They were as childish, as passionate, as cruel, as deceitful and as immoral as any Greek or Trojan.

In a council of the gods:

> "Juno's (Hêrê's) breast
> Could not contain her rage."
> (*Iliad*, Bk. IV, ll. 26-27)

Hêrê is absolutely relentless. Through the whole epic she will do anything, give anything, to wreak her vengeance on the Trojans. After Ulysses has endured a long period of suffering and toil the gods were moved with pity:

> "save Neptune (Poseidôn); he alone
> Unceasing and implacable pursued
> Godlike Ulysses to his native shores."
> (*Odyssey*, Bk. I, ll. 27-29)

Athênê, "caerulean-eyed," at one moment gloats over the

"vengeance heaped" that has fallen on Aegisthus, but at the next:

> "with a bosom anguish rent I view
> Ulysses, hapless chief."
> (*Odyssey*, Bk. I, ll. 62-63)

They deceive not only men and women but even amongst themselves there is no code of honour. Hêrê descends to the meanest subterfuge to mislead Zeus. She lies to Aphroditê and obtains the Cestus. She bribes Sleep; and then "with deceitful speech" lures Zeus to slumber while Poseidôn succours the Grecians.

The morals of the majority of the gods were of the lowest order. The armours of Zeus are almost too numerous to mention. Arês seduces Aphroditê. Poseidôn, her outraged husband, catches the guilty pair in the very act. Frantic with indignation he summons the other gods. They stand in the porch and

> "infinite arose
> The laugh of heaven."
> (*Odyssey*, Bk. VIII, ll. 404-405)

4. Arts and crafts had made some considerable progress. Weapons and clothes were carefully and richly made. The shield of Achilles, probably described from some masterpiece of contemporary work, was:

> "vast and strong
> With rich adornment...
>
> . . . .
>
> And on its surface many a rare design
> Of curious art...
> Thereon were figured earth and sky and sea"
> (*Iliad*, Bk. XVIII, ll. 539-545)

and much else intricate and beautiful.

Ulysses, moving to the palace of Alcinous, the Phæacian king, saw:

> "a light
> As of the sun or moon illumining clear
> The Palace of Phæacia's mighty king:
> Walls plated bright with brass, on either side
> Stretched from the portal to the interior house
> With azure cornice crowned; the doors were gold
> Which shut the palace fast: silver the posts
> Reared on a brazen threshold, and above
> The lintels, silver, architraved with gold."
> (*Odyssey*, Bk. VII, ll. 100–108)

Such might be the luxury of some Grecian chiefs and kings, especially in places where Phoenician influences were strong. The life of the peasant was probably rude and simple, although food and coarse woollen clothing would be generally in sufficient abundance. Iron was not greatly used, although a lump of iron—possibly a meteorite—is mentioned as a prize which would supply the owner of even a large estate with so much metal that for:

> "five revolving years
> It will his wants supply: nor to the town
> For lack of iron with this mass in store
> Need he his shepherd or his ploughman send."
> (*Iliad*, Bk. XXIII, ll. 964–967)

Brass alloyed with tin was the substance commonly used for weapons and armour.

5. Forms of social organizations were various. Hereditary chiefs, claiming descent from the gods, led the men of various tribes to battle, and in many cases were apparently rulers in time of peace. They were essentially soldiers—a military aristocracy—who had emerged during the early invasion and conquest of Greece. Their rule was at its best benevolent and patriarchal. Telemachus refers to Ulysses as:

> "A noble father, who as fathers rule
> Benign their children, governed once yourselves."
> *(Odyssey*, Bk. II, ll. 59–60)

The hereditary right both of Ulysses and Telemachus is freely admitted by the suitors. Eurymachus admits their fault, blames Antinous, who was aiming to make himself supreme, and concluded with the prayer:

> "Now, therefore, spare thine own,
> Thy people."
> *(Odyssey*, Bk. XXII, ll. 60–61)

Despite reference to:

> "Nor council here, nor session hath been held
> Since great Ulysses left his native shore"
> *(Odyssey*, Bk. II, ll. 33–34)

it is fairly evident that the rule of Laertes' son was practically absolute in the island of Ithaca.

Agamemnon, "lord of the largest hosts and chief of chiefs," ruled a State much larger and more complex than the Ithacan community. His position probably corresponded with that of a great feudal overlord of medieval times. The description given of the shield of Achilles points to the existence of self-governing cities:

> "A busy throng the forum filled"
> "to the public one appealed"
> "in solemn circle sat the rev'rend elders"
> *(Iliad*, Bk. XVIII, ll. 560–570)

to hear a cause and give a judgment.

Such, then, is the picture Homer draws of the Greeks at the time of the Trojan War. Whatever credence we may or may not give to the alleged facts on which the narrative is built, the general descriptions of the unity of all Greeks as opposed to the trans-Aegean peoples, of the method of social organization and the state of religious belief are probably a true reflex of popular feeling at the time when the poems emerged in their present form.

The account given of Troy and the Trojans is unlikely to be of any value. If the poems were written before the period of the Greek colonization of Asia Minor the knowledge possessed by the poet would in such an illiterate age be slight. There would be, too, the natural tendency of a writer labouring under such difficulties to project his own beliefs for the sake of balance and dramatic effect. If, on the other hand, the period of composition was later than that of the Greek migration he would describe a Hellenized Troy differing not at all from any city of Greece. We must turn to other sources than Homer to get some idea of the peoples with whom the Greeks so fiercely clashed in that darkness which lies just before the real dawn of history.

Greece was the nucleus of Europe. A struggle which may have been a petty one, fought on a trivial issue, and sung by a bard who could perhaps neither read nor write formed at the very beginning of European history a barrier which the passing of centuries seemed only to pile higher and stronger.

(b) HESIOD

Hesiod lived about 735 B.C. and wrote the *Works and Days* and the *Theogony*. His whole thinking is set in a framework of pessimism. The great days lie in the past, and as history proceeds life becomes poorer and ever more infected with evil.

Gods and men arose from a common source. In the time of Chronos men "lived like gods without sorrow of heart; remote and free from toil and grief: miserable age rested not on them; but with legs and arms never failing they made merry with feasting beyond the reach of all evils. When they died it was as though they were overcome with sleep, and they had all good things, for the fruitful earth unforced bore them fruit abundantly and without stint. They dwelt in ease and peace upon their lands with many good things, rich in flocks, and loved by the blessed gods" (p. 11).[1]

From the idyllic picture of a Golden Age—strongly resembling the Eden of the writers of Genesis—there is a sharp declension to the time of the Silver Race. "They lived only a little time, and that in sorrow, because of their foolishness, for they could not cease from sinning and from wronging one another; nor would they serve the immortals; nor sacrifice on the holy altars of the blessed ones as it is right for men to do wherever they dwell." Zeus, angry with the sinful and impious race, destroyed the men of Silver and created the Brazen Race, which "was terrible and strong. They loved the lamentable works of Arês and deeds of violence; they ate no bread but were hard of heart. ... These were destroyed by their own hands and passed to the dark house of chill Hades and left no name" (p. 13). The Godlike race of Hero Men which fought at Thebes and Troy was passed over lightly, and Hesiod proceeded to draw a frightful picture of the men of his own time—the men of the Iron Race. "Men never rest from labour and sorrow by day, and from perishing by night. The future is black and hopeless. The father will not agree with his children, nor the children with their father, nor guest with his host, nor comrade with comrade: nor will brother be dear to brother as aforetime. Men will dishonour their parents as they grow quickly old ... hardhearted they, not knowing the fear of the gods ... might shall be their right and one man will sack another's city. There will be no favour for the man who keeps his oath or for the just or the good, but rather men will praise the evildoer and his violent dealing. Strength will be right and reverence will cease to be, and the wicked will hurt the

[1] *Hesiod*, Loeb Classical Library. White.

worthy man. . . . Envy, foulmouthed, delighting in evil, with scowling face will go along with wretched men" (p. 17). At last the time will come when the gods will withdraw altogether from relationships with men. There will be no help against evil, and in the long run Zeus will destroy the race of man.

Hesiod's conception of Zeus is in many ways similar to the ideas concerning God which were being expressed at about the same time by Hebrew writers. Zeus was the creator of men. He was all-powerful. "For easily he makes strong and easily he brings the strong man low: easily he humbles the proud and raises the obscure, and easily he straightens the crooked and blasts the proud" (p. 3). He upholds righteousness, "for whoever knows the right and is ready to speak it far-seeing Zeus gives him prosperity" (p. 25). The Almighty keeps sleepless watch over the race of men. Ten thousand spirits clothed in mist keep watch on all the doings of men and make report to Zeus, who punishes with vigour the crimes of men. "But for those who practise violence and cruel deeds far-seeing Zeus, the son of Chronos, ordains a punishment" (p. 21). His judgments are severe and pitiless. We have seen how in his anger at their iniquities Hesiod represents him as having already blotted out the race of Silver and the race of Brass. When Prometheus sinned for the sake of men, Zeus "planned sorrow and mischief against men" and sent Pandora scattering plagues so that earth became full of evil, "and diseases came upon men continually by day and night" (p. 9). The evil deeds of a single man were sometimes sufficient reason for a whole city to suffer.

The conception of a world that was steadily growing worse, and yet in which an all-powerful deity rigorously punished evil deeds, produced an ethical system which was lacking in inspiration and purely utilitarian in outlook. The times were very evil and would become worse, but the Judge was ever at the gate and his stern punishments were inescapable—therefore it were better to do righteously. Men should be careful to avoid the anger of the deathless gods by refraining from violence and unnatural sin, from offence against orphan children or neglect of parents. These inhibitions having been duly observed there remained but to "sacrifice... purely and cleanly, and burn rich meats also, and at other times propitiate them with libations and incense" (p. 29). The result of right relationships with the gods was that "you may buy another's holding and not another yours."

The main incentive in life was the acquisition of wealth. Men should not be idle. "A man grows eager to work when he considers his neighbour, a rich man, who has to plough and to plant and to put his house in good order—and neighbour vies with his neighbour as he hurries after wealth" (p. 5). Men became famous and renowned according to their wealth, but "shame is with poverty."

Between man and man there is an element of suspicion and calculation with little impulse towards generous actions. "Call your friend to a feast, but leave your enemy alone. Give to one who gives, but do not give to one who does not give." Men should be courteous in business dealings, but even with a brother it was wise to have a witness. Women were deceivers.

(c) THE GREEK MIGRATIONS TO ASIA MINOR

The Aryan conquest of Greece was no doubt a slow process extending over several hundred years. Fresh tribes from the Danube would ever and again be turning their faces toward the sunny southern lands. Sometimes, no doubt, they found empty spaces and settled. At other times bloody wars, resulting in the extermination or submergence of considerable populations, were waged not only with men of alien race but with tribes of the same blood, who had settled as a result of a previous migration. The continuation of this pressure from the north, and the normal growth of population in communities with no outlet save the sea, could have but one result. At a very early period the Greeks were on the sea probably ravaging the islands of the Aegean and raiding the Asiatic coasts. Settlement followed. In the Homeric catalogue (*Iliad*, Bk. II) there are contingents from Crete and Rhodes, but no mention of any from Asia. In all probability the Trojan War itself was the direct result of a determined attempt on the part of the Asiatics to throw back a wave of Greek migration no longer content with the islands but determined to establish itself on the mainland. If so, the attempt was unsuccessful, for at the opening of the historical period we find the whole of the Mysian, Lydian and Carian coastline in the possession of Greeks. Three great migratory movements—the Aeolic, the Ionic and the Doric—were responsible for the settlement.

1. The Aeolic migration was, according to the ancient legend, led either by Orestes himself or some other of the descendants of Agamemnon. Commencing from Laconia they journeyed through Arcadia, Boetia, Thessaly and Thrace, and so across the Hellespont into the Troad. Working by degrees farther to the south, they occupied Tenedos, Lesbos and the mainland to the south of the Gulf of Adramyttium, for some little distance across the River Harmos. Cities were built: Mitylene, and five others on Lesbos; Cymé, Larissa, Neonteichus, Temnus, Cilla, Notium, Aegiroëssa, Pitane, Aegæa, Myrina, Gryneia and Smyrna. The last-named was, however, taken by the Ionians and its population dispersed. The eleven remaining cities of the mainland drew together in a close federation.

2. The Ionic migration was composed of some Ionians mixed with the representatives of many other Greek States. They settled in the Cyclades, on Samos and Chios, and then founded ten cities on the mainland, from Phokaea in the

north to Milotus in the south. They regarded Athens as their parent town. From these States was formed the Pan-Ionic Amphiktyony with the Panionium as a common meeting-place. Herodotus says of the Ionian territory that "the air and climate are the most beautiful in the whole world; for no region is equally blessed with Ionia, neither above it nor below it, nor east, nor west of it" (Herodotus, Bk. I, c. 142).

3. The Dorian colonies were founded, according to legend, by certain Lacedaemonians and Argives with some Miniae from Lemnos, descendants of the Argonauts. Their settlements were Malos, Thera, Crete, Rhodes, Cos, Cnidus, and Halicarnuss.

The first definitely historical interaction between East and West is a migratory movement from Europe to Asia. This could hardly have been carried out without fighting and the expropriation of existing populations. Probably few Asiatics were greatly affected, but it was an act of aggression which, symbolized by the Trojan War, gave ground for the Persian contention "that the Greeks were greatly to blame, since before any attack had been made on Europe they led an army into Asia" (Herodotus, Bk. I, c. 4).

(d) THE DEVELOPMENT OF THE GREEKS FROM 776 B.C. TO THE OUTBREAK OF THE PERSIAN WARS

At the beginning of the historical period—about 776 B.C.—the Greeks occupied not only Greece proper but also the islands of the Aegean and a narrow strip of territory along the western coastline of Asia Minor. Over this considerable area they had established themselves in some three hundred cities.

There was an almost complete absence of any sort of political unity. Each city was a law unto itself. There were ties of friendship. The Ionian Greeks on the Asian coast regarded themselves as especially related to the Athenians. "Athens was the metropolis or mother city of them all" (Grote, I, c. xviii, sect. iii, p. 2).

Definite alliances were sometimes made. Chalkis and Eretria fought for the possession of the fertile plain which lay between them. The former were supported by the Samians and Thessalians, the latter by the Milesians (Grote, II, c. xii, p. 2). Speaking generally, however, there was no sort of political organization of all the Greeks. The reasons for this state of affairs were:

1. The fact that from the Trojan War to the Persian Invasion the Greeks as a whole were engaged in no great offensive or defensive operations. For a period of five hundred years their development was not interfered with by any outside people. No migratory horde crossed their frontiers. They were for the time being beyond the reach of the great empires that were developing in the East. In consequence a national muster was neither needed nor anticipated.

2. The economic condition of the country was primitive. The cities for the most part lived on the produce of their own fields. The volume of external trade was small. In

consequence highly developed road systems, adjustments of tariffs and the development of great market centres, were at that time quite unnecessary.

3. During this period no Greek State became in any large way ambitious to dominate at the expense of its neighbours. There were no doubt innumerable quarrels between cities. The age was a wild and turbulent one. "They looked on war as a trade and a living and loved it accordingly" (Schlegel, "Philosophy of History," Lecture VIII, p. 230). The whole organization of the Spartan State was calculated to make for the greatest possible efficiency in war. And yet in the early period of history, despite the wars with Messene, Arcadia and Argolis (Grote, II, c. vii & c. viii), Sparta cannot fairly be described as a disturber of the peace. The Spartan prided himself on being the first of all Greeks in arms, but this pride did not make him at all desirous to subdue other Greeks. "However, it was not the design of Lycurgus that his city should govern a great many others" (Plutarch Lycurgus, p. 90). Nor was it the design of the Spartans. There was then little need for the Greeks as a whole to organize against some powerful challenge to the common freedom.

4. There was latent in the Greek temperament a passion for free development which was outraged by any attempt to impose authority from above. Even after a victorious war the conquered, if they were Greeks, should be regarded with respect; and whatever might be the fruits of victory, the liberty of the vanquished should not be interfered with.

SOCRATES: "Do you think it just that Greeks should enslave Greek cities? or rather . . . to be sparing of the Grecian tribe?"
GLAUCO: "It is . . . best to be sparing."

(*Republic*, p. 169)

This free feeling crystallized itself in the growth of cities, each one independent of all others. The city is the unit of Greek society. Its foundations are strong in heroic legend. History and tradition make it venerable. Some god guards it with special care, and generations of men pay tribute of their finest loyalty to the highest they know. One city may have kingly rule; another an oligarchy; while in a third there may be established an advanced democracy, but each is free to develop in such fashion as seems most right and natural to its citizens. "Nothing short of force will efface in the mind of the free Greek the idea of his city as an autonomous and separate organization" (Grote, II, c. xxviii, p. 233). Even when the great age of Greece had long passed, St. Paul, a Hebrew of the Hebrews by birth and training, one of the greatest internationalists of all time, and Greek only by early environment, bursts out in a great moment with the proudest declaration possible to any Greek, "I am . . . a citizen of no mean city" (Acts xxi. 3). This supreme love and loyalty for the city rendered it difficult, even under conditions of the greatest strain and stress, for all Greeks to act together as an organized whole.

Despite political disunity, however, Greece was able to reach a union of a far higher and nobler sort. Before Platæa Sparta trembled for fear that ruined Athens might conclude peace with the Persian invaders and thus destroy every hope of freedom. The Athenian reply to the Spartan envoys is one of the noblest in history:

"Not all the gold that the whole earth contains—not the fairest and most fertile of all lands—would bribe us to take part with the Medes and help them to enslave our countrymen. . . . There is our common brotherhood with the Greeks; our common language, the altars and the sacrifices of which we all partake; the common character which we bear—did the Athenians betray all these, of a truth it would not be well" (Herodotus, Bk. VIII, c. 144). This brotherhood of the Greeks was the result of a common tradition, a religion firmly—indeed passionately—believed and practised, and a great and growing literature.

Between the period of the appearance of the Homeric poems—say 776 B.C. and the Persian War—the religious opinions of the Greeks remained practically unchanged. The prevailing belief in the anthropomorphic nature of the gods was scarcely questioned until the time of Xenophanes of Kolophon (*circa* 570–480 B.C.), who "denounced as abominable the descriptions of the gods given by Homer and Hesiod" (Grote, II, c. xxxvii, p. 95). Back of all human affairs, even of the smallest, stood the immortal gods demanding obedience and sacrifice, initiating action, overruling events both great and small, sometimes jealous, vindictive, passionate and cruel, at others benign and friendly. They revealed themselves to men through visions, in signs, omens and auguries and by catastrophe. In every part of Greece they were greatly feared and reverenced, and in the worship devoted to them all Greeks were one. In the historical period we see this attitude working out into great national institutions.

In the *Iliad*, games are a definite part of the religious ceremonies in connection with funerals. They were evidently closely associated with all assemblages of a public nature. Probably every Greek village had its sacred tree or spring or shrine devoted to the worship of some god or hero who was believed to specially favour that place. The inhabitants would gather round this spot for the purpose of prayer, sacrifice and games. As time went on people from neighbouring cities or villages, anxious to share in the benefits conferred by the god, attracted by the splendour of the ceremony or the fame of the games, sought admission. They were welcomed with the simple cordiality and hospitality characteristic of primitive peoples. An Amphiktyon, or religious brotherhood, was formed. Some of these groupings continued to grow in popular favour until they were recognized and frequented by the whole Greek community.

In a valley of great natural beauty, near the west coast of the Peloponnesus, was an ancient oracular temple dedicated to Zeus. On the foundation of Pisa by the Achaeans this worship was combined with that of the hero Pelops and later still of Hêrê. Games were instituted with appropriate religious ceremonies. For some time Elis and Pisa remained in joint control until the latter was crushed by the Spartan power. The Eleians became responsible for the general control of the games, which gradually commenced to have a Pan-Hellenic character. From a simple foot race the programme was gradually enlarged to include every kind of athletic competition known to the Greeks. While no competitions in music or poetry were arranged, yet lectures and recitations were frequently given, and it is even said that the history of Herodotus was read during the celebration of the games. The festival was attended by crowds from every city and state of Greece. Open to all Greeks but closed to all barbarians, it became the supreme expression of Greek unity and brotherhood. During the month preceding the celebration a truce was proclaimed by herald through all the cities of Greece, rendering sacred and inviolable the territory of the Eleian State. While no other festival commanded such universal respect and adherence, it was by no means the only one of its kind. The Pythian, Nemean and Isthmian Games all obtained great popularity. Occurring as they did in the years intervening between the Olympiads, they served to keep alive the feelings generated on the banks of the Alpheius.

The ties of a common faith were felt not only in the large assemblages wherein great multitudes assembled for celebrations and competitions, but also in the attraction of those sacred spots where were established the most famous oracles of the gods. The intense belief in the power and overruling authority of the divine personages pervaded the whole of Greek life. All matters great or small were referred to their judgment, and no Greek would commence an undertaking without sanction from the immortals. Temples were established at places rendered venerable by the legends of antiquity and the continued worship of succeeding generations. Here came all those seeking advice. After due ceremony and sacrifice the questions were propounded. Replies, usually of an exceedingly ambiguous sort, were given. One or other of the possible meanings would, in the light of after-events, probably prove true and the prestige of the oracle would thereby be maintained. The most famous of all these shrines was the temple of Apollo at Delphi. Here came inquirers from every part of Greece, and indeed from other countries as well.

During this period the Greeks were coming into touch with the outside world. Phoenician ships touched at their ports. Egypt was thrown open in 660 B.C. The colonies in Asia Minor were in direct contact with Thrace, Phrygia and Lydia. As a result we find the introduction of new ideas concerning the gods. While these were in no sense revolutionary they did have considerable effect. Dionysus and Demeter, who were not much mentioned in *Homer* and *Hesiod*, and whose names are identified with Osiris and Isis, are prominent in the Orphic *Theogony*. There was an increasing diffusion of special mysteries, orgies and ecstasies accompanied with manifestations of frenzy. The Eleusian mysteries were established. The sense of sin and the need of cleansing became stronger.

From the beginning of their history the Greeks possessed a great and abundant literature. Before any record of war, legislation or emigration we have existing the *Iliad* and *Odyssey*, the *Works and Days* and a number of other poems of which only the titles, and in some cases a brief *précis*, still remain. These poems were the expression of the historical and religious beliefs of a people active, warlike, passionate but unreflecting and little given to critical and constructive thinking. Public recitations rendered the subject-matter of the epics familiar to all men. Though Greek literature was to produce no poetry more splendid or enduring than *Homer*, it was not to cease with the production of a great epic but rather from such a root to widen and diversify and spread itself abroad until beneath the wide-spreading boughs there was room for every child of the human mind.

The Greek mind was plastic, not static. Old forms, however venerable, could not give full satisfaction to new modes of living and thinking. As all Greek poetry was sung or chanted to the accompaniment of music the introduction by Terpander of the seven-stringed in place of the old four-stringed lyre (676 B.C.) was revolutionary.

From this time new metres of every kind were introduced and new themes. The old poet had been a story-teller, the new was critic, lover, lawgiver, teacher, philosopher and preacher. His aim was to concentrate thinking on a point and to give vent to the feeling of the moment. His concern was not with the past but the present. The lyric, with its intensity, concentration and capacity for passion, became the new means of expression.

Archilochus (720–680 B.C.) wrote not only hymns to the gods but moralizing verse and lampoons. Kallinus and Tyrtaeus composed marching-songs to fire the valour of soldiers going into battle. Their songs were intended for a single voice accompanied by the flute.

Alkmann wrote for the chorus in various measures. Arion (*circa* 600 B.C.) travelled throughout Greece singing at the festivals and making large gains. Alkaeus of Lesbos (*circa* 610–580 B.C.) was the first to use poetry for a definitely political purpose. Sappho, a Lesbian also and of the same date, was the first great writer of love-songs. Some approach to prose was made by Simonides of Samos about 670 B.C., who moralized on the character of women, was concerned with the reward of industry and had a pessimistic outlook upon human affairs. Solon (*circa* 638–554 B.C.) used verse for comment on political affairs, as also did Theognis. These poets were the popular writers of the time. Their songs were on the lips of all men.

Despite, however, the popularity of the new form of expression the old was by no means forgotten or even reduced to secondary importance. At every public gathering there would be found some rhapsodist reciting the old epics. Solon and Peisistratus were both anxious for the preservation of a sound text of the *Iliad*. Old and new alike were the common property of all Greeks, and the stream of popular poetry was thus broadened and deepened.

Not so popular in its appeal, but destined to bear the greatest fruits, was the work of Thales (640–546 B.C.), the founder of Greek geometry, astronomy and philosophy; Pythagoras (582–500 B.C.), an ethical teacher who expounded the metempsychosis or transmigration of souls, and Xenophanes of Kolophon (570–500 B.C.), the first great sceptic. The work of these men stands at the beginning of European science and philosophy.

The literature of a people, next to its religion, is the strongest of all unifying agencies, and in it there is often a stronger tie than in any bond of political organization.

The Greeks, then, prior to 500 B.C., though politically disunited and economically undeveloped, were bound closely together by the strongest ties of a common religion and culture. While they were by no means isolated and were in touch with Asia Minor, Egypt and Phoenicia, they were practically a self-contained people, and the influences of the East, although by no means unimportant, were as yet insufficient to produce any great changes in Greek life and thought. The influence of Greek thought was unfelt outside Greece.

CHAPTER XI

ROME

Tribes of the Aryan race had at some early period poured in over the Apennines and settled the Italian peninsula. While historical records of this migration and the subsequent settlement are completely lost, the identity of the Italian dialects with Greek and Sanskrit is proven by the common roots which form the base of them all. "The Greek and the Italian are brothers" (Mommsen, c. ii, p. 12). Certain tribes calling themselves Latins settled on the plain of Latium. Some thirty clans of these people drew together to form for religious and probably also defensive reasons what was known as the Latin League.

Three of these clans—the Ramnians, Tities and Luceres—amalgamated to form a single commonwealth on a group of hills some fourteen miles from the mouth of the Tiber. The city thus founded was Rome. The site, though neither particularly fertile, well-watered nor even healthy, was the natural trading centre of the Latin community. Ships could both ascend and descend the Tiber. The inland situation was a safeguard against the attacks of pirates. The fortification of the hills on the river-banks was a sure defence for the whole of the northern part of the Latin Territory. The original settlement on the Palatine Hill grew by slow degrees until the Servian Wall linked scattered urban groups into one great city, which emerged clearly into history as the head of the Latin League.

The Roman family was the model on which was formed the Roman State. The family consisted of the father, the wedded wife, sons, daughters (while unmarried) and dependants. The "paterfamilias" was absolute head of the house. He, only, had the right to control and dispose of property, and not property only but the liberty and even the life of any member of the family. At his will the new-born babe might be exposed, the son might be sold into slavery, the slave might be put to death. During the whole course of his life this authority remained unimpaired. The sons remained subject to him not only in boyhood and youth, but even in manhood, after they had established houses and families of their own. The death of the father gave to the sons in their turn complete authority over their households. The women of the house were dependent absolutely on the will of the master. Legally, indeed, they had no standing apart from him. They were part of the family. The State was concerned with unit families, and of these the "paterfamilias" was the responsible head. Although politically and legally practically non-existent, the wife was generally the honoured mistress of the home. Daughters were in the power of the father until they passed on marriage into the hand of husband or father-in-law. In addition to the wife, children and children's children there were two dependent classes under the control of the family head. The clients were freed men or refugees who, not having any standing as burgesses, were in need of protection. They were retainers who, while not in a strict sense free, were yet actually so in fact. Slaves, on the other hand, were the chattel property of the household in a like manner to the domestic animals.

Households related to each other in blood formed the clan. The federated clans in their turn formed the State. All those who were born in legal marriage within the clan were citizens of Rome. As "sons of the fathers" they called themselves patricians in contradistinction to clients and slaves, who had no standing in law and therefore no traceable descent. All such patrician citizens were free, possessed of equal rights and privileges and liable to render the same service to the State.

As the father was the supreme head of the household, so the king was supreme head of the community of households forming the State.

The ruling king nominated his successor, but on his death the one nominated had to challenge the allegiance of the whole assembly of free citizens capable of bearing arms. Ratification given, his power was for life. Although he had no authority to alter or initiate legislation, his power in an administrative and executive way was enormous. As the head of the state religion he not only conducted the most inportant religious ceremonies but also appointed priests and priestesses. He had the control of foreign policy and the command of the army. The keys of the Treasury were in his keeping, and he administered justice. Every official in the public service was appointed by the king and was responsible to him. While, however, the sovereign was the executive head, the assemblage of citizens was the final court of appeal. The ruler might propose new legislation, but before any such law could be enforced it had to be ratified by the whole assembly voting by "curies" or wards. The citizens were in every legal and political sense equal. Wealth and noble descent gave no advantage. Only executive rank in the service of the state conferred power, precedence or even the right to wear any garb except the simple white toga.

The Senate, originating probably as a gathering of clan chiefs, developed into a council of elders who sat in a circle round the king and on whom he called for advice. The number of senators was fixed at three hundred. They were considered to be the guardians of the constitution. Even resolutions proposed by the king and ratified by the assembly could be vetoed by the Senate if in the opinion of that body the proposal was in conflict with the law as already established. For the creation of new burgesses their consent was necessary, and, most important of all, it was imperative that before operations commenced their sanction was given for a war of aggression.

Such was the early organization of the Roman people. Extraordinary freedom in the private affairs of life was combined with a rigid obedience to the authority of the state represented in the person of a king administering a definite system of recognized law, which in its turn was jealously guarded by the senatorial body. The population of the city was composed of citizen clients, who were free but without civil rights and slaves.

Rome was primarily a commercial city and depended for its greatness and prosperity upon the free flow of trade. This meant very considerable intercourse with other states. Many outsiders were from business reasons drawn to the city. Refugees and all manner of other folk naturally drifted to so cosmopolitan a place. While these men received the full protection of the state as clients of the king or even of private persons, they were naturally without civil rights or defined duties. They grew rapidly in numbers and frequently acquired considerable wealth. The citizens or patricians were in course of time heavily outnumbered. Possessing as they did a final authority in all matters of government, they developed into a ruling aristocracy. In course of time the mass of clients or the plebs naturally became impatient with a system which gave them no voice in the control of affairs. On the other hand, the patrician body found that the responsibilities of the system pressed very heavily upon them, as they alone were liable for direct taxation and for military service. Some adjustment was obviously necessary. Under one of the early kings—possibly Servius Tullius (570-535 B.C.), every landholder became liable to appear in arms and to pay taxes without distinction of class. This necessitated a new division of the people into four tribes, the taking of the first census and the reorganization of the army. The plebeian now had duties even if as yet he had no political rights except that of protection. This arrangement gave no real stability, but the development of the constitution took, for the time being, another direction. The last of the Roman kings, Tarquinus Superbus, acted in a most tyrannical and overbearing fashion. A rising led by Brutus and Valerius expelled him from the city. His allies were defeated and the consulate established in place of the kingship. The new office was held not for life but for a single year, and the power was divided between two consuls. The flight of the king took place about 509 B.C., and from that time for nearly five hundred years the very idea of kingly rule was abhorrent to the people of Rome.

At this period the Romans had produced no single great book nor had they any considerable body of mythology. They were profoundly religious. Their gods were less purely anthropomorphic than those of the Greeks and were to a greater extent personifications of abstract qualities. Every operation, every person, every household, every community had its own particular god or gods demanding prayer and sacrifice. They were jealous gods, and if the rightful ceremonies were not observed disaster followed.

There was little love between the gods and men. The relation was rather that of debtor and creditor. The deities were just but hard, and demanded their full dues under penalty. No action great or small was ever entered upon without an attempt to ascertain the mind of the god concerned. Morality was associated with the gods. Certain actions were pleasing, others highly displeasing, to them. There was no speculation into the nature of the divine beings. Roman religion in consequence rapidly became stereotyped and degenerated into "an anxious and dreary round of ceremonies."

The Carthaginians and the Sicilian Greeks at some early period established contact with the city. What volume of trade was carried on there is no means of knowing. Greek influence is observable in the Roman standards of weight and measurement.

The alphabet is a variation of the Greek. Hellenic influence is observable in the architecture of the walls, sewers and public buildings, some fragments of which still remain.

By 500 B.C. Rome had behind it some two hundred years of development. Roman character had emerged. Religion was established in permanent form. The main lines of the constitution had been laid down. The citizens had shown themselves in a high degree capable of organization and discipline while at the same time preserving a maximum of personal freedom and self-respect. At the same time Rome was practically unknown in the Mediterranean world, and the influence of its people was felt for but a few miles beyond the city gates.

CHAPTER XII

THE INTERACTION OF THE EASTERN AND WESTERN PEOPLES TO 500 B.C.

By the year 500 B.C. the main racial types had been established and many of the major racial movements had taken place. China was occupied by the people whose decendants, with few modifications, are the Chinese of to-day. They had records of a civilization that was then 2,000 years old. So long had they been settled upon the soil that their earliest legends contain no records of migration. In India the wave of Aryan conquest had swept across the peninsula and merged itself with the darker-skinned aborigines. Other waves of the Aryan race had swept down into the peninsula of the Mediterranean and in Italy and Greece were laying the foundations of the greatest empire and the greatest school of philosophy the world has yet known. Just as our period closes the Persians reached Babylon and the Teutonic branch of the world wanderers would be completing their great trek from the Caucasus to the shores of the German Ocean. The Egyptians were a stable race whose history lost itself in the immemorial mists of time. There are no records of a period when the long-robed fellaheen were not breaking the dark surface with the primitive share, guiding the Nile-water into its appointed channels, and three times a year gathering in the harvest. In Palestine, Asia Minor and the valleys of the Tigris and Euphrates there was a state of greater flux, and great changes were to come in the composition of the races; but even in this area permanent types had evolved, the most notable being the Jewish nation, whose existence as an independent political unit ended before the close of our period. It has been no part of our task to trace in detail the origins of these people or the movements by which they came to be settled. Our concern is to take them as they merge into the clear light of History and to study their developments, economic, social, political, intellectual or religious, in so far as these are actual or potential influences in the great interaction of the East and West which has resulted in the world situation of our own day, with its complex problems, its terrifying dangers, and its marvellous opportunities of developing a great brotherhood of peoples amongst whom life shall be a grand fellowship of good will.

The first general conclusion we reach as a result of our detailed studies is that of the enormous importance of the various developments that had taken place prior to 500 B.C. When we consider, for instance, that the religion of Israel had reached its loftiest conceptions concerning the being of God and the nature of morality; that Zarathustra had proclaimed the universe to be an ever-increasing kingdom of righteousness; that Brahmanism had formulated its philosophy and established its social system; that Buddha had taught the way of enlightenment; that Confucius had summed up the orthodoxy of China; that Homer had enshrined Aryan polytheism in its most magnificent poetry; that Phoenician sailors had circumnavigated Africa; and that the pyramids of Egypt and the palaces of Babylon were antiquities in the eyes of the men of that time—when we consider all these things, we see what far-reaching developments had taken place and how far the race had emerged from its infancy. There is often a tendency amongst those of us whose immediate traditions are European to think that before Socrates there was but a rude confusion of thought—a sort of chaos without form and void. Such a view becomes almost a provincialism when an attempt is made to get a balanced idea of the speculations that had been elaborated throughout the whole world, and of what an influence these have had on the life of countless millions of the human race who never heard the names of the Greek sages.

Our second and indeed our main conclusion is that all these developments in thought and experience were isolated, and that the races whose history we have considered interacted only to the slightest extent the one upon the other. The reasons for this were: (1) The need that some peoples had for consolidation. (2) The complete isolation of others. (3) The primitive economic developments of nearly all ancient peoples. (4) The lack of established trade routes, means of transportation and communication. (5) The generally hostile feelings entertained toward all strangers, especially those of another colour or race. The world was still a very large place; its peoples for the most part dwelled in isolated corners and had few contacts with one another.

All the peoples whose developments we have studied lived in the Torrid Zone, or the southern part of the North Temperate Zone—that is to say, within the latitudes where the maintenance of life with more or less primitive tools is most easy. From the shores of the Pacific Ocean to the Pillars of Hercules there were few large towns but innumerable villages, each one of which would be, as far as the necessities of life were concerned, an independent economic unit. Modes of living would vary with conditions. Some communities would be purely pastoral, and here the people would be clothed in skins, and would subsist almost entirely on meat and milk. In others again, where agricultural pursuits predominated, clothing would be woven from fibre, and food would consist of corn and the fruits of the soil. Usually, however, as cattle, goats and sheep were widely spread, there would be a combination of the two. Each village would have its cultivated fields and flock of sheep or herd of cows, and within its borders there would be some division of labour, but it would be sufficient to itself. Men lived mainly upon what they themselves could

THE INTERACTION OF THE PEOPLES

produce, or on what they could procure by the simplest form of barter with their neighbouring communities. The necessities of life were too bulky and likewise too perishable to exchange unless distances were short and means of transport good. The Phoenicians were probably the only people of the time who did not produce a sufficiency of food from their own soil. They imported a quantity of corn and oil from the Hebrews, and exported timber in return. Such an exchange is the commonplace of to-day, but it was then the rarest exception, and was only made possible by the ease of communication both by land and sea. The beginnings of international trade are to be traced to the exchange of luxuries. Articles of great intrinsic value and of relatively small bulk could be brought thousands of miles by pack-camel, or hundreds of leagues by sea, providing they could be exchanged for something of equal or greater value, and again of a size that could be readily handled. The swordblades of Damascus, the spices of Arabia, the silken garments of China, the worked gold and silver of India, the priceless vases of the Greeks were easily carried and eagerly exchanged for whatever was most desired by the travelling merchant, but except for the very shortest distances the common articles of food or clothing could not be profitably packed. They were too heavy and far too perishable. When the navies of Hiram and Solomon sailed home from Ophir and Tarshish they were laden not with wheat and coal, or meat and common cloth, but with gold, silver, and precious stones, ivory, apes, peacocks and rare woods. From the farthest East there was a straggling line of connection with the coast towns of the Eastern Mediterranean and so to Egypt and Europe. From China and India to Bactria, from Bactria to Babylon, from Babylon to Tyre, from Tyre to Heliopolis rare and rich goods were carried by the camel trains over the ancient tracks. This traffic, however, would not be regular. For long periods parts of the long highway of trade would be closed by war. One has only to consider the disturbing effect that the civil wars between Judah and Israel must have had on the spice trade to Egypt to see what conditions of insecurity prevailed. The whole route was probably never open long enough for any regular international exchange of even luxury articles to develop between countries widely separated. The physical difficulties of crossing wide deserts were very great. When food and water for the transport animals, the drivers, and the not inconsiderable escort had been allowed for, the actual bulk of merchandise available for exchange in the markets was not high, even in proportion to the carrying capacity of the mule or camel. As the determining factor in the exchange value of products has ever been the labour power required for their production and distribution, the wages cost of the transportation of goods across the caravan routes was too great to allow of the carriage of any quantity of the more ordinary commodities. The economic relationships established were therefore superficial, and the periodical breaks caused by war and disorder would not seriously affect standards of life. This was further accentuated by the fact that while craftsmanship had in some cases reached a high standard of excellence, there was none of the labour-saving machinery which to-day makes the mass-production of certain high-grade articles so cheap and easy a process. A Damascus blade was a Damascus blade—the work of a craftsman who was an artist. Its value in the market was the value of professional time plus the cost of transport. There was a sale for such blades wherever men fought in war, but they were the arms of aristocrats, of the men who could pay for a weapon of great strength and beauty. Foot-soldiers of the line were not armed with such. Their blades were the work of local smiths which probably could not in most cases have found a profitable market a week's journey from the anvil on which they were forged. Direct economic contact between the Eastern and Western peoples was confined to the Phoenician trade with Greece and that of the Greek colonies with the inhabitants of Asia Minor.

Political and social systems varied in outward form, but they were essentially one in spirit. Everywhere the strong and the rich ruled and the humble and poor submitted to that rule, not questioning its rightfulness. Society everywhere was based on authority, sometimes that of the sword, at other times that of religion or superstition. Democracy emerged only in its most rudimentary forms. Where communications are difficult the maintenance of a strong central executive is impossible. The local chieftain and the priest loomed larger than all others. United action with other villages or clans was only called for in some such emergency as war. In primitive communities there is no well-defined hierarchy of nobles. In consequence the chiefs coming together with little exact knowledge of each other's powers and resources naturally formed a deliberative assemblage in which the presumption was that all stood on something like a common level. Such a council would as a rule not proceed farther than to elect a war chief, into whose hands it would resign its powers or to support or reject the proposals of an established king. This rough-and-ready council with its power of election was probably common to nearly all Aryan peoples in the periods of their migration, conquests and early settlements. Rude as they were, limited in their scope and aristocratic in their composition, these councils were the nearest approach to democracy then known. In Rome then a small city of relatively little importance—the council consisted of free citizens who had a considerable power of veto; Greece, a country and not a State, was a loose federation of clans and cities where the forms of government ranged from the direct control of tribal chiefs to oligarchies of leading citizens. In every case there were large subject-masses whose will was never consulted, and from whom the aristocracy, whether hereditary chieftains or free citizens, drew their wealth, power and prestige. From the earliest times great monarchies had been established in the East. Egypt had a complex social and political development. The Pharaoh was supreme. His power was exercised through great Ministers and a highly developed Civil Service in the interests of a priestly class and a landowning nobility. The common labourers of the fields and a large slave class enabled minorities to live a highly cultured and luxurious life. The kingdoms of Judah and Israel were military aristocracies. Priestly influence was strong, but by no means dominant. The brutal oppression and exploitation of the poor was the constant theme of the prophets. Assyria and Babylon developed the first great imperialisms of history. Their armies marched in triumph from the borders of India to the banks of the Nile. Shalmaneser III, Tiglath-Pileser, Sargon II, Sennacherib, Essar-Haddon, Assur-bani-pal and Nebuchadrezzar are the first outstanding names on that roll of conquerers whose lust for dominion and power has devastated wide areas, driven whole peoples from their homes to captivity and exile, and deluged the earth with unavailing slaughter. The "Bloody City," with its lies and robberies, its pomp and power, richness and beauty, was built by the violent and the strong upon the spoil of the poor and the labour of the defenceless. On such foundations no power can endure. At first the debauch of blood gives apparent strength, but in the end comes weakness. The fierce clans of the Medes and the Persians overthrew the Empire, and possessed its vast spoils. The tyrants were overthrown, but not tyranny. In India the Aryan kingdoms were established throughout the north. The aboriginal inhabitants were either driven out or became the hewers of wood or the drawers of water for their "Twice-Born" conquerors. The Kshatra class of fighting nobles and the

THE INTERACTION OF THE PEOPLES

Brahman priests shared power and wealth with one another, but as time went on the latter class tended to become predominant as the religious conceptions of Brahmanism took firmer hold on the people as a whole. China possessed a monarch no less authoritative and far more venerable than any except that perhaps of Egypt. Here, as elsewhere, the strong ruled, but with an entirely different outlook. Power was ordained of God for the welfare of the people. While the people were not to be consulted, and had no voice in their own government, the rulers were bound by their allegiance to heaven to consult, not their own desires, but the good of their people. Amongst the Chinese the conception of absolute monarchy reached its most idealistic development. All over the world, then, the idea of authority imposing itself from above was universally accepted. The soldier by the power of the sword, the priest by the conviction that he was the oracle of the gods or the gateway of salvation, bound the souls and bodies of men to subjection and toil. The multitudes of humble poor toiled for the enrichment of master classes with scarcely a thought but that this was the divinely ordered rule of life. This almost universal acceptance of imposed external authority was a development from the raw material of human nature and was not in any way due to the interaction of influences.

Three great national movements, ultimately of the greatest international importance, preceded the close of our period. The Phoenicians, cut off from the Red Sea and the Indian Ocean, commenced to plant their trading-posts and then their colonies throughout the north of Africa, Sardinia, Sicily, and the south of Spain. This movement brought them face to face with the Europeans on a wide front. With the rise of Carthage to pre-eminence in the Mediterranean they threatened to subdue and possess Europe, not only by the means of the new force of economic penetration, but by the might of their navies and the strength of the mercenary armies which their wealth could assemble and which their naval supremacy enabled them to deploy at any threatened point. Their ships at some time or other entered every port of the inland sea, and wherever they went they carried something of the culture and the arts and crafts of Egypt and Assyria. The provision of markets gave a tremendous impetus to the production of surpluses which could be exchanged for the luxury wares of the merchants. Wherever the Phoenicians touched, economic life became more complex and the process of civilization was accelerated. The Greeks overflowed from the peninsula, took possession of Crete and the Aegean Islands, and after at least one tremendous struggle established themselves on the Asian shores. By degrees also they planted their settlements in Cyprus, the south of Sicily, Corsica and the south of France. They thus invaded the East, challenged the leadership of Europe and deflected the Phoenicians to the South and still farther to the West. As a result of these two movements we have a definite beginning of interaction between the East and West. Although the contacts were still slight, yet outpost lines had been established and there was some skirmishing at the outposts. The immediate results were not great, but the stage was set for the vast actions of the future. One other movement, pregnant with possibility, remains to be considered. The downfall of Assyria made the once subject Medes and Persians the most powerful people of the Middle East. They took Babylon and so entered into possession of the old Assyrian Empire. More important, however, in its ultimate results than this conquest was their previous victorious march upon Sardis. The fall of this great city brought the power of their developing Imperialism face to face with the growing might of the Greeks, then at the zenith of their vigorous expansion.

Whilst in Egypt and Assyria there had been some considerable development in scientific thinking in which many blind alleys had been explored and many discoveries of permanent value made, religious speculation was the field which was most eagerly explored and in which the ancient peoples made their strongest and most enduring mark. The importance of this on the subsequent history of the race cannot be over-estimated. Men's convictions concerning the existence or non-existence of a Divine Being, the nature and quality of such a Being, the ultimate destiny of human life and the content of ethical codes have the most direct bearing on the life of the individual and on the organization of society. Belief in the existence of the gods was almost universal, but there was the utmost diversity of opinion concerning the nature and effectiveness of their operations. In India, as we have seen, certain conceptions of Brahman definitely lacked personality. That indefinite vagueness, that misty ocean of being may have had consciousness, but it certainly did not have personality. Vast and inert, it contained all things but conditioned none. Such gods as are occasionally portrayed in the Buddhist scriptures were ineffective and shadowy beings, as helpless, as burdened and as much in need of salvation as the poorest and weakest of mankind. Throughout the rest of the world, however, beliefs were much more anthropomorphic, and it was generally felt that men were like the gods in that both were essentially personal, possessing intellectual capacity and passion. Polytheistic conceptions were general, but were rapidly moving toward Monotheism. There is a difference in this respect even between Homer and Hesiod. In the *Iliad* and the *Odyssey* Zeus is certainly the father of the gods and the president of the council. He is represented as being omnipotent, but he does not fill the whole earth with his majesty and might as he does in the greater passages of *Hesiod*. Among the Egyptians Isis was developing in importance while other gods were receding into the background. The Chinese paid great reverence to the deified spirits of their mighty ancestors, but Heaven ruled over all, and although the person of the Deity was remote and removed far from common men by hierarchies of priests, nobles, kings and spirits, yet he was in the last analysis the sole and absolute ruler of all beings and men. In the case of the Hebrews and the Zarathustrians the idea of the unity of God had definitely prevailed. The move towards Monotheism was of tremendous importance in so far as in the ultimate it provides a unifying idea. Polytheism, with its tendency toward the patron god and the favoured class, tribe or nation, tends towards disintegration. When there are many gods the qualities of divinity can be held to be various and contradictory, but when the Divine is thought of in the terms of One Person the whole field of thought must be rationalized. In the being of God there must be an essential unity. The process of rationalizing polytheism was a difficult and painful one, not because of logical difficulties, but because the unifying process was also a moralizing one. In the clash of direct opposites there could often be no compromise. Pleasant vices that could be justified when practised under the auspices of Dionysos or Aphroditê became impossible when the existence of these deities was denied and the whole question of conduct referred back to the being of a god who must be consistent within himself. The prophets of Israel and the teachers of the Mazdean faith in proclaiming that there was one God of all the earth visible in nature and living in history, who judged men in righteousness, laid tremendous stress upon the fact that He Himself was moral and holy. In both religions God was conceived as struggling with the evil of the world and moving ever to great goals, to a holy mountain of lasting peace and a heaven of endless light and everlasting song. All religions, except the Brahmin and the Buddhist, represented God or the gods as being directly concerned with the welfare of men and therefore with men's conduct. To a large extent this was expressed in denunciations of existing wickednesses in pursuance of the view that the evil in the world is to be removed by the punishment or destruction of the wicked. For their frightful enormities Hesiod even says that Zeus will destroy the Race of Iron as he has destroyed others before it. The stern imagination of the Hebrew prophets ran continually upon the terror of God's judgments. His wrath flamed upon the guilty, and in passage after passage of tremendous power they proclaim the doom of the idolaters, the proud and cruel oppressors of the poor, the greedy extortioners, and the violent shedders of blood. Nothing is so high and so great that it can stand before the righteous judgments of Almighty God. The continual stressing of the wrath of God, the horror of the judgments, which the prophets see as coming directly from him, tend to obscure the essential principle that lies behind. God is concerned with evil because it destroys the happiness of the humble poor. The prophets are in revolt against the principles on which the society of their time was built. They were rebels and revolutionaries, and if there was often more condemnation in their utterances than constructive social thinking they had nevertheless made a tremendous advance in associating God, because of His essential righteousness, as being of necessity on the side of the oppressed and down-trodden. It is this intensity of God's feeling that is the particular contribution of Hebrew thought. The content of Mazdean thinking about the Divine Nature is perhaps wider and deeper; Chinese conceptions approached more nearly the ideal of Our Father Which Art in Heaven, but both lack the blazing passion that runs like a fire from Amos and Hosea to Zephaniah and Jeremiah. The utter sincerity of the feeling at last enables it to rise above crudities and misconceptions, and in its mood of greatest exultation to reveal, not the implacable and relentless judge, but a God agonizing over the wicked and suffering for their redemption.

The destiny of human life is regarded variously. The Hebrews, strangely enough, seem scarcely to have considered any question of a life beyond. Most of the prophetic thinking was concerned with the nation or the race as a whole. God was unquestionably working toward a perfect State, and a society in which life as a whole was to be righteous and holy. The individual as an end in himself, as indeed anything more than a link in the chain, was not greatly considered. A man's immortality was in that continuing process of life that issues from him. His children and children's children were his fulfilment. By some train of thought, impossible for us to follow, the Aryan conquerors of India developed the idea that life with personality and individuality was an insupportable evil. Their search was continually for a way of escape from the dreadful succession of rebirths to the formlessness of Brahman. This quest was pursued anxiously and without any ceasing from the way of mortification of the flesh and subjugation of the spirit. Buddhism advanced a further stage and strove for utter annihilation—complete escape from the burden of life. Both religions laid down foundations of pessimism which have largely conditioned Indian life to our own day. While the Greeks did not believe in the cessation of personality, their outlook as far as the future was concerned was gloomy. Love and joy and light and life were to be had here and now on the green earth beneath the blue sky. When the soul left the body it became but a pale wraith without ardour or the capacity for a full life of joyous expression. The Egyptians believed in the immortality of the soul, and that the life of the future was the greater life. To win this in its fullness was the desire of every Egyptian. For the Chinese, too, there were blessed fields. The belief in immortality, however, rose to its finest height amongst the followers of Zarathustra. Eternal life meant a growth and an enlargement of the soul. Only those whose souls had been guided by the desire for goodness, whose minds had been purified by holy thinking and whose lives had been full of right actions could hope to cross that narrow bridge that led into the presence of God; but when they did enter His home of song they were enlarged and purified, made capable of greater expression and of deeper joys.

In most cases, although not in all, a religious system includes an ethical code as an integral part of itself. Brahmanism is here a notable exception. Some other religions we have considered did not greatly stress any definite principles of living even although in a general way they admitted the necessity of such. The Greeks were utilitarian. Hesiod seems to have considered that one should be moral because it paid to be so. If a man were unjust or dishonest, the anger of Zeus would be upon him. His morality did not consist in a love of virtue for its own sake. The Egyptians were far more concerned with laying hold on eternal life by means of words of magical power through which they could command the gods than with the practice of moral living. Mazdaism, while stressing the necessity for good life, defined it in vague terms similar to the familar "Beauty, Goodness and Truth" formula so common in our own day. The Hebrews, on the contrary, promulgated a comprehensive code expressed in the clearest terms and with the utmost directness. The short summary, commonly known as the Decalogue, covers practically all problems in conduct likely to arise between a man and his neighbour. This and the general conceptions in the prophetic books are largely negative, condemnations of evil rather than definitions of what is good. Their intention is the usual one of restraining the evildoer, not of encouraging men to take positive and perhaps adventurous attitudes in a spirit of brotherhood and co-operation. This ancient code has been enormously influential and is to-day the real standard of most modern civilized States. They have certainly not gone beyond it, but they may be said to have accepted it as a highest common ideal. The ethics of Buddhism were extremely high. They inculcated the utmost reverence for life in all its forms, the definite refusal to use any way of violence, the practice of mercy and compassion, temperate and sober living, chastity, utter truthfulness and honourable life. No method of obtaining a livelihood that could in any way be harmful to other men could possibly be countenanced. Friendship had always to be fostered, and the Buddhist had to be a peacemaker with a passion for peace. If any criticism can be levelled it is that the system itself is not positive enough and has a tendency to renunciation for the sake of renunciation's sake. The disciple of Gotama must do nothing which conduces to the harm of himself or others. He lacks—as of course he is bound to do by his whole conception of life—an enthusiasm for making greater and grander ways of expression open to the children of men. Confucian standards were not less high and sprang from a more humanistic spirit. If indeed any man lives in such a manner as to regard those about him with respect, to be generous in his attitudes, to be sincere in all his dealings, conscientious in all his actions, and to be unendingly kind in all his ways, there is a little more that he as an individual can do towards making a great society. Uprightness and moral living was the goal of life. There is perhaps no greater tragedy in history than that the philosophers of ancient China, with their very lofty conceptions of the nature of God and the meaning of morality, turned back from exploring the channels of mystical experience along which alone can flow those tides of the spirit which inspire men to live very passionately to the height of their ideals.

The period before 500 B.C. is predominantly one of preparation in comparative isolation. The fundamental ideas in religion and philosophy had been formulated and had developed into considerable systems. In very few cases, however, had there been any interaction. It was as though the snow had commenced to melt upon some rugged peak, and the streams, running off at all angles, were finding channels through the long and winding valleys that cut through into the plains beyond. Some few of these streams were to disappear into dry and barren wastes of sand, some, very shortly after our period ends, were to meet and mingle, while others were to flow separately for great distances before they flowed into the wide river of human life which to-day flows on toward the ocean. The tendencies and influences which go to the making of the international life of our day had established themselves but had hardly commenced to weave themselves into the warp and woof of history. Yet the stage was set for the mighty movements which to-day are culminating in the most marvellous opportunity the human race has ever had of achieving the great society which its most inspired dreamers have always pictured as its real destiny.

BIBLIOGRAPHY

CHAPTER I
(*a*) Outline of History, Wells
(*b*) Herodotus, Rawlinson. (Everyman)

CHAPTER II
(*a*) E. B. (Encyclopædia Britannica), 10th Edition
(*b*) Legends of Gods, Budge. (Kegan Paul)
(*c*) Annals of Nubian Kings, Budge. (Kegan Paul)
(*d*) Egyptian Magic, Budge. (Kegan Paul)
(*e*) Genesis   (*f*) I Kings
(*g*) Exodus   (*h*) Herodotus

CHAPTER III
(*a*) E. B.
(*b*) Odyssey, Cowper. (Everyman)
(*c*) Herodotus
(*d*) Peake's Commentary, Peake. (T. C. & E. C. Jack)
(*e*) Judges   (*f*) Joshua
(*g*) II Samuel   (*h*) I Kings
(*i*) Ezekiel

CHAPTER IV
(*a*) E. B.   (*b*) Peake's Commentary
(*c*) Nahum   (*d*) II Kings
(*e*) II Chronicles

CHAPTER V
(*a*) Peake's Commentary
(*b*) Introduction to the Literature of the Old Testament (9th Edition), Driver. (T. & T. Clark)
(*c*) The Bible, Peake. (Hodder & Stoughton)
(*d*) Ideas of God in Israel, Pace. (George Allen & Unwin)
(*e*) Old Testament (A. V.):
    Genesis, Exodus, Leviticus, Numbers, Deuteronomy, Joshua, Judges, Samuel I and II, Kings I and II, Chronicles I and II, Amos, Hosea, Micah, Isaiah I and II, Zephaniah, Jeremiah, Ezra, Lamentations, Ezekiel.

BIBLIOGRAPHY

CHAPTER VI
(a) E. B.
(b) Peake's Commentary
(c) Herodotus

CHAPTER VII
(a) Zenda Avesta, Sacred Books of the East

CHAPTER VIII
(a) Cambridge History of India, Vol. I
(b) Hinduism and Buddhism, Eliot. (Arnold)
(c) Christianity and Buddhism, Estlin Carpenter. (Hodder & Stoughton)
(d) Rig-Veda, Sacred Books of the East, Vols. 32 and 46
(e) Satapatha Brahmana, S.B.E., Vols. 12, 26, 41, 43
(f) Upanishads, S.B.E., Vols. 1 and 15
(g) Ramayana and Mahabharata, Dutt. (Everyman)
(h) Sacred Books of Buddhists, Vols. 2, 3, 4, 5, 6, Ed. Muller and T. W. & C. A. F. Rhys Davids. (Oxford University Press)
(i) E. B.

CHAPTER IX
(a) E. B.
(b) Texts of Confucianism, S.B.E., Vols. 3 and 16
(c) Analects of Confucius, Soothill
(d) The Four Books, Legge
(e) Christus, Manuel d'histoire des Religions, Huby. (Gabriel Beauchêsne, Paris)

CHAPTER X
(a) E. B.
(b) History of Greece, Grote. (Everyman)
(c) Iliad, Derby. (Everyman)
(d) Odyssey, Cowper. (Everyman)
(e) Hesiod, White. Loeb
(f) Herodotus

CHAPTER XI
(a) E. B.
(b) History of Rome, Mommsen. (Everyman)
(c) History of Rome, Merivale. (Everyman)

INDEX

Aahmes, 21
Abednego, 116
Abel, 65
Abimelech, 69 f.
Abraham, 67–70
Absolom, 61
Achaens, 288
Achilles, 269, 271, 273
Adam, 65, 111
Aegisthus, 275
Agag, 83
Agamemnon, 268, 272 f., 277
Agni, 165, 167, 169 f., 179, 183, 185, 191, 199
Ahab, 50, 53
Ahaz, 53, 90
Ahaziah, 50, 90
Ahitophel, 61
Ahura Mazda, 130–161
Ajax, 269
Alcinous, 276
Alexander, 266
Alkaeus, 290
Alkmann, 290
Amalek, 49
Amaziah, 53, 88
Amen, 19
Amenemhat, 119
Amenra, 21
Ammonites, 49, 53, 86 f., 98, 103, 121
Amorites, 41, 78, 98
Amos, 85–88, 92, 309
Amsa, 167
Anâhita, 150, 160
Analects, 256, 261
Ananda, 210, 211
Angra Mainyu, 144, 145, 148, 149, 153
Antariksha, 191
Antinous, 277
Aolic Migration, 282
Apep, 25 f.
Aphroditê, 270, 273, 275, 308
Apoasha, 151
Arabians, 53
Arahants, 210, 228
Archilochus, 290
Arês, 269, 272, 275, 279
Argonauts, 266
Artaxerxes, 117
Aryan, 15, 18, 43, 127, 152, 153, 155, 160, 162, 165 f., 167 f., 170, 173, 198, 204, 281, 292, 298, 310

Aryan Eightfold Path, 221
Asa, 52
Asha, 131, 142, 152
Ashi, 154
Assurbanipal, 43, 304
Assyria, 40, 44, 50 f., 52, 96, 121, 127, 306
Astyages, 128
Asuras, 186
Asyamedha, 174
Athaliah, 53
Athênê, 270, 271, 274

Baal, 104
Baasha, 50
Babylon, 40–44, 128 f., 235, 301, 304
Bactria, 301
Balaam's Oracles, 60
Barbarians, 16
Bendva, 139
Benhadad, 50
Benjamin, 50, 52
Berbers, 15
Bharati, 167
Bimbisara, 209
Binothris, 18
Book of Gasher, 59
Brahmanism, 167, 175–202, 208, 210, 217, 229, 231, 279, 305–311
Brazen Race, 279
Brihadaranyaka, 190–195
Brihaspati, 189
Brutus, 296
Buddha (Gautama), 204–211, 212–231
Buddhism, 204–231, 307 f., 312
Budge, 26
Bunyan, 200
Burmese, 15

Cain, 65
Carthaginians, 296, 305
Causation, 217
Celts, 16
Chaldeans, 40, 54, 107
Charlemagne, 166
Ch'en Heng, 260
Chi-chi, 254
China, 15, 16, 232–265, 298, 301, 305, 310
Ching, 261
Christian Missions, 16
Chronos, 278, 280
Chryses, 272

316

INDEX

Chusharishatháim, 48
Confucius, 250, 252 f., 255 f., 259 ff., 299, 312
Court History David, 51, 63
Creation and Fall, 65 f.
Cretans, 266
Croesus, 128
Cyaxerxes, 127 f.
Cyrus, 44 f., 116 f., 122 f., 128 f.

Daêvas, 134, 143, 145, 148 f.
Dagon, 82
Damascus, 94, 103
Danites, 34
Darius, 117
Dasyus, 168, 170
David, 34, 35, 48 ff., 55, 61 f., 80 ff.
Deborah's Song, 58
Decalogue, 73, 75, 98, 311
Deioces, 127
Demeter, 289
Deuteronomy, 78, 96-99, 102
Devas, 183, 186, 191, 194
Dharma, 192, 200
Dhritanashtra, 166
Diomed, 271
Dionysos, 289, 308
Doeg, 81
Dorian Migration, 283
Dravidians, 15, 162
Driver, 61, 64, 68 f., 71, 74, 76, 78, 97, 123
Drug, 145 ff., 148
Dualism, 157
Duryudhan, 66
Dyú, 191

Edomites, 53, 86 f., 103, 121
Edward III, 267
Egypt, 15, 18-31, 42 f., 50 f., 54, 71 f., 74, 77, 82, 94, 96, 103-107, 235, 289, 298, 301 f., 305, 310 f.
Ehud, 48
El, 47
Elah, 50
Elamites, 103
Eli, 83 f.
Elkanah, 84
Elohim, 70
Ephraim, 88 f.
Esau, 68
Essarhaddon, 22, 43, 304
Esthonians, 15
Ethiopians, 53, 94
Eurymachus, 277
Eve, 111

Evil One, 132 f., 159
Exile, 115 f.
Exodus, 71-76
Ezekiel, 38, 119-122
Ezra, 122

Finns, 15
Flood, 66
Fravashis, 153

Gâthas, 130
Gautama, 197, 312
Genesis, 64-71
Ghurkas, 15
Gideon, 48
God, 55 f., 58 ff., 62 f., 65-126 (as Mazda), 130-161, 198, 200, 246, 250, 280, 305, 308 f.
Golden Age, 279
Gordon, 100 f.
Gôs, 151
Gotama, 202
Great Learning, 261 f.
Greeks, 14, 16, 28, 36 f., 50, 266-291, 296, 306

Hadadezer, 49
Hammurabi, 41
Hang, 249
Hannah, 83
Haoma, 143, 154
Harmless Livelihood, 227
Hathor, 23
Hazael, 51
Heaven, 240, 250
Hebrew, 27, 40, 52, 75, 82, 108, 117, 301, 307, 309 f.
Hector, 269, 273
Helen, 266 f.
Heliopolis, 18
Hêrê, 270, 274 f., 288
Herodotus, 16, 25 f., 28, 32, 36, 127 ff., 143, 266 f., 283, 288
Heru-khent a-moati, 22
Hesiod, 278-281, 287, 289, 307, 309
Hexagram, 240
Hezekiah, 53, 96
Hindrances, Five, 213, 214
Hiram, 35, 52, 301
Hiranyagarbha, 184
Hittites, 42 f.
Homer, 267 f., 287, 289, 299, 307
Horus, 24 f.
Hosea, 88 f., 92, 309
Hoshea, 51
Hsia, 235 f.

317

Huns, 15
Hyrksos, 20

Iberians, 15
Ida, 167
Iliad, 287, 289
Indo-Aryans, 16
Indra, 167, 168, 183 ff., 189, 191, 199
Intelligent Activities, 227
Io, 266
Ionic Migration, 282
Iron Race, 279
Isaac, 67
Isaiah I, 92–96
Isaiah II, 122–125
Isana, 191
Isis, 22 f., 24 f., 289
Israelites, 20, 34 f., 45–124, 302, 304, 307
Italians, 16

Jacob, 20, 67 ff.
Jehoahaz, 51, 54
Jehoash, 51
Jehoiakim, 54, 119
Jehoida, 53
Jehoram, 51, 53
Jehoshaphat, 53
Jehovah, 55, 117, 119
Jehu, 51
Jeremiah, 102–107, 309
Jeroboam I, 50 ff.
Jeroboam II, 51, 85
Jew, 56
Joash, 53
Jonathan, 81
Joseph, 20, 69
Josephus, 32
Joshua, 34, 47, 78 f.
Josiah, 54, 96, 101
Jotham, 53, 90
Jotham Fable, 59
Judah, 49 f., 52 ff., 86, 89, 94, 102, 104, 108, 302, 304

Ka, 26
Kalama, 206, 208
Kallimus, 290
Kandramas, 191
Kao, 244
Karma, 230
Kassites, 42
Kau, 241 ff., 244, 248
Khanghui, 236
Khan-hsia, 239
Khang, 236, 242

Khau-hsia, 242
Khepera, 22
Khi, 236
Khin, 232
Ki, 252
Kieh, 236, 237
King Arthur, 166
Kingdom of Ahura (God), 157, 160
Kista, 153
Kolarians, 162
Kshatra, 174, 180, 191, 192, 194, 198
Kurus, 166

Lamech's Song, 58
Lamentations, 118 f.
Lao-tze, 252 f.
Lapps, 15
Latins, 292
Legge, 254
Levites, 52 f., 63
Libya, 18
Lu, 245
Luceres, 292
Lycurgus, 285

McFadyen, 122
Mahabharata, 166
Maitreyi, 193
Manasseh, 54, 96, 97
Mara, 206
Maruts, 168 f., 191
Mazdaism, 129, 130–161, 308 f., 311
Mazdayasnian Confession, 142
Medes, 16, 44, 127–129, 286, 304, 306
Memnon, 28
Menahem, 51
Menelaus, 271
Menes, 18
Menkira, 19
Meshach, 116
Miao, 234
Micah, 90 f., 92
Michal, 82
Midianites, 48
Mills, 141
Mindfulness, 219
Miriam's Song, 58
Mithra, 144, 151, 152, 160
Mitra, 167, 189
Moabites, 48 f., 51, 53, 86, 98, 102, 121
Mommsen, 292
Mongols, 15
Moses, 29, 46, 71 f., 73 f., 77, 97
Mrityu, 191
Mu, 244 f.

318

INDEX

Aabal, 81
Nadab, 50
Nahash, 80
Nahum, 53, 100 f.
Nakoketas, 196
Nakshatras, 191
Nanda, 209
Nathan, 62 f.
Neb-er-tcher, 22
Nebuchadrezzar, 22, 38, 39, 54, 102, 104, 105, 115, 117, 128, 304
Necho, 37, 54
Nepthys, 22
Nimshi, 51
Nine Virtues, 234
Nineveh, 21
Nirvana, 206, 219
Noah, 66, 112
Noah's Curse, 58
Nut, 22, 23

Odyssey, 166, 289, 307
Og, 78
Old Testament, 33, 57, 63, 76, 108, 124
Omri, 50
Osiris, 19, 22, 24 ff., 289
Othniel, 47

Paganism, 269
Pan Kang, 238 f.
Pandora, 280
Parganyas, 191
Paris, 271
Patroclus, 273
Paul, 286
Pautrayana, 180
Peake, 118
Peisistratus, 291
Pekah, 51
Pekakiah, 51
Pelops, 288
Pentateuch, 41, 47
Pentecostal Church, 84
Pepi, 19
Persians, 44, 127-129, 298, 304, 306
Pharaoh, 20, 22, 29, 45 ff., 70, 74
Philistines, 48 f., 53, 80, 82, 93, 103, 121
Phing, 245
Phoenicians, 22, 29, 32-39, 52, 85 f., 121, 266, 276, 289, 299, 301, 305, 306
Phraortes, 127
Piankhi, 21

Poseidôn, 274, 275
Po-I, 261
Pragapati, 178, 183, 185, 191
Pre-Exilic Period, 57-110
Priam, 273
Prithivi, 191
Prometheus, 280
Psammetichus, 22
Ptah-hotep, 19
Purgatory, 214 f.
Purushadmedha, 176
Pushan, 191
Pythagoras, 291

Ra, 23 ff.
Rahula, 209
Rajasuya, 166 f., 194
Ramaputta, 206, 208
Ramnians, 292
Rashnu, 153
Rehoboam, 50, 52
Ribhu, 167
Rig-Veda, 162-172, 199
Right Aspirations, Conduct, Rapture, Speech, and Views, 222-227
Robinson, 90, 107
Roman Catholic Church, 160
Rome, 292-297, 303
Rudra, 167, 170 f., 191

Sacrificial System, 173-177
Sakka, 228 f.
Sakyas, 204
Samson, 48
Samuel I & II, 79-84 f.
Santrusita, 228
Sappho, 290
Sargon, 43, 304
Sarpedon, 271
Satapatha Brahmana, 174
Saul, 34, 48, 55, 80 f., 83
Savitri, 167
Scythians, 44, 156
Seb, 22
Semites, 15, 20
Senate, 294
Sennacherib, 22, 43, 54, 304
Senoferu, 19
Servius Tullius, 295
Set, 22, 25
Shabak, 22
Shadrach, 116
Shallum, 51
Shalmaneser, 42, 304
Shang, 238
Shepherd Kings, 20

319

A STUDY IN CREATIVE HISTORY

Shishak, 52
Shun, 233 ff.
Shu Shi, 261
Siamese, 15
Silver Race, 279
Simonides, 290
Slavonians, 16
Socrates, 285, 289
Solomon, 35 f., 49 f., 52, 55, 59, 301
Solon, 291
Soma, 171, 191
Spartans, 288
Sraosha, 152
St. Stephen, 29
Subhadda, 201
Suddhohana, 204
Sudra, 191, 198, 203
Sunimatra, 288
Swaraj, 16
Syria, 42, 49, 52 f., 85 f.

Taharqa, 22
Tao, 252
Tarquinius Superbus, 296
Tefnut, 22
Telemachus, 276, 277
Teutons, 16
Thang, 232, 237, 246
Theognis, 291
Theogony, 278
Thoth, 25
Three Main Duties, 258
Thucydides, 33
Ti, 235, 244
Tibeto-Burmans, 162
Tiglath-Pileser, 42, 51, 53, 304
Ting, 254
Tiresias, 273
Tistraya, 151
Tities, 292
Ti-Yao, 232
Torah, 47
Trojans, 266, 268, 274, 278
Turks, 15
Tvashtri, 167
Typhon, 25
Tyrtaeus, 290

Ulysses, 33, 273 f., 277
Ushasti Kakrayana, 173

Uzzah, 81
Uzziah, 53, 92

Vaisvanara, 180
Vaisya, 180, 198, 213, 217
Vaiyu, 179, 183, 185
Valerius, 296
Varuna, 167, 169, 185, 189, 191
Vasas, 190 f.
Vasavatti, 229
Vata, 171
Vedas, 167, 194, 228
Vendîdâd, 144–149
Verethragna, 153
Vishnu, 167, 189
Vistapa, 138, 155
Visvedevas, 184, 191

Wai Ting, 239
Wai Wu, 244
Wan, 248
Wardle, 122
Wars of Yahweh, 59
Works and Days, 278, 289
Wu, 240 f.

Xenophanes, 287, 292

Yagnavalka, 190–194
Yahweh, 47, 70, 72, 85, 109 f.
Yama, 191, 196
Yasna, 141–144
Yasodhana, 209
Yen, 237 f.
Yî, 250
Yin, 236, 238
Yu, 232, 234 ff.
Yudhishthir, 166 f.
Yueh, 239
Yui, 240

Zachariah, 51, 53
Zarathustra, 129, 130–172, 299, 308, 310
Zedekiah, 104, 115
Zend Avesta, 130–172
Zephaniah, 101, 102, 309
Zeus, 270, 272 f., 275, 279 f., 307, 309, 311
Zimri, 50